Penguin Handbooks
The Penguin Bicycle Handbook

Rob Van der Plas was born in the Netherlands and educated in the
United States. For many years he lived in the Midlands and the north
of England, where he learned to love and understand the bicycle.
He holds advanced degrees in both engineering and economics and
brings to cycling a 'scientific' as well as a practical background.
His earlier books about the bicycle have appeared in Germany and
Holland; in addition he has been a regular contributor to bicycling
publications in the United States and Europe. He is married and has
two children.

The Penguin

Bicycle Handbook

How to Maintain and Repair Your Bicycle

Rob Van der Plas

illustrated by Bryan Marsh

Penguin Books

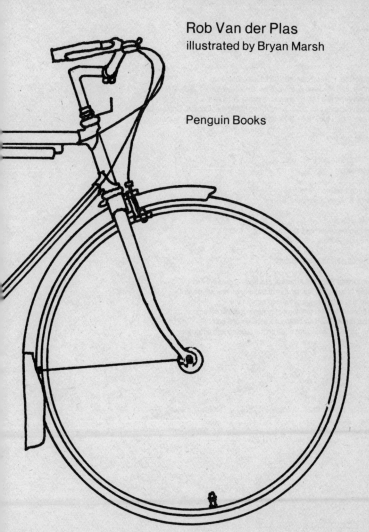

Penguin Books Ltd, Harmondsworth, Middlesex, England
Penguin Books, 625 Madison Avenue, New York, New York 10022, U.S.A.
Penguin Books Australia Ltd, Ringwood, Victoria, Australia
Penguin Books Canada Ltd, 2801 John Street, Markham, Ontario, Canada L3R 1B4
Penguin Books (N.Z.) Ltd, 182–190 Wairau Road, Auckland 10, New Zealand

First published 1983

Made and printed in Great Britain by
Hazell Watson & Viney, Aylesbury, Bucks

Set in Helvetica Medium
by Rowland Phototypesetting Ltd
Bury St Edmunds, Suffolk

Designed by Philip Hall/Michael Scott

For my parents

Contents

Part 3 The Bicycle Extraordinary

Part 4 Maintenance and Repairs

Part 5 Appendix

Tables and Graphs

Part 1

YOU AND YOUR BICYCLE

Thank God for the bicycle. In the days before universal motoring the 'pushbike' was the working man's ticket to freedom, and we are still riding it, faster and farther than anyone would have thought possible in the early days. Now we have no need to cycle, for we can drive a car or take a bus instead, although petrol and bus fares are expensive. So most people who cycle today do so not because they *have* to but because they *choose* to.

One of the major aims of this book is to show you how to use a bike to its greatest advantage. You will discover that your bike lends itself to more uses than you may originally have thought. The Sunday ride to the park and the evening jaunt after work are not the end of the road for the cyclist – you will discover your bike's half-forgotten *alter ego* as a viable means of transport.

Another aim of the book is to show you how to know the bicycle itself – what Oxford University's Stewart Wilson, in his fascinating article in *Scientific American*, called 'the human machine'. After taking a close look at the operation and construction of all the major components of the bicycle I will describe how to maintain, adjust and, if necessary, repair them. You will get to know your bike intimately, even the complexities that mystify many experienced cyclists. There is much more to the bicycle than meets the eye.

In the late seventies the bicycle took on another role, as a political tool. It became a symbol of ecological awareness, a chal-lenge to the almost universally accepted economic priorities of the motorist. This seems to be part of an international trend; beginning in the USA in the early seventies, it reached Holland in 1975 and is now sweeping through the British Isles. When I went to live in Germany in 1979 protesting cyclists were taking to the streets there as well. The phenomenon could be called the movement of the *policyclists* – the political cyclists – or the *unicyclists*, since the protagonists often seem to be associated with some institute of higher learning. It's a movement with which one feels some sympathy, but in a way it is also alarming, because the typical participants are often insufficiently experienced as *cyclists* to know what is good for cycling and what isn't. Only too often they demand cycle paths, bike lanes, traffic relief and a general rebuilding of our cities. But experienced bicycle-users have learned to live with what we have and have found that it can work well. In fact, it often has advantages over many of the schemes thought up by well-meaning political cyclists.

For this reason, ways of planning for the bicycle as a means of transport will be considered – the best ways of reducing the risks and increasing the benefits that the bicycle has to offer. We shall see that the car and the bicycle can exist side by side and that, indeed, the bicycle could be substituted for the car without the need to rebuild every road and demolish every underpass. I am not against traffic relief or special provisions for the bicycle, but I shall indicate where these provisions can be used to the advantage of the cyclist and where not.

It is probably not necessary to point out that the bicycle is good for the cyclist and for society. Nevertheless a little moral support may be in order, if only to help the cyclist to defend his chosen means of transport. Having spent over ten years in the world's most car-oriented society, the USA, I have been forced to defend my cause often enough to know all the pros and cons.

I cycle, oddly enough, for the same reason that the motorist uses his car – to get around quickly and comfortably. Cycling *is* quick – often considerably quicker than the car. By the time my neighbour has driven his car out of the garage and put it into gear, I've got a mile's start on him. When I arrive at my destination, I walk straight in, chaining my bike to the front gate or a lamp-post, while the motorist is still cruising round the neighbourhood looking for a parking place. According to data published by the Transport and Road Research Laboratory, the bicycle is faster than any other means of transport for trips of up to about five miles in urban areas. On really short journeys – up to about four hundred yards – the pedestrian wins, so don't use your bike for trips to the garden shed!

The bicycle provides gentle exercise but wastes very little energy. According to data from Wilson's article in *Scientific American*, the average energy consumption is 15 calories per kilogram per kilometre; that is, about 92 Btu per passenger mile, or 4 per cent of the energy required to take a car passenger over the same distance. If you were powered by petrol you could say that you were getting 1,600 miles per gallon on your bike.

The remarkable efficiency of the bicycle – it travels eight times as far as the pedestrian with the same expenditure of energy – is an indication of the genius that lies behind its development. Instead of exploiting resources, it makes much better use of the human energy at our disposal than was previously possible. It combines two major inventions in the field of mechanics – the wheel and the cantilever – with the principles of ergonomics. The product of this combination is now sold from Greenland to Peru and from China to Washington. Surely this must be man's greatest triumph in engineering.

Many of the principles of engineering first developed for the bicycle have since been applied in other areas of engineering: ball-bearings and the pneumatic tyre, the various forms of brakes and the space frame, to mention but a few. It is not a coincidence that the first aeroplane was built by the Wright brothers, who originally made bicycles, or that the bicycle formed the basis for that remarkable contraption, the 'Gossamer Albatross', which Bryan Allen flew across the English Channel one morning in May 1979 propelled by his own power, proving that man was meant to fly after all!

On that remarkable flight, Allen used no more than a quarter of a horsepower (0.18kW) for almost three hours; his trip provided him with good exercise, the kind of exercise that would keep anyone fit. However, such benefits are not confined to those who fly across the English Channel: every cyclist can enjoy such exercise if he wants. All he needs do is ride faster. This gives the cyclist an advantage over the runner or almost anyone else who wants to keep fit. He can take his exercise in the course of his daily routine, on his way to work or while getting the groceries. The runner (who insists on calling himself a 'jogger' nowadays – the word sounds as exhausted as the man himself) has to change his clothes and he soon gets bored; at five miles an hour he doesn't see much of the world. Other sportsmen are in an even worse position, since they have to travel some distance even before they begin. If they cycled to the tennis court, they would probably derive more benefit from the journey there than from the game itself.

I am often asked, 'Surely you wouldn't take your bike to go shopping?' Indeed I do, and so do thousands of others. A bike will hold quite a lot of luggage when properly loaded and there's no reason to feel that groceries present a worse problem than a two-man tent and a few cooking pots. You may not want to use your bike for every shopping trip, but you will soon find that you make fewer really bulky purchases than the car shopper supposes.

I'm a little reluctant to mention the economic advantages of the bicycle lest anyone should think that the bicycle is a poor man's substitute for a car, making the cyclist a kind of second-class citizen. Indeed, there is a certain amount of truth in this – in Germany, for example, people usually ride bicycles because they cannot afford to do otherwise. The English, however, have never hesitated to use a bike at the weekend, leaving their car in the garage, and they do not think of the bicycle as a sign of poverty.

Nevertheless we should not ignore the economic advantages of the bicycle, both to the individual and to society as a whole. For the individual, it is a case of saving the expense of owning and running a car, or of using public transport. What does it cost to ride and maintain a bicycle? About a month's pay every ten years or so. The cost of a good touring bicycle is about 3 per cent of the annual income of a factory worker – as it has been ever since the twenties – and the bike should still be in good condition ten years later. Over those ten years the bike will probably have cost its owner about the same amount again in maintenance if he rides about two

thousand miles a year (eight miles every working day). Special clothing – a waterproof cycling cape or anorak and possibly cycling shoes, trousers and some form of head protection – could amount to another week's pay. It all adds up to about four weeks' pay for twenty thousand miles, a small fraction of the cost of any other form of transport.

Society as a whole also benefits from the use of the bicycle rather than the car. The capacity of roads, bridges and so on is significantly increased; the parking space required is much less. The bicycle requires a much smaller consumption of the earth's non-renewable resources both to make and to run. *The Bicycle Planning Book*, for example, claims that for the energy required to manufacture a single car between seventy and a hundred bicycles can be produced. A rough comparison of weights gives some idea of the savings – a medium-quality bicycle weighs thirty pounds, a car seventy times as much.

Finally, of course, there is the question of pollution. If there were fewer internal combustion engines there would be less carbon monoxide, nitric oxides, hydrocarbon vapours, and heavy metals (particularly lead) released into the atmosphere. The noise level, particularly in urban areas, would be dramatically reduced, a welcome relief. (According to the Transport and Road Research Laboratory over 60 per cent of the population of Britain is subjected daily to noise levels that are unacceptably high.)

There are, of course, a few drawbacks to cycling, but they are not as serious as they are often made out to be. Take the weather, for instance. It is certainly less fun riding in the rain – but it doesn't rain quite as often as is generally assumed. Richard Ballantine, author of the excellent book *Richard's Bicycle Book*, has found that, on average, at any particular spot in the UK, rainfall is recorded between the hours of 8 and 9 a.m. and 5 and 6 p.m. on only twelve days in the year. And if it does rain? There are excellent waterproofs available that will keep you dry even if it rains all day.

Cold is even less of a problem, for cycling will keep you warm even in the most dismal weather. I cycled every day during the exceptionally bad winter of 1978–9, having just returned from sunny California, and felt a lot more comfortable cycling than I did on the odd occasion when I left the bike at home. You will find that what seems, from behind the windscreen of a car, to be miserable weather, turns out to be quite bearable when you are out on your bike.

Use your bicycle and you'll learn to love it more every day!

2

The Parts of a Bicycle

Let's take a closer look at the subject of the book, and establish what the various bits and pieces of a bicycle are called (fig. 2.1).

Not every bicycle looks quite like the one pictured here, nor are the names for the different parts the only ones used. The bicycle illustrated is a ten-speed touring machine; real racing cycles are somewhat lighter and less cluttered, while other bikes are equipped rather more elaborately. You will be shown what differences you are likely to encounter in this respect in the next chapter, which covers choosing the right bike. As for terminology, the main differences will be pointed out as we go along.

Let's start with the *frame*. Quite simply,

it is an assembly of metal tubes joined together at the ends to form a structurally sound geometric design. It is usually like the one shown here, but is sometimes slightly different. In the traditional English ladies' frame, the horizontal top tube between the saddle and handlebars is replaced by a sloping tube to make room for long skirts (although it unfortunately weakens the frame). Some other variants are the *mixte* frame and the *berceau*, both using double bracing tubes from the handlebars down to the rear axle. There is also the small-wheeled bicycle which has been with us since Alec Moulton introduced his delightful, sprung, portable bike in the early sixties. It usually has a frame made up of fewer and thicker tubes, which

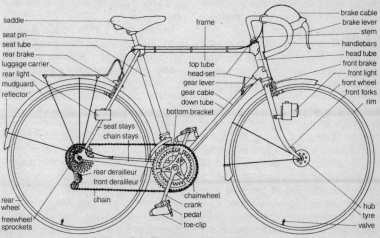

2.1 *The parts of the bicycle*

2.2 Frame variants

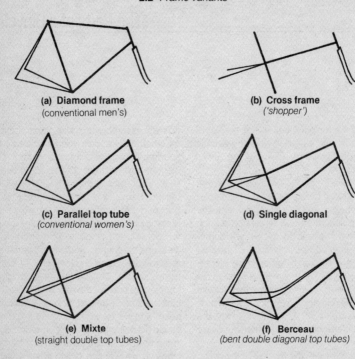

(a) Diamond frame
(conventional men's)

(b) Cross frame
(*'shopper'*)

(c) Parallel top tube
(*conventional women's*)

(d) Single diagonal

(e) Mixte
(straight double top tubes)

(f) Berceau
(*bent double diagonal top tubes*)

makes it less bulky but not as strong nor as rigid. Fig. 2.2 depicts some of the more common frame designs.

The *front forks* are held through the front tube of the frame (called the *head tube*) by a set of ball-bearings known as the *head-set*. The *handlebars* are connected to the forks through the same tube by means of a *stem*, which allows for adjustment of the bars. The *saddle* is attached to another one of the frame tubes, the *seat tube*, by means of a similar device, called the *seat pin*. It too can be adjusted by means of a *binder-bolt*, which clamps the split end of the seat tube together. Further saddle adjustments are possible by means of the clamp that holds the saddle to the seat pin. Americans and some manufacturers refer to the seat pin

as the *seat post*; others call it the *seat pillar*.

The *wheels* are attached to the frame and to the front forks at the flat ends of the frame and fork tubes, called the *fork-ends* or *drop-outs*. They are held in place either by means of axle-nuts or handy little gadgets called *quick-release levers*, which you usually find on good quality road cycles. The wheels themselves consist of the *hubs*, the *spokes*, the *rims* and the *tyres*. The tyre may consist either of the conventional outer cover with a separate inner tube, called a *wired-on* or sometimes (incorrectly) a *clincher* tyre, or of the lighter and more fragile *tubular* ('tub' or 'sew-up') tyre used on competition bicycles, where a very thin tube is sewn inside a light casing, the whole thing being cemented on to the (special) rim.

The rear wheel has one (or more in the case of a derailleur gearing) toothed *sprocket* and usually a *freewheel* to allow forward motion even when the rider is not pedalling. The sprocket is driven via the *chain* from the *crank-set*, which is mounted with ball-bearings in the *bottom bracket*. This is the short cross tube at the point of the frame where the seat tube and the down tube join. The right-hand crank has a larger toothed *chainwheel* which drives the chain (although on ten-speed bikes there are two chainwheels, and on fifteen-speed bikes there are three). The *pedals* are screwed into the ends of the cranks and these are often fitted with *toe-clips* to hold the feet in place.

Then there are the *brakes*. They are usually hand-controlled rim brakes and they may be either *callipers* (on lighter bikes) or pull-rod-operated *roller-lever* or *stirrup brakes* (which are pulled up from the inside of the rims). Other kinds of brakes are seldom seen this side of the English Channel; *back-pedalling brakes* (also called *coaster brakes*) and *hub brakes* (which work very well and are actually made by Sturmey–Archer) are sold mainly abroad. Two types of brake common in Japan are the *disc brake* and the *band brake* (also known as the *contraction brake*). The familiar calliper brakes come in two versions, called *side-pulls* or *centre-pulls*. It's hard to say which is better, since their quality depends more on how well they are made than on their type. However, the aluminium versions are invariably superior to the steel models.

Finally, there are the trimmings and accessories. Some are essential and some are trivial; only the important ones are mentioned here. *Mudguards*, called *fenders* across the Atlantic, are a must for touring in wet weather, and plastic ones are light enough not to add much extra weight. The *luggage carrier* on the back is useful for anything that won't fit inside a saddlebag. *Lights* are so important (and so often ignored) that I've devoted an entire chapter to them. Use them and keep them in operating order – they can extend not only your cycling day but your life too! Then there are *bells*, *pumps*, *water bottles*, and, on most touring machines, a *chainguard*, a totally useless device (like the prop stand, which is not even worth mentioning), unless it fully encloses the chain on all sides.

All this adds up to a large number of accessories. However, unlike the motorist, you may be able to choose all or most of them for yourself. In fact, most bicycle manufacturers don't make all these components themselves. They often just build the frame, buying the other parts from specialist suppliers and mounting them in their factory. Consequently, you can just buy your own frame and choose the other components to suit yourself, getting a bicycle mechanic (if you can find one) to put it all together or getting all the fun – and frustration – from doing the job yourself.

If you are unprepared for the task – that is, if you don't know how all the parts fit together – you will almost certainly get into trouble. One of the major reasons for this is that many bicycle parts are made to any one of three different national standards. This is explained in more detail in the chapters that follow but what it means is that components (especially those that are threaded, like the various bearings and freewheels) may be built to either French, Italian or British standards and are often not interchangeable. On top of all this, many cheaper and simpler components, specifically made to fit one bicycle manufacturer's range, may also turn out to be incompatible. Seat pins seem to be available in sizes that don't fit your seat tube; and tyres, rims and spoke-

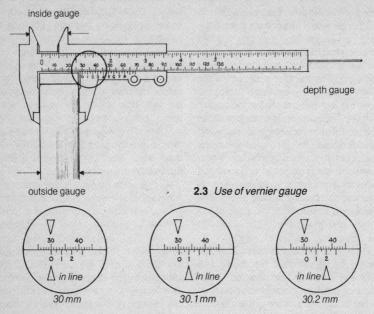

inside gauge

depth gauge

outside gauge

2.3 *Use of vernier gauge*

in line

30 mm

in line

30.1 mm

in line

30.2 mm

lengths confuse even the most experienced cyclists.

The way to cope with this confusing mass of dimensions and details is to know what you're talking about. First learn to use a *vernier*, a remarkably accurate measuring tool that will help you determine dimensions with an accuracy of ± 0.1 mm or 0.005 in. Fig. 2.3 shows you how it's done. You might also do well to become familiar with the metric system, since it's used for most of the dimensions that are worth checking – even those on entirely English bicycles.

Fig. 2.4 shows the most important characteristics of a *screw thread*. Each

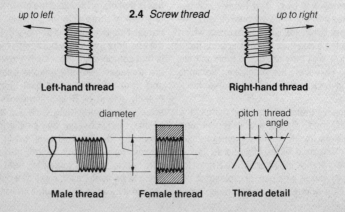

up to left

2.4 *Screw thread*

up to right

Left-hand thread

Right-hand thread

diameter

Male thread

Female thread

pitch   thread angle

Thread detail

threaded connection consists of two parts: one with a *male* thread; the other with a *female* thread. Depending on which way the spiral is wound, the thread will be either *left-handed* or *right-handed*. The right-handed thread is more common in the case of ordinary screws. But on every bike there are a number of threaded connections that are subjected to rotating forces, and some of these require a left-handed thread. An example of this is the left pedal.

When dealing with screw threads, other common terms are the nominal *diameter*, which is always measured across the male part, and the *pitch*, which is the number of threads per inch of thread length. Pitch is expressed in tpi (threads per inch) or, in the case of metric threads, it is simply measured in millimetres. Two screws with the same diameter may well have a different pitch.

There is just one more detail which I have to discuss – the *ball-bearing*. Ball-bearings are essential to the bicycle. On every bike there are at least twelve sets of them, and their adjustment, accuracy and state of lubrication probably has more effect on the quality of the bike's performance than any one other factor. Fig. 2.5 shows a typical ball-bearing assembly on a bicycle. It is an adjustable type (unlike the ones found on most cars and other pieces of machinery) and it is extremely light and versatile, reducing friction and

absorbing forces in several different directions. Bearing assemblies are lubricated with light grease which fills the space between the balls. Adjustment is often required to compensate for wear – possibly every thousand miles or so. To adjust the bearing assembly, loosen the *lock-nut*, lift the little *lock-washer* and turn the adjustable *cone* a fraction until it is tighter or looser as required. Then hold the cone in place with one spanner, while tightening the lock-nut with another. If the balls are held in a retainer, they must be

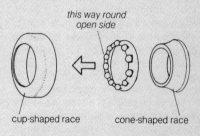

*this way round
open side*

cup-shaped race   cone-shaped race

2.6 *Installing a bearing retainer*

installed as shown in fig. 2.6: i.e., with the open side towards the cup-shaped race.

So much for those items that are common to all bicycles; the following chapters will examine the specific characteristics and parts of one particular machine: your own bicycle.

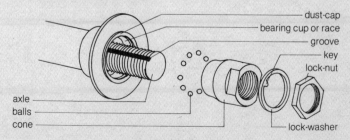

dust-cap
bearing cup or race
groove
key
lock-nut

axle
balls
cone

lock-washer

2.5 *Ball-bearing detail*

There are as many different kinds of bicycle as there are fish in the sea. This chapter describes the various models available and their advantages and disadvantages. I'll deal with the questions of weight and comfort, and of speed and image. Unfortunately I can't tell you very much about the most interesting factor of all – the cost. That, of course, is because of inflation. By the time this manuscript reaches the printer, every price I might quote would be out of date. So all that can be considered are the relative prices.

The first principle of bicycle economics could be that what is heaviest is cheapest. Fortunately, there's a good side to this: it means that you can save yourself a lot of money if you're willing to expend the extra energy necessary to ride a somewhat heavier bike. Of course, excess weight can be eliminated by gradually substituting more expensive light materials and components for cheap, heavier ones, but there is a lot more to the selection of a bicycle than weight alone. There are, in fact, distinct and recognizable categories into which a bicycle can fall, each with its own special uses.

THE 'ROADSTER'

Though it is really only the name of one particular Raleigh model, 'Roadster' is also the general term for just about every bike that is associated with everyday, dull

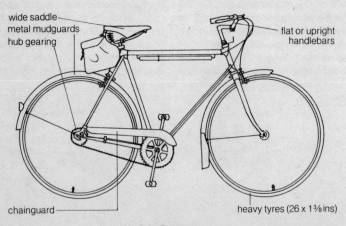

wide saddle
metal mudguards
hub gearing

flat or upright
handlebars

chainguard

heavy tyres (26 x 1⅜ ins)

3.1 *Roadster*

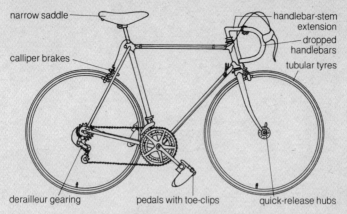

narrow saddle

handlebar-stem extension

dropped handlebars

calliper brakes

tubular tyres

derailleur gearing

pedals with toe-clips

quick-release hubs

3.2 *Road-racing bicycle*

cycling. Yet it's by no means a bad bike, especially in the more elaborate and expensive versions. These, however, seem to be built primarily for export to the continent, where they are regarded as excellent for day-to-day cycling and touring with any amount of luggage.

The 'roadster' has a conventional frame, and there is a parallel bar model for women. The wheels usually measure 26 ins (the diameter measured across the inflated tyre) with rather wide tyres and quite a solid tread pattern. Flat handlebars and a wide 'mattress' saddle make this bike suitable for short trips, but rather tiring for a long run. It comes equipped with mudguards, chainguard and often a luggage carrier. On superior models, the chainguard fully encloses the chain and sometimes the normal calliper or stirrup brakes are replaced by hub brakes, which are more reliable. Gear-change – if provided – is accomplished with the simple and reliable three-speed hub. This kind of bicycle usually weighs between 35 and 40 lb.

THE ROAD-RACING BICYCLE

If you want this kind of bike, you will have to pay for it! There are, however, versions of this type of machine that cost little more than a good 'roadster' and ride very well. Unlike the 'roadster', it has no mudguards, no carrier, no chainguard and no lighting. Handlebars are dropped and the saddle is narrow and hard. It has derailleur gearing – usually ten speeds – and the pedals are equipped with toe-clips. The wheels are slightly larger in diameter (27 ins) and very narrow. They are held in the frame by means of the quick-release levers that I described earlier. Many of the parts on this bicycle are of aluminium or, to be more correct, *light metal* or *aluminium alloy* (a 'mixture' of aluminium and several other metals which is as light as aluminium but much stronger). This results in a total weight of about 22 lb (10 kg) for the entire machine and significantly less for the most exclusive versions, which may cost up to ten times more than a simple 'roadster'.

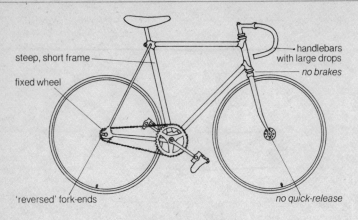

steep, short frame

handlebars with large drops

no brakes

fixed wheel

'reversed' fork-ends

no quick-release

3.3 *Track-racing bicycle*

THE TRACK-RACING BICYCLE

This is another version of the racing bicycle but one that is used for racing on a track instead of on the open road. It differs from the road-racing machine, in that it has no derailleur and does not even have brakes. Since changes of terrain which call for gear changes do not occur on racing tracks, this bicycle has a simple *fixed wheel*: no gear-change mechanism and no freewheel. Although there are some other differences, it can be said that the track bicycle has the appearance of a stripped-down version of the road-racing bicycle.

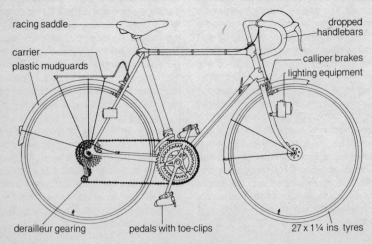

racing saddle

dropped handlebars

carrier

plastic mudguards

calliper brakes

lighting equipment

derailleur gearing

pedals with toe-clips

27 x 1¼ ins tyres

3.4 *Touring bicycle*

THE TOURING BICYCLE

I do not want to be accused of trying to persuade anyone, but this is probably the machine that will suit you best, unless you have a delivery round (in which case you might prefer the 'roadster') or unless you plan to race. This bicycle looks like a cross between a 'roadster' and a road-racing machine, and that is just what it is. It makes use of the lighter and more precise technology developed for the racing bicycle and applies it to a design that lends itself to touring and everyday use. Because of its slightly different frame geometry, it is considered rather more comfortable than a bicycle built strictly for racing, but it is made according to the same general principles. It has narrow 27-in wheels, light components, derailleur gears, dropped handlebars, and everything else. It is equipped with plastic or light metal mudguards, a luggage carrier and lighting. The weight of this machine may be as little as 22 lb (10 kg), but it is usually about 30 lb (13–14 kg). Although there are women's models with some form of lowered crossbar design or the *mixte* frame, most women tourists prefer to ride the conventional men's design, which is more rigid.

THE 'SHOPPER'

Once more I am using the name of a Raleigh model in place of a general term. I am doing this because there is no better universally accepted description. The first bicycle of this kind was the Moulton. This was designed as a portable machine with rubber spring elements to overcome the effects of the roughness of the road – very necessary when wheels are as small as they are on this kind of machine. Today's 'shopper' models all lack the springs that made the original Moulton so comfortable. There are several brands available. An interesting example is the Bickerton portable bicycle which is made largely of aluminium. It is very compact and is really easy to carry. Wheel-sizes on 'shopper' bicycles vary from 14 ins to 22 ins (the latter being preferable if no suspension is used). Some versions of this cycle can be folded or parted so that they can be stored and handled easily, and saddle and

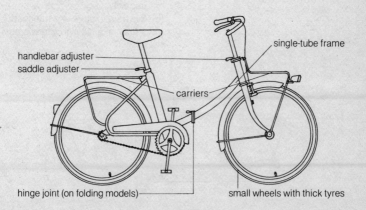

handlebar adjuster
saddle adjuster
carriers
single-tube frame
hinge joint (on folding models)
small wheels with thick tyres

3.5 *'Shopper' bicycle*

handlebar heights are readily adjustable. They are ideal for shopping, but hardly suitable for longer tours. Though British Rail is no longer quite as unkind to the cyclist as when Moulton designed the first portable model, it is probably fair to say that the cycling commuter still has enough problems to justify investing in a portable bicycle.

CHILDREN'S BICYCLES

Bicycles for children are made in about as many different styles as adult models. And there is also the monstrosity that probably saved the British bicycle industry from total disaster in the sixties – the 'chopper'. The 'chopper' is the only bicycle that I truly abhor. Even the unicycle makes more sense than this design. It combines all the elements that make cycling less efficient and less safe, and it was built as an imitation of something else, not as an original bicycle. The other kinds of children's bikes will be dealt with in detail in chapter 10.

THE TANDEM

Yes, 'Daisy' could still look 'sweet' today. In fact, the tandem is becoming increasingly popular as more and more people are going back to cycle-touring. Several major manufacturers now offer quite satisfactory simple tandems at reasonable prices. But the tandem is also available in more sporty versions, including the original racing tandems designed to be short (and therefore rather uncomfortable) and made by specialist frame builders.

The tandem is a lot of fun and has some significant advantages:

(a) It is faster than a single bicycle on the level or downhill.
(b) It allows partners of different strengths to stay together.
(c) It makes riding with children safer.
(d) It can be ridden by blind or otherwise handicapped partners.

But it also has its drawbacks:

(a) A tandem may be more expensive than two single bikes and you'll still need these as well.
(b) It is hard to ride uphill.
(c) It is difficult to brake.
(d) It has a limited luggage-handling capacity.
(e) It is hard to store and transport.
(f) It may be difficult to find spares.

3.6 *Tandem*

3.7 *Tricycle*

THE TRICYCLE

Probably the most typically English of all forms of cycle, the 'trike' still has hundreds of supporters. Many of these are members of the *Tricycle Association*; they ride their 'barrows', as they fondly call their machines, with determination and with surprising skill. The problems involved in riding a trike are not those that you might at first imagine. A good tricycle is essentially a modified touring bike as far as the quality of its components are concerned. There are kits available for converting a bicycle into its threewheeled form, but a better solution is to buy one that was originally designed as a trike. At least one frame-builder (Ken Rogers, see Appendix for address) specializes in building and equipping fine quality tricycles.

4

I have no wish to send you out immediately to buy yourself a new bicycle. It is quite likely that the one you have is good enough. But, in case you are thinking of buying a new cycle, this is as good a time as any to discuss how to go about it. I have already described the different kinds of machines available, how they differ from each other and what to look for, so that now leaves only the pleasant task of choosing and purchasing a bike.

American bicycle books usually advise you to go to what they describe as 'your local pro-bike shop'. Unfortunately, things are not so straightforward in the country where the modern bicycle was born; in many parts of Britain, you will probably head for the nearest shop selling toys, radios, hardware and a few cycles. But the advice has some justification: the more professional the bicycle dealer, the better will be your chances of finding what you need. And he may even give you sensible advice as well. So the most important thing is to find the shop with the most bicycles, and the minimum of other merchandise.

Once again – as in the days before the decline of the bicycle industry – it is possible to find many different makes and models. Besides Raleigh, there are several other domestic manufacturers, such as Dawes, Viscount and Mercian. There is also a steadily increasing range of imported bicycles from France and several other countries. If what you are looking for is a more unusual and special-ized machine, you will be interested in the products of the many independent frame-builders and manufacturers of small series.

Whatever your eventual choice, the catalogues of the major manufacturers are a good place to start your search. Study the brochures, and list what you are looking for as regards style, weight, components and accessories. You may find it helpful to fill in the form on pages 186–7, but be prepared to revise your list as you progress with your selection, since you may find reasons to change your mind about the desirability of certain features. As a rough guide, you may find table 4.1 (pp. 30–31) helpful. It lists the major advantages of the various types of machines and components.

JUDGING QUALITY

Even if you have decided not to buy a new bicycle but to try to pick up a second-hand one, you may be confronted with a choice between two or more machines that look very similar. You can usually get a fair idea of the quality of a bicycle by comparing some simple details. Here is what you should look for.

First, compare the frames, in particular the lugs connecting the different frame tubes (fig. 4.1). The appearance of these lugged connections is a clear indication of the quality of the frame. They must be cleanly finished, without any coarse edges, splutters of brazing metal around

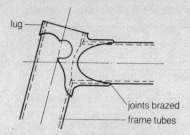

4.1 *Lugged frame-joint*

them or gaps between tubes and lugs. It is worthwhile noting here that on some frames the tubes are brazed or welded together without lugs. Here, too, smooth surfaces indicate good quality.

Another important detail is the quality of the drop-outs (the flat plates at the ends of the forks and stays in which the wheels are held, fig. 4.2). The thickest drop-outs

'Reynolds 531' (five-three-one, not five-thirty-one) or of a similar material such as Columbus, Ishiwatha, Vitus, Falk or Tange. In chapter 11, I'll discuss the implications of these details, but the best frames, for lighter bicycles at least, are those made with either 'plain-gauge' or 'butted' alloy tubes. Slightly less impressive are those made with other cold-drawn seamless tubes. Anyway, it is a good idea to look for a label, read it carefully and ask the person you're buying from, assuming that he knows what he is talking about.

In addition to the frame, it may be worth checking the materials used for most of the other major parts, such as the wheel rims, hubs, brakes, cranks, chainwheels, handlebars, seat pin and so on. These parts will almost invariably be of a higher quality if they are made of aluminium rather than simply of steel. Here, too,

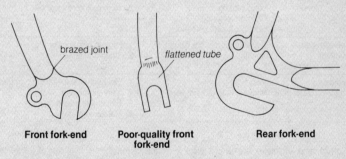

Front fork-end   **Poor-quality front fork-end**   **Rear fork-end**

4.2 *Drop-outs or fork-ends*

are usually the better ones and, once again, the attachment welding must be smooth. Bicycle frames on which the ends of the forks and stays are simply flattened are of poor quality.

Next, you should find out what the bike is made of. There may be a label on the seat tube telling you what material has been used for the frame. It may, for example, be made entirely or partly of

appearance is often a good indication of quality. A smoother finish often means better quality.

SECOND-HAND BICYCLES

The best bicycle I have ever owned was second-hand. It was a superbly equipped Carlton which had been specially built and which weighed a mere 24 lb complete with

Table 4.1 *Advantages and disadvantages of different types of bicycle equipment*

TYPE	ADVANTAGES	DISADVANTAGES
Weight of complete bicycle		
Very light: less than 24 lb (11 kg)	1. Usually of the highest quality 2. Easy to ride and handle	1. Usually expensive 2. Rather fragile 3. Not suitable for heavy loads
Light: 24–32 lb (11–15 kg)	1. Usually of high quality 2. Reasonably priced 3. Comfortable to ride and handle	1. Rather fragile 2. Not suitable for the heaviest loads and roughest terrain
Moderately heavy: 32–38 lb (15–18 kg)	1. Reasonably priced 2. Sturdy, suitable for carrying loads and for rough terrain	1. Quality unpredictable 2. Rather hard to handle
Heavy: over 38 lb (18 kg)	1. Cheap 2. Sturdy	1. Quality often uncertain 2. Rarely comfortable to ride and handle
Wheels		
27 × 1¼ ins or narrower (French size: 700 × 32 mm)	1. Low rolling resistance 2. Comfortable 3. Light-weight	1. Fragile 2. Unsuitable for poor road surfaces 3. May not last long 4. Often quite expensive
26 × 1⅜ ins (French size: 650 × 37 mm)	1. Less fragile 2. Long-lasting 3. Comfortable ride 4. Suitable for rough roads	1. Rather heavy 2. High rolling resistance
Small wheel sizes of up to 22 ins (French size: 550 mm)	1. Suitable for transportable bicycles	1. High rolling resistance 2. Uncomfortable
27-in tubulars (French size: 700 mm)	1. Very light 2. Minimal rolling resistance	1. Only suitable for racing bicycles 2. Very expensive 3. Extremely fragile 4. Hard to repair

mudguards and luggage carrier. It was later stolen by a discriminating thief and probably went back to the second-hand bicycle market! There are at least three conclusions to be drawn from this: first, you can often pick up an excellent bike second-hand; second, beware of bicycle thieves; and, third, take care, when buying a second-hand bike, that it is not 'hot'.

The first thing to check on a second-hand bike is the frame number, usually found underneath the bottom bracket. The second thing to do is to ask for evi-

dence of purchase. If either of these give cause for suspicion, you'd do better to contact the police rather than to buy the bike, however great a bargain it may seem to be.

Buying a second-hand bicycle also differs from buying a new one in that you need to check for wear and tear. Normal wear must be expected as a result of age, but any bike that looks or feels neglected probably is. Although it may, in fact, be all right, it will require very close inspection.

If a bicycle has been in an accident, it may be beyond repair and no longer safe

Rims

Aluminium	1. Light-weight 2. Improved braking	1. Fragile 2. Expensive
Chrome-plated steel	1. Less fragile 2. Cheap	1. Very poor braking when wet 2. Heavy
Stainless steel	1. Moderately good braking 2. Sturdy and durable 3. Moderate weight	1. Expensive

Brakes

Centre-pull callipers	1. Effective 2. Easy to centre 3. Light 4. High quality available 5. Usually reasonably priced	1. Less prestigious than top-quality side-pulls
Side-pull callipers	1. Effective 2. Very light 3. Available in very prestigious versions (recommended for racing only)	1. Quality varies greatly 2. Good ones very expensive 3. Hard to centre
Stirrup (roller-lever)	1. Reliable because of absence of cables	1. Very heavy 2. Less effective than callipers 3. Hard to adjust and maintain 4. Makes changing a wheel difficult
Hub brakes (internal expansion)	1. Extremely reliable 2. Effective even when wet	1. Rather heavy 2. Hard to maintain

Gear-change mechanism

Derailleur	1. Allows flexibility in spread of gears 2. Light-weight	1. Fragile 2. Requires frequent adjustment and maintenance
Hub gear (3-speed)	1. Easy to operate 2. Easy to maintain and adjust 3. Very reliable	1. Rather heavy 2. Not flexible 3. Allows only few gears which (in currently available models) are spread too far apart for most types of terrain

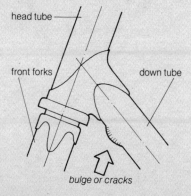

head tube

front forks

down tube

bulge or cracks

4.3 *Frame damage*

to ride. In order to tell whether or not this has happened, you have simply to check two points. These are the alignment and distortion of the forks and frame. Distortion of the frame is usually shown by the presence of bulges or cracks in the paintwork just behind the head-set on the down tube (fig. 4.3). The forks will appear to be

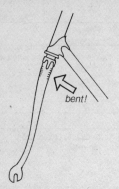

4.4 *Bent front forks*

bent back (fig. 4.4) or, if the damage is in their upper section, the steering will be stiff and uneven. Wheel alignment can be checked by looking along both wheels from behind (fig. 4.5).

wheels at different angles

4.5 *Wheels not aligned*

I would definitely advise against buying any bicycle with frame damage. It may be possible to replace the forks if they are the only parts that are damaged but, on an expensive bike, this will be quite costly.

Similarly, other parts can be replaced, but this, too, may not be cheap, especially if you can't do the job yourself. You would be well advised to check the cost of all individual parts that need replacing, noting the type and quality of the components, before you commit yourself to buying.

CHOOSING THE RIGHT SIZE

With the exception of the small-wheeled 'shopper', bicycles are supplied in various sizes, measured down the seat tube of the frame, between the centre of the bottom bracket and the top of the seat lug. This 'frame-size' may be expressed either in inches or – as is becoming more and more common with racing frames – in centimetres. Typical frame-sizes are 19–22 ins (48–56 cm) for women's bikes and 21–25 ins (53–64 cm) for men's models. Some shops make the selection easier by having a frame-fitting stand (fig. 4.6) to determine frame-size and extension length.

To decide which size you need you may use one of several methods. For a standard men's frame the easiest is simply to

stem-length adjustment

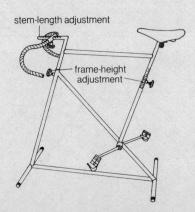

frame-height adjustment

4.6 *Frame-fitting stand*

straddle the bike (or, if you are buying just a frame, to straddle the frame when it is fitted with a pair of wheels of the appropriate size). You should be able to stand astride the frame, just clearing the top tube when your feet are resting on the ground. A more abstract method – one that will tell you what frame-size you need before you even set foot inside a shop – is to measure your inside leg length and deduct 9 or 10 inches (23–25 cm). Table 1 on page 253 summarizes the frame-sizes that are usually recommended according to this method, as well as data for the seat-height adjustment, discussed in the next chapter.

5

Someone cycling for the first time will probably ride his machine around the block and then collapse with exhaustion. Yet an experienced cyclist may think nothing of riding a hundred miles or so. And there are enthusiasts who cycle non-stop from Land's End to John o' Groats and who, afterwards, instead of understandably refusing to ride ever again, vow to do better next time. Is it the level of physical fitness that varies or does the difference lie in their bikes? Has the novice chosen a bad model, while the long-distance enthusiast has managed to patent a self-propelling secret design?

Of course not! The cycling enthusiast has, as likely as not, also been reduced to sweating and panting in his time, but now he would probably manage almost as well on the old bike left in the garden shed by his father since the Second World War. The difference, then, is neither in the man himself, nor in the machine – it's in knowing how to use the machine. Of course, much of this knowledge can only be gained through practice and from your own experience and mistakes, but you can reduce the entire process to something that can be mastered within a few weeks by following some simple advice. That is the purpose of this chapter. It should show you how to get the most out of your bicycle with less pain and more comfort.

Assuming you have a bicycle that is not far too large or far too small, probably the most important single factor determining the ease and comfort of cycling is the correct adjustment of the seat and handlebars. We'll consider the saddle first. You have a choice between two methods of adjustment. One is according to scientific experiment, while the other is more practical. The scientific method was developed at the Loughborough College of Physical Education and is known as 'the 109 per cent rule'. The scientists at Loughborough simply took a number of cyclists and made them try different saddle positions, each time measuring their physical efficiency. It was proved that the most efficient position was generally the one in which the distance from the pedal-axle to the top of the seat (measured along the seat tube) equalled 109 per cent of the inside-leg measurement. Fig. 5.1 illustrates this, and the results for many

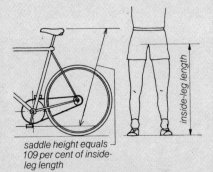

saddle height equals 109 per cent of inside-leg length

5.1 *Determining saddle height (using 'the 109 per cent rule')*

common leg lengths together with the recommended maximum frame-sizes are summarized in table 1 on page 253.

For the practical method, you will need a helper who will hold your cycle while you are testing it for size and who will check that you do it properly. The saddle is at the right height if you can sit on it and reach the pedal in its lowest position with the heel of the foot (as shown in fig. 5.2).

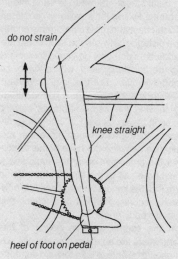

do not strain

knee straight

heel of foot on pedal

5.2 *Determining saddle height (using the practical method)*

The actual adjustment of the saddle height is done by loosening the binder-bolt (fig. 5.3) and sliding the seat pin up or down, then tightening the binder-bolt again when the saddle is in the correct position. Two other adjustments can be made to the saddle. They are both done by means of the saddle clamp, which holds the saddle to the seat pillar. To tilt the top of the saddle to a different angle, loosen the clamp-bolt and move the clamp until it fits into a different serration and the seat is at a more desirable angle. To adjust the forward position of the saddle, loosen the bolt and push the saddle clamp forwards or backwards along the wires or rails that support the saddle cover. Special seat pins will be discussed in chapter 13.

To determine just how far forward the saddle should be, consult fig. 5.4 (p. 36). What is usually recommended is that the knee-joint should be vertically above the front pedal-axle when the cranks are in a horizontal position (assuming that the saddle has previously been adjusted to the correct height).

Now for the handlebars. Once more, we will want to adjust the height, the horizontal position and the angle. The range of possible adjustments depends on the kind of handlebar you are using. On the

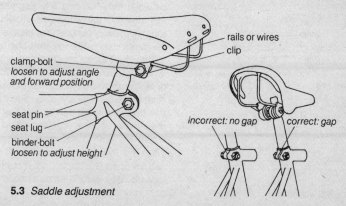

rails or wires
clip
clamp-bolt
loosen to adjust angle and forward position
seat pin
seat lug
binder-bolt
loosen to adjust height

incorrect: no gap   *correct: gap*

5.3 *Saddle adjustment*

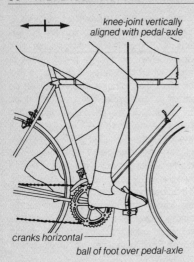

5.4 *Determining saddle position*

top of the handlebar stem is a bolt, some-times (on the slightly more sophisticated models) in the form of a recessed Allen-head screw which requires the use of a special small hexagonal spanner. Loosening this *expander-bolt* will loosen the bar-stem inside the steering-head and allow the handlebars to be moved up or down. A second bolt, the *binder-bolt*, must

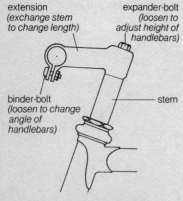

5.5 *Handlebar adjustments*

be loosened to allow adjustment of the angle of the handlebars (fig. 5.5).

The handlebars should preferably be no higher than the saddle, and most cyc-lists would agree that on a touring cycle the highest part of the bars should be one or two inches lower than the top of the saddle. The ends of the handlebars should point downward slightly. In the case of dropped handlebars, this should be quite steep – between ten and fifteen degrees. Riding for a while will soon tell you the best and most comfortable angle. The distance between the saddle and the handlebars can only be varied by replac-ing the handlebar stem with a longer or shorter version. But this is an important measurement and it should not be varied by moving the saddle from its correct position (see above). Though some people take it as a rough guide that the distance between the nose of the saddle and the cross-portion of the handlebars must be equal to the length of the lower arm with the fingers outstretched, the only really accurate method is to check the cyclist's body-angle.

If the saddle and the height of the handlebars are adjusted properly, the rid-er should be able to lean forward comfort-ably with his arms outstretched to grip the top of the bars, resulting in a body angle of between forty-five and fifty degrees. In this position the shoulders should be roughly midway between the saddle and the handlebars, while the arms should be slightly bent to act as shock absorbers. When you use the drops on the handle-bars, the shoulders will come forward a little. Fig. 5.6 will give you an idea of how this might look, but don't forget that ulti-mately only your own comfort will tell you whether or not the adjustment is right for *you*. The seat angle, in particular, may require some fine-tuning: tilt the saddle forward just a little if it remains uncomfort-able after some use.

5.6 *Correct riding position*

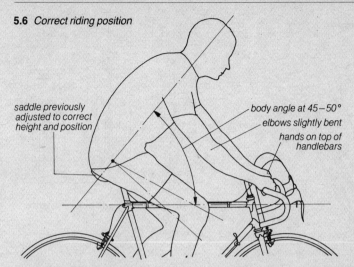

saddle previously
adjusted to correct
height and position

body angle at 45–50°
elbows slightly bent
hands on top of
handlebars

Now that we have made the most important adjustments to the bicycle, it is at last time to take it out for a ride. Of course, the *way* you cycle will also affect whether or not you get a comfortable ride, and I have briefly summarized below the most important points of good cycling technique.

1. Pedal with the ball of your foot directly on the centre of the pedal-axe – cycling shoes and toe-clips make it easier to achieve this position.

2. Do not simply push your foot up and down, but aim at a 'rounded' or circular motion, pushing down and forward at the top of the stroke and down and back near the bottom taking the weight off your foot on the way up. The easiest way to learn this motion is to ride a bicycle with a fixed wheel.

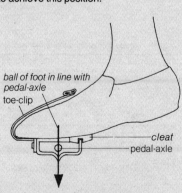

ball of foot in line with
pedal-axle
toe-clip

cleat
pedal-axle

5.7 *Correct foot position*

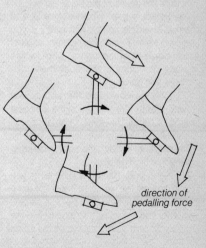

direction of
pedalling force

5.8 *Correct pedalling movement*

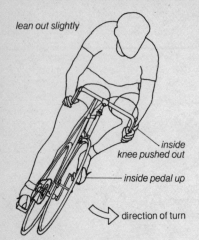

lean out slightly

inside knee pushed out

inside pedal up

direction of turn

5.9 *Cornering at speed*

5.10 *Body profile and wind resistance*

3. Avoid 'bottoming out' your inside pedal when taking a sharp bend (or when making a wide-radius turn at high speed). Keep your inside pedal up and transfer your weight away from it by pushing your inside knee away from the bike and keeping your upper body bent low and leaning towards the inside of the bend.

4. Select a gear which allows you to spin the pedals lightly, especially if you have to travel over a long distance. Most beginners select too high a gear – which results in discomfort, because they have to push too hard.

5. Change down into the appropriate lower gear before you reach the steepest part of a climb. However, try to approach short hills at high speed, since you may be able to gather enough momentum to keep going in a high gear.

6. Keep your body low whenever you cycle against the wind. Do the same thing when you are aiming to cycle fast, since – whether you are riding into a head-wind or not – your own speed will create the effect of one.

7. When travelling in a group – especially if riding at high speed or against the wind – use the technique which racers call riding in a 'bunch' or an 'echelon'. Stay very close together in a formation that will increase the shelter from the wind provided by the rider in front.

8. Keep your tyres well inflated to minimize loss of power and to protect both tyres and rims from bumpy road surfaces.

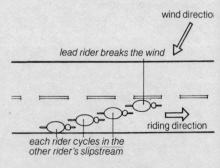

wind direction

lead rider breaks the wind

riding direction

each rider cycles in the other rider's slipstream

5.11 *Bunching to minimize wind resistance*

9. Wear comfortable clothing. Do not wear anything that chafes or pinches or anything that flaps in the wind or might get caught in the moving parts of the cycle.

10. Eat and drink in moderation, preferably little and often rather than large meals and large quantities of liquid.

11. Rest before you become exhausted, but not too often or for too long. One ten- or fifteen-minute break every one to two hours is quite sufficient.

12. Beware of sunburn, even in our part of the world. Only clothing or sunscreen (e.g., zinc oxide) will do any good. Most sun-tan lotions offer no protection at all.

13. Don't set out without a pump, a lock, tools and some money – it's very reassuring to know you can get home or at least get help if things do not go according to plan.

14. Check your bicycle regularly to ensure a proper state of adjustment and maintenance. Have all urgent work done immediately or, with the aid of Part IV of this book, learn to do these jobs yourself.

6

Few bicycles are sold these days without some form of gear-change mechanism, whether this is a three-speed hub or a derailleur system offering anything up to twenty-one speeds. Do I really need them and how do I use them? you may ask. I will try to answer these questions in the present chapter and at the same time also try to come to some conclusions regarding the choice between a hub or a derailleur system.

The purpose of the gear-change mechanism is to allow the cyclist to adapt the 'drive-train' of the bike to varying weather and road conditions. Imagine riding a single-speed bicycle on a level road with no headwind. You might be pedalling at a rate of about sixty crank-revolutions per minute (this is known as 'cadence') and it might require a noticeable but not uncomfortable amount of effort. Your cycling speed would perhaps be about 12 mph (19 km/h). But as soon as you came to a hill or encountered a sudden headwind, you would have two possible ways of adapting to the changed conditions. You could either push harder, continuing to ride at the same speed, or you could pedal more slowly. In the second case, you would avoid having to increase your effort, but of course your speed would be reduced. However, like most machines, the human body operates to produce energy most efficiently within a rather narrow range of speeds. For the human body the most efficient cadence while cycling appears to be anything upward of 60 rpm,

although it is higher when the effort is spread over a longer period and closer to the 60 rpm figure for short bursts of greater energy. Purely for convenience, I'll use the 60 rpm figure here.

To maintain the cadence of 60 rpm while also maintaining the same road-speed when climbing a hill, you will need to increase the pressure on the pedals quite considerably and exert a lot more effort, which is less comfortable and more tiring. So you're in a predicament: either option, whether you choose to pedal more slowly or push harder, will result in less comfort and more fatigue. Gears exist in order to solve this problem. Although your road-speed will inevitably be reduced, they allow you to continue pedalling at a comfortable rate, without increasing the pedal pressure unacceptably.

What applies to an uphill ride, where you must change into a lower gear, also applies to a downhill ride. In this case, you must change to a higher gear in order to reach a higher road-speed without increasing the cadence to an uncomfortable rate. It is also worth mentioning that you should choose a *low* gear when accelerating from standstill.

Gear-change mechanisms make it possible to get the best use out of the energy and effort that you put into cycling. Whatever the conditions, they enable you to pedal at a comfortable rate and exert a comfortable amount of force on the pedals while achieving the maximum speed possible without having to push yourself beyond the human body's most efficient range of operation. Gears mean that you get more mileage for fewer aching muscles.

HOW MANY GEARS?

Depending on the range of conditions you expect to encounter, you may require a large or a small number of gears. While three basic conditions – 'normal', 'easy' and 'hard' – may make it seem, on the surface, that at least three gears are needed, the differences between these three categories may be either a great deal or only very little. Furthermore, you may encounter very different conditions within the range of extremes catered for by only one gear – for example, 'hard', 'very hard' or 'impossible'. To cope with the greatest number of these conditions, it might seem best to have the highest possible number of gears, but then having more gears also means spending more money and can often give more trouble. We can therefore only conclude that the number of gears and the differences between them must be chosen to suit the range of conditions which you will encounter.

For mountainous terrain, or perhaps for hilly districts with strong winds, your gears should be spaced further apart than if you usually ride on level roads without excessive winds. For this reason, a racer may want his gears closer together than a touring cyclist carrying luggage. The racer will also be more likely to concentrate on fine-tuning his gears to ensure that he achieves the maximum possible speed – and this calls for the highest possible number of gears placed quite close together.

HUB OR DERAILLEUR GEARING?

The different gears on a bicycle may be provided with either a built-in hub gear or a derailleur system, which is delicate, in spite of its crude appearance. Before we become involved in examining the intricacies of the two gearing systems, let's consider the advantages and disadvantages of each set out in table 6.1.

It should be clear from this that derailleur gearing is the way to achieve the greatest efficiency within the widest range of differing conditions. Hub gearing answers the need for a reliable all-weather system that requires very little maintenance. The difficulty with the three-speed hubs currently available is that the three gears are spaced too far apart to

Table 6.1 *Advantages and disadvantages of derailleur and hub gearing*

SYSTEM	ADVANTAGES	DISADVANTAGES
Derailleur	1. Allows many different gears 2. Allows flexibility in gear spread 3. Light-weight	1. Fragile 2. Expensive if of good quality 3. Needs frequent adjustment, lubrication and maintenance 4. Sensitive to snow, mud and dirt
Hub gear	1. Hard wearing 2. Requires little maintenance 3. Relatively insensitive to the elements 4. Rather heavy 5. Easier to shift and adjust	1. Offers a limited number of gears 2. Inflexible in gear spread 3. Expensive to install 4. Harder to repair if this is ever necessary

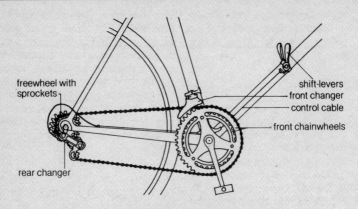

freewheel with sprockets

rear changer

shift-levers
front changer
control cable
front chainwheels

6.1 *Derailleur gearing system*

meet normal conditions. The Sturmey–Archer S5 five-speed hub – though difficult to find and very expensive – is the answer to all our problems. It has the right number of different gears and they are better spaced than on the three-speed hub. The S5 also has all the advantages of the hub gear regarding toughness, reliability and ease of maintenance. What I use myself, however, is the derailleur. I like the flexibility of gear selection that this offers, and I have learned to cope with its disadvantages, which I can reduce by keeping the equipment clean, well-lubricated and properly adjusted.

Derailleur Gearing

On a bicycle with derailleur gearing, the rear wheel is equipped with a 'cluster' of several sprockets, each with a different number of teeth. A shift-lever is connected to the changer or derailleur by a 'Bowden cable' and this may be installed either on the down tube of the frame, at the handlebar ends or on the handlebar stem. Changing the position of the shift-lever will cause the derailleur to move the chain from one sprocket to another, provided that you are pedalling forward with

reduced force. The right-hand shift-lever controls the rear derailleur; the one on the left controls the front derailleur.

To engage a low gear, the chain is put on a large rear sprocket, which usually means that the shift-lever is pulled towards the rider. When the lever is pushed forward the derailleur moves sideways and pulls the chain on to a small sprocket – thus selecting a higher gear. To shift to a higher gear with the front derailleur, the left-hand lever is pulled back towards the rider so that the chain moves on to the larger front chainwheel. The smaller front chainwheel is selected when the lever is pushed forward, giving a lower gear. Most changes are made, however, with the rear derailleur and only a few with the front one.

A ten-speed bicycle has two chainwheels in front and five sprockets in the rear, which in theory at least gives ten (two sets of five) different speeds or gears. However, two of these combinations are not recommended. When the chain crosses over from the large chainwheel to the largest sprocket or from the small chainwheel to the smallest sprocket, the system is impractical, be-

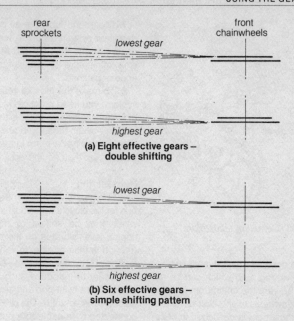

rear
sprockets

front
chainwheels

lowest gear

highest gear

**(a) Eight effective gears –
double shifting**

lowest gear

highest gear

**(b) Six effective gears –
simple shifting pattern**

6.2 *Possible gear combinations on a ten-speed derailleur*

cause there is excessive chain torsion and derailleur interference. This leaves a mere eight gears, not all of which may be significantly different from one another. In fact, there are often only six gears which are easily distinguishable. Fig. 6.2 demonstrates the different combinations possible with a ten-speed derailleur system. Depending on the selection of the chainwheel and sprocket sizes, you may have up to eight different gears, and the sequence in which they are engaged may also vary.

The method of selecting chainwheels and sprockets with the right number of teeth is a matter of gearing theory, and this will be discussed in the next chapter. Here, we will concentrate on how to use the derailleur gearing system to its greatest advantage.

1. Start off in a low gear: you'll become much less tired if you do this. Change down while slowing down to stop in order to be ready in a low gear again.

2. Always continue to pedal forwards with reduced force when shifting. This means that you must change down to a lower gear *before* you have lost too much momentum.

3. Shift only one derailleur at a time – either the rear derailleur alone or only the front derailleur. If two shifts are required, they must be done separately.

4. The shift-levers must be moved quickly but not further than necessary. Since most derailleurs have no set positions for the different gears, precise shifting has to be learnt. Listen for tell-tale signals: if the chain 'grinds' or sounds rough, you haven't yet found the correct position for the lever.

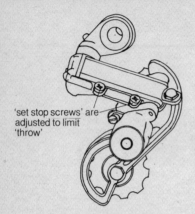

'set stop screws' are
adjusted to limit
'throw'

6.3 *Derailleur adjustment*

5. Each derailleur has at least two 'set stop screws' (fig. 6.3) which can be adjusted to prevent the chain from jumping off the chainwheels or sprockets. The process of adjustment is described in chapters 31 and 32.

6. The screws or wing-nuts on the shift-levers are there for a purpose. Keep them tightened to ensure that the levers stay in the position you want.

7. Clean and lubricate all parts of the derailleur system regularly, including the chain and the shift-cables. At the same time, make sure the cables are not damaged or pinched.

8. To make the most of your derailleur system, you need practice. Make a habit of shifting whenever there is the slightest reason – since those who are lazy in the use of gears never learn to derive the full benefit from their equipment.

Hub Gearing

The hub gear is essentially a rear-wheel hub for the bicycle with a built-in gear box, which may be shifted by means of a control-lever situated on the handlebars (though in their attempt to vary the basic design of bicycles, Sturmey–Archer felt it necessary to introduce such alternative controls as a twist-grip and an awkwardly placed console-shift). The control-lever is connected by a cable to a push-rod that runs through the centre of the axle. The adjustment mechanism is situated at the connection of the cable and the push-rod.

The built-in gears allow the hub – and with it the entire rear wheel – to run at a

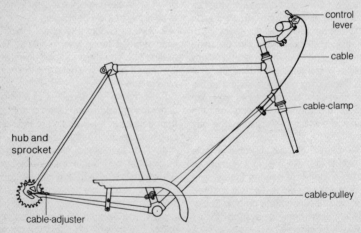

control
lever

cable

cable-clamp

hub and
sprocket

cable-pulley

cable-adjuster

6.4 *Hub-gearing system*

different speed from the sprocket. The wheel turns more slowly in a low gear and faster in a high gear. the 'normal' gear speed occurs when the hub is turning at the same speed as the sprocket. The method of operation will be outlined in chapter 16.

Here is a short list of points to note when riding a cycle with hub gearing.

1. The hub gear is best shifted while pedalling forwards with reduced force, which means that you should shift before you lose momentum.

2. Check the adjustment occasionally. You will be shown how to do this in chapter 32.

3. Lubricate the hub with light mineral oil. It needs about a teaspoonful once a month.

4. Check regularly that the control-cable (or cables in the case of a five-speed hub) runs freely and is not pinched, damaged or frayed.

7   Gearing Theory

It is useful, and indeed often necessary, to have a measure of comparison for the different gears on a bicycle. In a car you have first, second, third, fourth and often more gears, and once you are familiar with the engine's flexibility you will easily know in which gear you should be driving at any time. But since the energy stored in a moving bicycle is not very great, you will find that gear-changes on a bicycle are needed more often than in a car. In addition, you will notice a considerable difference between gears that may be quite close to one another and you will need some means of measuring *how high* or *how low* a gear is, especially in the case of derailleur gearing, where no fixed positions are marked.

The difference between the various gears can be seen as the ratio between the pedalling speed (or cadence) and the road-speed. Several methods are used to express this relationship. Perhaps the simplest of these is an expression of the number of teeth on the chainwheel and on the sprocket. The normal gear for a level road, in the case of an inexperienced cyclist using a bicycle with 27-in wheels, might mean a 50-tooth chainwheel and a 20-tooth sprocket. This could be called a 50×20 gear. A higher gear might be 50×14 or a lower one 50×26.

However, the problem with this method is that it is not easy to imagine in practice and harder still to use for comparison. You might not immediately realize that 45×18 has the same result as 50×20. (In fact, it

is the same, since for every pedal revolution the rear wheel turns $50/20$ or $45/18$ which equals 2.5 times.) And how do you compare bicycles which have different wheel-diameters? A 50×20 gear on a cycle with 27-in wheels gives a much higher speed than the same gear on one with 20-in wheels; in other words, the expression indicates a higher gear in one case than in the other.

Two different methods have been developed which take wheel-size into account. The first method expresses the gear in terms of 'equivalent wheel-size' — that is, as the diameter of the wheel if it was being driven directly, without gearing. For example, a 27-in wheel with a 50×20 gear would be equal to a directly driven wheel with a diameter of $50/20 \times 27$ ins = 67.5 ins. The same gear on a 20-in wheel would give you $50/20 \times 20$ ins = 50 ins. Fig. 7.1 illustrates this. Obviously, the larger wheel-size indicates a higher gear. Thus, we can talk about a 100-in gear as being high. (Such a wheel would be enormous if it actually was a directly driven wheel, and this clearly illustrates the advantage of the chain-driven bicycle over the directly driven version of the past.) A 'normal' gear would be perhaps 65 ins and a 'low' one 35 ins. The resulting *gear numbers* or *inch-gear* sizes (which are the correct terms and are both preferable to 'equivalent wheel-sizes') for almost any combination of chainwheel and sprocket are given in table 2 on pages 254–5.

DEVELOPMENT

Although I would be the last to deny that it's charming to see your bicycle as a penny-farthing, this is hardly a realistic basis for the comparison of gears. Consequently, I favour an alternative method of comparison, based on the distance travelled per crank revolution. This method is the one used by most of the world's racers today, although the British and Americans have been a little slow to adopt it. The distance travelled per crank revolution is called 'development' and can easily be calculated by multiplying the gear number by 3.14, that is, the constant π. This would give you a development in inches, but unfortunately it is customary to express development in metres (see table 3 on pages 256–7). Fig. 7.1 illustrates this, if it is not already clear enough, and table 5 on page 259 shows corresponding developments for various inch-gear sizes.

A high gear, for example 50 × 14, gives a high inch-gear number (96.4 ins) and a long development (7.69m); a low gear, for example 50 × 26, has a low inch-gear number (51.9 ins) and a short development (4.14m). However, as shown in table 2 (pp. 254–5), a variety of high or low gears can be achieved with several different combinations of chainwheel and sprocket. What matters most is which gears you can achieve, expressed either in development or in inches, within a given range of chainwheels and sprockets. Alternatively – and this may be the case if you want to prepare your bicycle for different conditions – you may want to know which sprockets and, perhaps, which chainwheels (though changing chainwheels may become rather expensive) you need to select in order to have the range of gears you require. For mountainous areas, you will need a wide-range

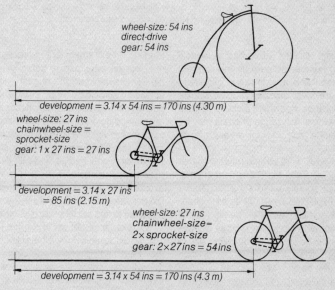

7.1 *Gear number and development*
('development' is the distance travelled per crank revolution)

Table 7.1   *Choosing gears for different terrain conditions*

TERRAIN TYPE	RECOMMENDED GEARING RANGE			SUGGESTED CHAINWHEEL AND SPROCKET SELECTION		
	Inch-gear numbers	Development		Full-step	Half-step	Crossover
Mainly level	60–105 ins	4.8–8.3 m	Chainwheels:	53/47 (*Diff. 6*)	53/49 (*Diff. 4*)	not recommended
			Sprockets:	14/15/17/19/21	14/15/17/19/22	
Slightly hilly	50–105 ins	4.0–8.3 m	Chainwheels:	53/46 (*Diff. 7*)	53/48 (*Diff. 5*)	not recommended
			Sprockets:	14/16/18/21/25	14/16/19/22/26	
Hilly	45–105 ins	3.6–8.3 m	Chainwheels:	53/45 (*Diff. 8*)	53/47 (*Diff. 6*)	53/40 (*Diff. 13*)
			Sprockets:	14/16/19/23/28	14/16/19/13/28	14/15/17/20/24
Very hilly	35–105 ins	2.8–8.3 m	Chainwheels:			53/37 (*Diff. 16*)
			Sprockets:	not recom-mended	not recom-mended	14/16/19/23/28
Mount-ainous	27–105 ins	2.1–8.3 m	Chainwheels:			53/33 (*Diff. 20*)
			Sprockets:	not recom-mended	not recom-mended	14/16/20/26/32

Notes

1. Given the total range required, the most important measurement is the *difference* between the larger and the smaller chainwheel, rather than the *absolute* chainwheel-sizes.

2. Fifteen-speed systems (triple chainwheels) should combine the *full-step* or *half-step* system (for the difference between the largest and the middle chainwheel) with the *crossover* system (for the difference between the middle and the smallest chainwheel).

3. Racing cyclists will generally choose slightly higher and more closely spaced gears. For loaded touring, slightly lower and more widely spaced gears may be preferred.

freewheel cluster (this has a widely varying number of teeth on the different sprockets) and a wide-range derailleur. For more level ground, you will want a narrow-range freewheel cluster. To help you decide which range of gears may be appropriate for particular areas, refer to table 7.1.

This looks more straightforward than it actually is, since there are certain limitations of equipment to consider. These will be explained in greater detail in chapters 15 and 16, but I will mention a few now. Not all makes and models of freewheels can be equipped with every size of sprocket; most can be obtained with sprockets having between 14 and 28 teeth, but larger and smaller sprockets may present a problem. Many derailleurs have a limited capacity and may not function on extremely large sprockets or may not be equipped to cater for wide differences between the largest and the smallest sprockets and chainwheels. Finally, cranksets do not necessarily accommodate very small chainwheels; most makes will take a range between 42 and 54 teeth, but smaller or larger chainwheels may only be installed with certain makes and models. The best way of avoiding this difficulty is to write down all the relevant information and ask the sales assistant to find out whether it will work.

The examples shown in the left-hand column of the table show what is known in the trade as 'full-step' gearing. The three lowest gears are all selected with the chain on the same chainwheel (the smaller one) and can be shifted with the rear derailleur. The next shift is accomplished by shifting once to the larger chainwheel, which leaves the chain on the same (middle) sprocket at the back. The last two changes are made again using the rear derailleur, which leaves the chain on the larger chainwheel in the front. This method of shifting is easier to learn, but results in the 'loss' of up to two gears: you only have the use of six different gears.

The second method is known as the 'half-step' system. In this, the intermediate gear between each set of two rear-sprocket changes is engaged by shifting the front derailleur. This method is slightly more difficult to use, but it has the advantage that it releases the greatest number of gears for use. Racers are probably best advised to use this method, but tourists – and certainly the occasional rider – might prefer to stick to the simpler full-step method. Whichever method you use, it is worth remembering that the *percentage* changes between one gear and the next should be almost equal wherever possible. To put this in scientific terms, it is best to achieve a progression resembling a geometric series. In the higher gears, the differences between changes should be greater; in the lower gears, they should be smaller.

I feel that the ten-speed is overrated these days. It is possible to save yourself a lot of frustration (as well as money) by setting up a good five-speed system. Use just one chainwheel of anything from 44 to 48 teeth and a wide-range freewheel. This will give you five well-spaced gears, suitable for use almost anywhere. Although you'll have to sacrifice one or two really high gears, used only for riding downhill, you'll get a much simpler shifting pattern and less troublesome cycling.

HUB GEARS

Hub gears today mean big gaps between the individual gears. With the Sturmey–Archer three-speed hub, the high gear is a full 33.3 per cent higher than the normal gear, and the low gear is 25 per cent lower. Though that corresponds to the geometric series mentioned above, it also means you simply haven't the use of enough gears. Even in mountainous country, most riding is done in the 'normal' range, where gears between 60 and 85 ins (development 4.8 to 6.8 m) will prove most useful. If you choose a 50-tooth chainwheel and a 20-tooth sprocket, the direct or normal gear will be 68 ins (development 5.4 m) but, with a standard three-speed hub, both the high and the low gear will fall well outside the 60–85 ins range.

You can improve the situation by installing a replacement sprocket, selecting the number of teeth in such a way that you have two gears within the range preferred, or at least closer to it – but the gaps between the gears will remain very great. Table 4 on pages 258–9 gives you some idea of the various possibilities that can be opened up by selecting different sprocket-sizes for different wheel-sizes. It is even possible to put two (dished) Sturmey–Archer sprockets back-to-back and use a derailleur to expand the range, but that way you get all the disadvantages of both systems – hardly an improvement on just having a derailleur. Perhaps the best you can do is to use the Sturmey–Archer five-speed and pray that they will soon re-introduce some of the many other models they used to make before the advent of the derailleur. Several of these older models had much more closely spaced gears, as can be seen in the notes to table 4.

FASTER THAN YOU THINK

Finally, we might have a look at the speeds a cyclist can reach on a bicycle with well-selected gearing. The speed for a given gear and pedalling rate (or cadence) may be calculated from the following formula:

$$\text{road-speed} = \frac{\text{development} \times \text{cadence} \times 60}{1,000} \text{km/h}$$

or

$$\text{road-speed} = \frac{\text{inch-gear} \times \text{cadence} \times 60}{19,700} \text{mph}$$

or, easier still, it may be deduced from table 6 on page 260. Read off the road-speed along the appropriate inch-gear line, directly above the applicable cadence.

Earlier on, I talked about cadence and for convenience assumed a normal figure of 60 rpm. However, most trained cyclists maintain a far higher pedalling rate than that – more typically between 80 and 100 rpm. You will see from the table that even at a cadence of 80 rpm, combined with a gear of 80 ins – nothing unusual for an experienced cyclist – a road-speed of 20 mph (32 km/h) will be reached. You may bear that in mind when the bicycle is next publicly denounced as being too slow for today's distances and the modern pace of life!

The number of bicycle accidents in Britain, as reported by Mike Hudson in *The Bicycle Planning Book*, is significantly higher than that of cars for the same distance travelled. In fact, the risk of sustaining a serious injury for each mile travelled may be around ten times higher for the cyclist than it is for the motorist. Yet many of us ride our bicycles cheerfully, and some live to a ripe old age while continuing to do so – in fact, we've learned to handle ourselves and our machines safely in a wide variety of modern traffic conditions. We've managed to make our cycling comparatively safe.

The secret lies in conditioning, although this isn't as callous as it sounds. The figures are exaggerated in two ways: firstly, bicycle-use is restricted largely to short-distance trips in town, where accident rates are higher for *all* vehicles; secondly, many cyclists seem never to get enough mileage behind them to attain the level of competence that is required of anyone competing in traffic, whether using two wheels or four. The motorist, after receiving formal training, clocks up many miles very quickly. In fact, the average motorist probably drives as many as 10,000 miles within the first year, while many cyclists may never cover anything like as much in a lifetime of cycling. I maintain that there are relatively few incompetent motorists on the road, and a large number of incompetent cyclists. The fact that, according to one source, motor-

ists were more often at fault than cyclists in motor vehicle/bicycle accidents does not contradict this, since competence does not necessarily mean that you are any more or less in the right; it simply means you can keep out of trouble.

After all, with motor vehicles it has long been clear that the overwhelming majority of accidents were 'the other person's fault'; nonetheless, the experienced motorist has far fewer accidents than the inexperienced. Hudson's conclusion that 'bicycle accidents occur because of the mixing of cycles with motor traffic' makes as much sense as it does to say that car accidents occur because of the mixing of cars with cars. We will probably never – and certainly not in our lifetime – rebuild the road network so that it completely separates motor vehicles from bicycles. So far, this has been attempted only in isolated communities, most notably in Stevenage, but sooner or later the bicycle – if it really is used as a proper means of transport – has to return to the mixed environment.

There is nothing wrong with the Stevenage plan or with its initiator, Eric Claxton, but what can be done in a new, planned community can never be done in an existing environment without sacrificing the cyclist's safety, speed and convenience. So, if you want to cycle safely, you may be better advised to follow the example of other experienced cyclists who have learned to avoid accidents, rather than wait (or even campaign, as the new political cyclists do) for the millennium.

Some excellent educational programmes have been developed to shorten the process of learning. Probably the best known of these is the National Cycling Proficiency Scheme, organized by the Birmingham office of the Royal Society for the Prevention of Accidents (RoSPA), which aims to improve levels of proficiency and safety amongst young cyclists – although it must be said that too few children have benefited from it, since it is reported that the results tend to 'wear off'. For adults, few such programmes are available. Perhaps the best option open to them is to take advantage of the large body of experience to be gained by joining other, more experienced cyclists in the CTC (Cyclists' Touring Club) and the many local cycling clubs. As for literature, the best manual is John Forester's *Effective Cycling* (see Bibliography), even though it's written for the USA.

Probably the most important thing to learn is that the cyclist is bound as much by the rules of the road, as set out in the Highway Code and the Road Traffic Act, as is anyone else using a vehicle. If you ride your bicycle as you would drive a car, you'll be a lot safer and more predictable to other road-users than if you overtake cars on their left, ride on the extreme left of the road, refuse to ride in line with cars, dodge in and out between parked vehicles and forget to signal at turns and stops. A good description of the Highway Code as it affects cyclists may be found in an article by David A. Crick, the long-standing legal representative for the CTC, in *The Raleigh Book of Cycling*. Otherwise, simply reading through the Highway Code booklet and mentally reconstructing how the various situations described would apply to the cyclist is an excellent way of becoming a safer rider in

traffic. Here, you'll find just a few additional suggestions for things to keep in mind when cycling and things to check before you even set out.

SAFETY HINTS

1. Keep your bicycle correctly adjusted, as explained in chapter 5.

2. Check the correct operation of brakes, steering and lighting before you set off.

3. Take a few essential tools and minor first-aid equipment on every trip, however short.

4. Do not ride your bicycle when under the influence of alcohol, drugs or medication.

5. Abide by all the rules of the road. They make cycling and driving safer for all concerned.

6. Ride in the road, not on the pavement or on one of those rare but newly popular roadside cycle paths. Other road-users don't expect to find anyone moving at any speed worth mentioning anywhere other than in a traffic lane.

7. Do not ride too close to the shoulder on the left-hand side of the road, especially when approaching a crossroad (unless you are preparing to turn left). The left shoulder is often poorly paved, and near a crossing it is the place for vehicles turning left, not for cyclists carrying straight ahead.

8. Consider every traffic situation in its own right. Always think out the safest alternative open to you.

9. Never ride in the dark or at dusk without lights. You need them in order to be visible to others, as well as for your own convenience.

10. At night, wear light and bright clothing to make yourself visible to others.

11. Make sure your clothing does not hamper your movements or get caught up in any part of your bicycle.

12. Be extra careful in bad weather. Rain will increase the required braking distance dramatically and visibility will be reduced. Besides, the likelihood of skidding and falling is far greater on a wet road surface.

13. Try to cross kerbstones, railway tracks and other uneven road surfaces at a right angle so that you avoid falling.

14. Take luggage only on a properly constructed and firmly attached luggage-carrier; never hang anything on the handlebars – except a properly designed handlebar bag or basket.

15. A child should be taken as a passenger only in a proper children's seat safely attached to the bike (see chapter 10).

16. Do not rely solely on your rear brake. Use both, bearing in mind that the front brake is more effective.

17. In town traffic, it is wise to stay in a fairly low gear to facilitate sudden changes in pace.

18. Look well ahead, on both sides as well as behind you, *before* every manoeuvre you intend to make. Show by your position in the road what you intend to do. *Be predictable*!

EQUIPMENT SAFETY

Few bicycle accidents are the direct result of equipment failures, but it is quite possible that incorrectly functioning equipment may be a contributory factor to accidents that might otherwise have been avoided. So we'll take a look at the weak points on our bicycle. Apart from the balancing problem inherent in the two-wheel design, the major problems seem to be brakes and lighting. Oddly enough, the rules given in the world's first set of safety requirements for bicycles, the American CPSC (Consumer Product Safety Commission), virtually ignore these points, concentrating instead on some totally irrelevant items, such as lateral and forward reflectivity and protrusions assumed to be dangerous.

Of course, it will do no harm to be aware of the potential hazards of unnecessary protrusions (for example, excessively long cables or screws, gear-shift levers or pointed decorations), but the most attention ought to be paid to brakes and lights. There is a lot to be said for hub brakes rather than conventional calliper or stirrup types, especially in wet weather. But even conventional rim brakes can be made to work more effectively when the materials from which the brake blocks and rim are made are selected properly. Aluminium rims give you much better braking in wet weather than chromium-plated steel ones, whereas the serration sometimes added to the sides of steel rims have been proved to give no improvement in braking efficiency whatsoever – wet or dry.

Recent innovations in brake-block materials offer vastly superior braking. Fibrax and Raleigh offer brake blocks that give much greater wet-braking power when used with steel rims. My experience with these kinds of brake block is that cleanliness of the rims is extremely important if unpredictable braking action is to be avoided. Weinmann and other major brake manufacturers have also introduced designs that promise to give more effective braking.

Lighting, too, has undergone significant improvements in recent years. And, for once, it's British industry that's leading the way. The two British Standards for bicycle lighting equipment, BS AU–155 for headlights and BS 3648 for rear lights, have done more to improve the quality of lighting than almost anything else. Lights that conform to these standards promise the best in lighting and visibility without using an excessive amount of battery power. Make sure your lights conform to these standards. The much-maligned, plastic 'Ever-Readies' do conform (though, for the front, dynamo lights are brighter than battery units); the Hong Kong and Taiwan 'throw-aways' do not.

A few other things that will contribute to your safety should be mentioned briefly. Most importantly, your head should be protected. Concern for this is not without cause: a safety survey conducted during the massive cross-America cycling pro-gramme, *Bikecentennial*, found that the most common form of debilitating acci-dent involved head injuries that could have been prevented or minimized by wearing a crash helmet. Of course, kids in the USA are lucky: they can choose from at least a dozen hard-shell crash helmets specially designed or adapted for bicycle use (fig. 8.1). Our equivalent, on the other hand, is more like a hairnet than a helmet (fig. 8.2).

Should you fall off your bike, there are two other things that may minimize any injury: gloves and clothing. A pair of gloves will protect your hands when you try unconsciously or consciously to break your fall. The most useful are special bicy-cle gloves with padded palms and cut-off fingers, but an ordinary pair of leather

ventilation space

(a) Bailen

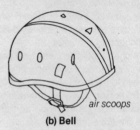

air scoops

(b) Bell

8.1 *Hard-shell helmets*

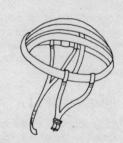

(a) Conventional leather type

8.3 *Cycling glove*

(b) Open hard-shell (Skid-Lid)

8.2 *Open crash helmets*

gloves will do. As for clothing, long sleeves on shirts and sweaters and long trousers can make a spill a lot less painful than it might otherwise have been. You may never fall – and indeed millions of cyclists go for years without an accident – but it is reassuring to know that you've minimized the dangers, should anything happen.

SAFETY COLOURS

Choice of colour is somewhat overrated as a factor affecting bicycle safety. Shocking pink, international orange and Van Gogh green are all promoted as means of being noticed and of preserving our safety. In the central field of vision, these colours are indeed the ones most readily noticed. This is a good reason for road-workers (who often step straight out into the line of traffic) to wear such monstrously visible garments. Typical bicycle accidents, on the other hand, are caused by insufficient early visibility in the *peripheral* range – despite most novice cyclists' paranoid fears of being stabbed in the back by the nose of a speeding Lamborghini or a roaring dust-cart. The peripheral vision does not respond to colours at all – merely to reflected light *intensity*: bright, shiny lights and dark shadows. That means that you'd probably be better off wearing light-reflective garb at night and dark clothing by day.

Apart from the limited use of bicycles in track racing and indoor training on rollers, it is clear that the bike's place is on the road, not in the attic, the basement or the boot of the car. Get out and ride! That's the only true way to appreciate the machine and the sport. You may think of the bicycle as having any number of primary functions: a means of getting to and from work; a vehicle for active racing; a tool for keeping healthy or for relaxing; a way of preserving the environment; or a means of touring. But none of this is of any use at all unless you actually get out and ride your bike. In this chapter, we'll consider some of the things that will help you make the maximum use of your bicycle. I'll describe luggage-carrying equipment, clothing and shoes, maps and ways of avoiding hills, and what you will need to prevent your machine from being stolen.

CARRYING LUGGAGE

Man has not yet devised a better way of carrying luggage on a bicycle than the traditional English touring *saddlebag*. The saddlebag puts the weight of the luggage near the centre of the bicycle where it least disturbs handling, is unlikely to interfere with the movements of the rider and does not create additional wind resistance. But, unfortunately, there are limits to the size of saddlebag you can obtain. The biggest I've seen had a capacity of 22 litres (about ¾ cu ft) – large enough for most weekend trips, but not for camping

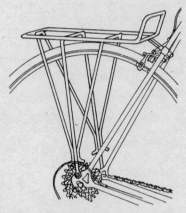

(a) **Rear carrier**

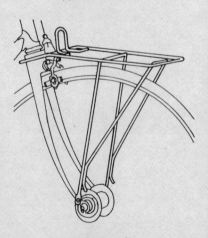

(b) **Front carrier**

9.1 *Luggage carriers*

nor for carrying a few days' supply of groceries if you want to use your bike for shopping.

To carry more, you will need *racks* or *carriers*. These are available both for the rear and the front (fig. 9.1). The ones that are most rigid and least likely to break are those made of tubular steel; the next best are the rigidly welded aluminium models, such as the Jim Blackburn racks, which are light and strong. Other light-weight carriers are those made by Pletcher (Switzerland) and ESGE (Germany). However, these are much less rigid than the welded ones. The most common carriers are the chromium-plated steel models, like the popular Claude Butler, which are both heavier and less rigid, though preferable by far to the collapsible aluminium varieties.

With carriers, the problem becomes not so much one of limited capacity but rather a danger of taking too much. I have in fact seen bicycles loaded up like the one in fig. 9.2 – useful as an illustration of the various possibilities for carrying luggage, but not a suggestion for putting into practice unless you aim to reach the other side of the globe or beyond. Rule number one of bike-packing should remain: 'if in doubt,

leave it out'. Otherwise, you will soon learn to hate the whole business.

The various bags shown in fig. 9.2 all have their uses, but not all at once on the same bike. The *handlebar bag* is handy for small items which need to be easily accessible on the road, like sunglasses, camera, rainwear and maps (for which a transparent top-flap may be provided). Disadvantages are the fact that the bag may interfere with steering and braking, and that it sits just at the point where I prefer to mount my light, which I like as high as possible. The installation of a support bracket will minimize problems of handling.

A second kind of bag to mount at the front is the *front pannier*, used in sets of two and mounted on either side of a front rack. This is a good place to carry relatively heavy items which take up little space, particularly if the rest of the weight is in panniers in the back. The low centre of gravity of panniers makes them almost unnoticeable, though they are placed where most people mount their front light. To solve this, I suggest you put the light either on the front rack or on the handle-bars.

The *rear panniers* are mounted on a

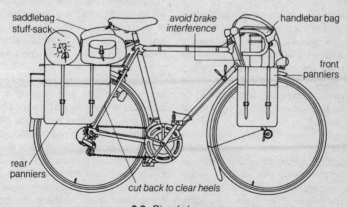

saddlebag
stuff-sack
avoid brake interference
handlebar bag
front panniers
rear panniers
cut back to clear heels

9.2 *Bicycle bags*

luggage carrier at the back. These are the work-horses of bicycle touring and can easily hold a tent, sleeping bag and cooking gear. Try to get a pair that have additional smaller pockets at the back or the side, but make sure the bags don't interfere with your leg movement or obstruct the rear light (which you can mount under the rear luggage carrier if necessary).

Even if you use rear panniers, there will be room for another bag on the back of the bicycle, either the familiar saddlebag or a *stuff-sack*, mounted on top of the luggage carrier. Saddlebags never seem to be big enough, but try to get a small one if you are combining it with other bags. If you do not have a rear carrier, you may find a bag-support useful for a heavily loaded saddlebag. Similar devices also exist to keep handlebar bags off the front wheel.

All bags must be made of first-class materials, such as canvas or heavy-duty nylon with leather reinforcement. The plastic-coated cloth or cardboard-backed ducking, and especially the plastic straps often found on cheaper bicycle bags, are extensions of a throw-away attitude which has no place in the world of cycling.

CLOTHING

Cycle clothing is not usually particularly elegant, but it *is* practical and is therefore highly recommended for all cycle-riding of any duration. The main points to look for are these: the clothing must be comfortable, flexible and light-weight, it should allow you to 'breathe', and it should be moisture-absorbent (except, of course, for rainwear).

Cycling shorts, though superbly comfortable and therefore highly recommended, are probably the most ridiculous-looking items you'll ever see on a grown man – especially if you get the best type of racing shorts which are black, tight-fitting, knitted woollen garments with a piece of

chamois liner in seat

(a) Racing shorts   **(b) Touring shorts**

(c) Touring trousers

9.3 *Cycling trousers*

chamois sewn in the seat. English touring shorts and trousers are almost as comfortable and have pockets, which makes them useful for more than just cycling. The chamois crotch is important, since it will absorb moisture and prevent all sorts of skin problems. Wash it without soap and treat it with special chamois cream. Fig 9.3 shows the three varieties of trousers available.

Cycling jerseys are long, tight-fitting, woollen garments with pockets in the back. The material has to be wool; acrylic, nylon and most other synthetics are no substitute because they do not absorb the body's perspiration. A snug-fitting woollen jersey (with long sleeves if you are sensitive to the sun or if the weather is cold) keeps the body temperature at a very comfortable level, whatever the conditions. If it gets really cold, you may add or

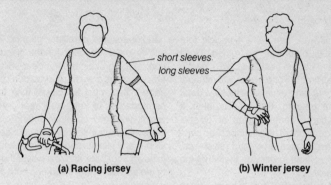

short sleeves
long sleeves

(a) Racing jersey   (b) Winter jersey

9.4 *Cycling jerseys*

substitute a thicker, equally snug, closely knitted sweater. Fig. 9.4 illustrates the two most common types of cycling jerseys. To protect your hands, you may want cycling gloves, as described in chapter 8.

SHOES

Cycling shoes are not for walking and they are not to be confused with shoes intended for any other sport, whether this be tennis, basketball or running. They differ in that they have a very hard, inflexible flat sole to help distribute the pedal-force over a larger area of the foot, thus improving the comfort and performance of the cyclist considerably. To derive maximum benefit from your cycling shoes, they should be equipped with a plate or 'cleat' which holds them in place on the pedal. It is sometimes recommended that new shoes be worn without cleats for a few days, so that the imprint left by the pedals will show where they should be mounted. Fig. 9.5 shows both the shoe and the mounting of the cleat.

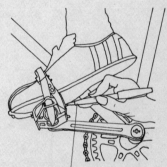

mark correct location on shoe

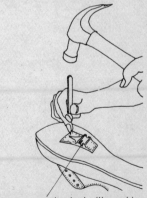

line up grove in cleat with marking

9.5 *Cycling shoe and cleat*

RAINWEAR

Good rainwear can save a bicycle tour that would otherwise be ruined. Don't hesitate to get the best and carry it on the bike at all times. For bicycles with straight handlebars (and especially those without derailleur gearing) the cape is ideal. It should be of coated nylon or plastic-coated cloth, not of fragile unbacked plastic. To avoid excessive wind-resistance, you are advised to get one that's not too generously cut.

A rain jacket with a built-in hood is more suitable for cyclists who use dropped handlebars and derailleur gearing, as it allows more freedom for the hands to control the brakes and the gear-shift levers. Leggings are a must if you don't use a cape. They must be close-fitting to be comfortable. To keep your feet dry and warm, you may consider putting plastic bags *inside* your shoes, over your socks. Capes and jackets should be long enough to cover your back and reach over the rear of the saddle so that they keep both *it* and your seat dry. Fig. 9.6 shows the most important rainwear.

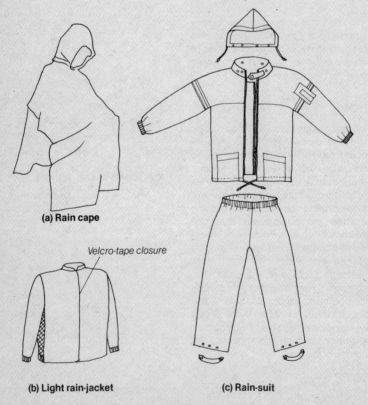

(a) Rain cape

Velcro-tape closure

(b) Light rain-jacket

(c) Rain-suit

9.6 *Rainwear*

MAPS

Since the best roads for cycling are often minor ones, the best cycling maps are those with the most detail. In Britain, that means Ordnance Survey or Bartholomew. These used to be available in 'one-inch' and 'half-inch' forms respectively, which meant that each mile in the field was represented by an inch or half an inch on the map. In recent years, they have been replaced by maps on a different scale, 1:50,000 and 1:100,000 respectively. I feel that the 1:50,000 maps are too detailed for cycling, since you can ride across the area covered by such a map in a matter of a few hours. For this reason, I recommend 1:100,000 maps (usually Bartholomew) for one-day and weekend trips, with smaller-scale maps, preferably 1:200,000, for longer journeys.

Alternatives to these are the 'quarter-inch' and 1:250,000 or 1:300,000 maps; however, these do not show all the roads and the details that are most useful to the cyclist. When you go abroad, you will find maps made by Michelin most suitable wherever they are available – i.e., in France, Belgium, Holland, Luxemburg and Italy. These maps are to a scale of 1:200,000. Other maps are best bought locally, provided that you plan your route with the help of some larger map of the country which may not show the actual roads you'll want to follow but which will give you a general impression of the entire trip. You can keep the map for handy reference if you mount a map-clip on the handlebars (fig. 9.7).

On a bicycle it is important to know which roads are steep and which are more suitable for cycling purposes. That's where the Ordnance Survey maps and similar ones in other countries have their greatest value. These maps show 'contour lines' – lines connecting all points at the same height above sea level. The more of these lines a road crosses, the

clamp to handlebars

9.7 *Map clip* (courtesy Andrew Hague)

greater the difference in height, and the closer together the lines, the steeper the road.

Other ways of avoiding great differences in height include choosing roads that run parallel to railway lines or waterways (although to cycle on the tow-paths along the British canals, a permit is needed from the Estate Office of the British Waterways Board; address on page 269). If all else fails, you may ask a local; but don't ask a motorist – they never seem to notice the hills that can break a cyclist's back!

BICYCLE THEFT

Buy a lock and a chain or cable and use them! You will hardly believe the figures for bicycle thefts: in some years, they exceed the combined value of all bank robberies. A good chain should be long and thick (with shackles or links that have a diameter of at least a quarter of an inch), case-hardened and enclosed in plastic to prevent damage to the paintwork. And don't just *lock* the bike. You must really *secure* it, to a tree or a post, with the chain through both wheels and the frame. Of course, it is better still not to leave the bicycle unguarded at all!

I read in one of the American cycling magazines how the former French ski-champion, Jean-Claude Killy – who is as keen on cycling as he is on skiing – looks forward to his son getting older so that they can go cycling together. How old, I wondered, would this infant be – three months perhaps? But no, Killy Junior was – at least at the time the article was written – thirteen years of age! This is quite ridiculous: you can take children of almost any age on an extended cycling tour, and they will not only enjoy it but will also hold their own remarkably well.

All the same, it should be realized that cycling with children involves problems not encountered when cycling with adults. However, with common sense and the necessary information, any additional difficulties will be of a very minor nature indeed. The main thing is to keep in mind the child's age, development and interests.

I suggest there are four periods in the child's development. First, there is the period before the child can hold his head and body upright. Here, of course, the best advice is 'don't'. Fortunately, this is a very brief period indeed – perhaps only six months or so.

Next comes the period when the child can be easily carried in a child's seat on one of the parents' bicycles – up to perhaps five or six years of age.

Between the ages of six and ten, the child will probably be able to ride a bicycle, and will often want to do so. However, this is perhaps the period with the most problems, since it is not safe to subject a child of this age to heavy traffic or rough terrain, except on a tandem.

After the age of ten, there isn't much difference between a healthy child and an adult when it comes to riding a bicycle, except that the child will ride a smaller machine.

CHILDREN'S SEATS

Certainly up to the age of six – and if you haven't a tandem that is adapted to the purpose, up to the age of ten – the safe way to take the child is on a child's seat, mounted on an adult's bicycle. For a very young child, a front-mounted seat may be desirable so that the parent can keep an eye on him. Otherwise it is preferable to fix the seat on to the back of the bike. Here is a list of standards to which a child's seat should conform:

1. The seat must be firmly attached to the bicycle.

2. It must have a level and comfortable seating surface and be the right size for the child in question.

3. It must have integral support to the sides and the back and, especially in the case of a younger child, some restraining harness or belt.

4. Firm and well-proportioned supports for the feet must be provided.

5. The seat must be mounted in such a way that neither it nor the child interferes

10.1 *Children's seats*

(a) Rear-mount **(b) Front-mount** **(c) Fibreglass rear-mount**

with the operation of the bicycle or the movements of the rider.

6. Be particularly careful that no sharp protrusions, such as a gear-shift lever or a bell, represent a danger to the child.

7. Finally, a note for the rider: never park a bicycle with a child in the child's seat; take the child out before you leave the bike.

CHILDREN'S BICYCLES

Perhaps the best aspect of the recent revival of interest in cycling amongst adults is the fact that children no longer need to compete with objects other than bicycles when they want to imitate adult behaviour. When adults were seen driving only cars or motorcycles, these were the things to copy – hence the 'chopper' and other similar monstrosities. Now that adults are once more riding bicycles without embarrassment, children will again ride machines that look and perform like what they really are – bicycles. Like the adult bicycle, the child's cycle of today is a remarkably efficient machine which it is a pleasure to ride. However, when choosing a bike for a child, the following points should be noted:

1. Be critical when buying a child's bicycle; it should be of the same quality as a good adult bicycle.

2. Make sure it is the right size (a further discussion of size will be found below). Never let children ride a bicycle that is too large for them on the assumption that they will 'grow into' the bike.

3. Continental and American 'coaster' (or back-pedalling) brakes are a good idea for young children up to the age of six, since they are not usually strong or co-ordinated enough to use a hand-brake effectively.

4. For the same reason, derailleur gearing is not recommended for younger children.

5. An adjusted 'shopper' bicycle is not necessarily suitable for children, because parts such as the cranks, handlebars, brake-levers and the seat will not be the right size for their smaller, different physique.

6. Keep your child's bike in good condition. Teach children to watch out for faults and what to do when problems occur.

7. Teach your child to care for his bicycle. A child of any age can learn to lock his bike and even quite young ones will willingly clean their own machines. A ten-year-old should be able to carry out many adjustments and repairs for himself.

THE SIZE OF
A CHILD'S BICYCLE

Many children ride bicycles that are too big for them. Just how dangerous this may be is suggested by American data which shows that the number of accidents amongst those riding a properly adjusted bicycle is only twenty per cent of the figure for those riding a bicycle that is not adapted to the proportions of the rider's body. The greatest danger, of course, is riding a machine that is too large. Yet many parents still seem to buy a bicycle with the idea that the child should 'grow into' it. This kind of economy may be reasonable when buying trousers or jackets, but it is highly dangerous when applied to bicycles.

To be safe on a bicycle, the rider must be able to control the machine in every conceivable circumstance, and a bicycle that is too large cannot possibly be adjusted to allow the rider full control. However, a bicycle that is too small cannot be recommended either, since the upward adjustment of the saddle and handlebars results in instability, while other important measurements, such as the length of the frame and the handlebar and crank size, do not match the rider's proportions.

Like the adult, the child must be able to straddle the crossbar comfortably if the bike has a conventional frame. If the frame has no crossbar, put the seat in the lowest possible position and check whether the rider can reach the ground with his toes. If the handlebars can also be easily reached in this position, and if they remain well below shoulder-level – preferably no higher than the saddle – the frame is of an acceptable size. For a child of average proportions, the following sizes will usually be satisfactory:

(a) up to the age of six: frame-size 14 ins (35 cm); wheel-size 16 ins (400 mm)

(b) aged six or seven to nine or ten: frame-size 16 ins (40 cm); wheel-size 20 ins (500 mm)

(c) aged nine or ten to eleven or twelve: frame-size 18 ins (45 cm); wheel-size 24 ins (600 mm)

(d) eleven or twelve and over: frame-size determined as for adult bikes (see chapter 5); wheel-size 26 ins (650 mm). Adult bicycles with 27-in wheels will not usually be suitable until the age of thirteen or fourteen.

BICYCLE TOURING
WITH CHILDREN

As I said at the outset, bicycle riding with children should be possible and enjoyable for both adult and child. But as with any other activity – whether it be motoring, visiting the zoo or even watching television – the special needs of the younger participant have to be taken into account. You must follow the general advice on touring given in chapter 9, but, in addition, the following points should be considered:

1. Consult the child before the trip as well as on the journey, so that he feels like a full participant – he may well have something to contribute to planning the trip.

2. Do not undertake terrain, traffic or distances that are beyond the child's capability. Revise your plans en route if necessary.

3. Include several stops for rest, play and diversion.

4. Try to create a reason for the trip which is other than the ride itself – perhaps a museum, a park, a playground or a cricket match will give the whole thing more purpose for adults and children alike.

5. Don't expect children to keep up the pace set by adults. But there is no need to dawdle: children can cycle reasonably fast if they ride at all regularly.

6. Divide any luggage sensibly. The strongest should carry the most and the weakest should perhaps carry enough to boost their self-image as load-carrying participants, i.e., something relatively light for its bulk.

7. Remember that the tour is supposed to be fun! Be loving, patient and relaxed.

BICYCLE MOTOR CROSS
(or What Will They Think of Next?)

The latest craze to have come across the Atlantic is *BMX* or *Bicycle Motor Cross*, and it seems to be gaining in popularity. It's actually not as outrageous as its name implies, and it provides a lot of clean, rough fun for· youngsters, riding across fields and down steep hillsides. According to participants, the number of injuries overall remains tolerably low, and perhaps the best attitude is to accept that 'boys will be boys', as they say.

The bike used for this outlandish pastime is based on a remarkably rigid, small frame, with straight forks and wide-tyred wheels, often even equipped with shock-absorbers (though these are as often as not mere fakes). BMX bikes look a bit like the absurd 'chopper' bicycles of the sixties, but they are available (if they are genuine models) as very high quality machines, with light and precise components and a correspondingly expensive price tag. If you want one that's worth the price you pay for it, you may judge it by its weight – the lighter it is the better. I can't recommend the cast-alloy wheels that come on the highest-priced models, since they are structurally inferior to the 'old-fashioned' spoked wheels.

reinforced handlebars

reinforced frame

straight forks

no gears

fat tyres on strong rims

10.2 *BMX cycle*

Part 2
A CLOSE LOOK AT THE BICYCLE

11

The frame is the backbone of the bicycle. Its quality, weight and geometry largely determine the quality, weight and handling efficiency of the entire machine. The conventional bicycle frame has the familiar diamond shape and is constructed of steel tubing welded or brazed together with lugs. Fig. 11.1 gives the names normally used for the various parts of the frame.

Although the diamond-pattern frame is by far the most common for quality bicycles, various other frame shapes are also used, particularly for women's bicycles, 'shopper' models and tandems. Some of the basic frame designs for women's and 'shopper' machines are illustrated in fig.

2.2 on page 18, while tandem designs will be discussed in chapter 28. The conventional men's frame has the best riding characteristics, but it is followed closely by the *mixte* frame, which is clearly the best of the women's designs available. Other designs, especially the cross frame and other variants used for 'shopper' models, are compromises that allow through-the-frame mounting and dismounting at the expense of more desirable handling.

The major components of the conventional bicycle frame (see fig. 11.1) are the *main frame* (consisting of *top tube* or crossbar, *down tube*, *seat tube* and *head tube*) and the *rear triangle* (which consists

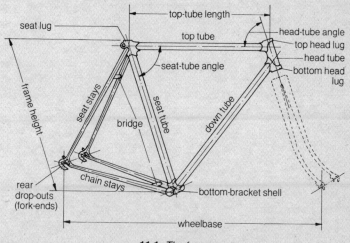

11.1 *The frame*

of two sets of parallel tubes called *seat stays* and *chain stays*). The front forks, though shown in the illustration, will be described in the separate chapter devoted to steering (chapter 12).

The tubes are usually connected rigidly by means of hollow *lugs*, into which the ends of the tubes are brazed. Contrary to popular belief, they are not welded, since in the welding process the material of the main tubes is actually melted – which would result in a much weakened frame. Brazing means that a rod of a material which has a lower melting point – usually bronze or silver alloy – is melted between the two parts to be joined, thus providing a far superior joint. The most important lug is the *bottom-bracket shell* (also called the *chain-hanger*), in which the bearings for the cranks (the *bottom-bracket bearings*) are mounted. The *seat lug* accommodates the seat pin and is split at the back to allow for tightening. Finally, the upper

and lower *head lugs* carry the races containing the head-set or steerer bearings.

The chain and seat stays end in flat plates, called *drop-outs* or *fork-ends*, which hold the rear wheel. To add rigidity to the rather thin tubes of the rear triangle, short bridges are installed to fix each pair together. One of these also serves to mount the rear brake. In addition, various small items may be brazed on to the frame: lamp brackets, tunnels or guides for the gear and brake cables and bosses to install gear-shift levers, a water bottle cage or cantilever brakes. A good look at such minor details will often reveal the quality of a frame more readily than any other easily visible aspect. Check not only the quality of these small items but also the workmanship apparent in their installation. Good workmanship shows itself in a clean finish to the joints and edges. There should be no roughness or gaps.

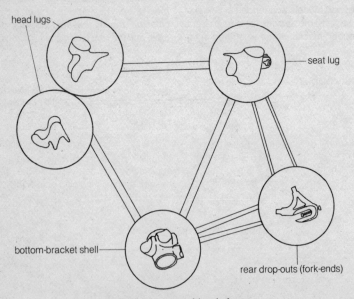

head lugs

seat lug

bottom-bracket shell

rear drop-outs (fork-ends)

11.2 *The lugs on a bicycle frame*

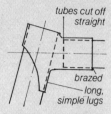

tubes cut off straight

brazed
long, simple lugs

(a) Cheap lugged joint

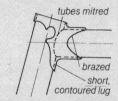

tubes mitred

brazed
short, contoured lug

(b) Good-quality lugged joint

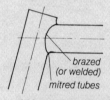

brazed (or welded)
mitred tubes

(c) Lug-less joint

11.3 *Frame-tube joints*

LUGS

As a rule, it may be said that the shortest and most elaborate lugs are usually those of the highest quality. Although all the different lug designs may be based on the same stamping (in the case of cheap, low-quality lugs) or forging or die-casting (in the case of more accurate and expensive ones), any embellishment, which may appear to be purely decorative, increases their contour length and this assures a better brazed joint on the finished frame. The longer lugs often serve merely to make a joint like the one in

fig. 11.3(a). In this case, the ends of the frame tubes are not shaped or 'mitred' in the fish-mouth pattern which is necessary to give the greatest strength, but are instead cut off straight.

In the opinion of some frame-builders, it is best to have no lugs at all. In other words, they favour the 'lug-less' construction method. In this case, the ends of the frame tubes must be carefully and accurately mitred and the brazing material must penetrate only the tiny gap between the ends of the tubes so that a smooth contour is built around the joint. Fig. 11.3 shows the three most common types of joint: a cheap lug without mitring, a good lug with mitred tubes, and a lug-less joint.

FORK-ENDS

Even fork-ends or drop-outs come in different shapes and sizes, and each has something to tell us about the quality and characteristics of the frame on which they are used. The simplest drop-outs are just plain, flat stampings about 3–4 mm ($\frac{1}{8}$ –$\frac{5}{32}$ in) thick. These do not give the rigidity needed for strenuous cycling, so a frame of real quality has forged or invest-ment-cast fork-ends which can be recognized by their rounded contours and by the precise method used to join them to the frame stays.

The four main designs of drop-out are the plain, the plain with gear-hanger, the adjustable and the vertical. The gear-hanger is an extension of the right-hand rear drop-out and it serves to accommodate a derailleur. This type of gear attachment is preferable to the method used on cheaper frames where the derailleur is clamped between the drop-out and the axle-nut by means of a little adaptor-plate held in the slot of the drop-out. Adjustable drop-outs allow you to make quicker and more accurate wheel-changes because they fix the position of the rear-wheel axle in the fork-ends. Finally, vertical fork-ends allow a closer clearance between the rear triangle and the rear wheel – thus producing a more rigid bicycle, preferable for racing because less energy is lost in the swaying and flexing of the machine.

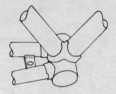

(a) Flat plate

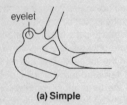

(a) Simple

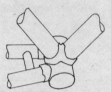

(b) Non-reinforced tube

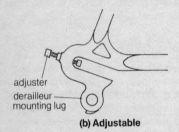

(b) Adjustable

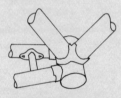

(c) Reinforced tube

11.5 *Chain-stay bridges*

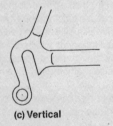

(c) Vertical

BRIDGES

On the very cheapest frames the necessary reinforcement between the pairs of chain stays and seat stays is provided by means of a flat plate which is brazed – or sometimes even welded – between the stays. Much greater rigidity is provided if the bridge takes the form of a short tubular section, possibly reinforced at the brazing points by means of flared ends. If the bridge between the chain stays (which takes very high forces indeed) is shaped like the example in fig. 11.5(c), it is a sure sign of a quality frame. On track frames, the rear triangle is often so short that no bridge can be used for bracing the chain stays; rigidity is then assured by the shortness of the stays themselves.

(d) Track racing

11.4 *Rear fork-ends (drop-outs)*

FRAME MATERIALS

For over a century the universally accepted material for bicycle frames has been steel tubing, a material that combines strength with lightness. The highest-quality frames use 'cold-drawn' steel alloys which have a greater unit-strength than even the strongest varieties of plain steel. This greater strength allows the manufacturer to use thinner-walled tubing, resulting in a frame of the same strength but lighter than could otherwise be achieved.

Such alloys are often made from steel with small percentages of either molybdenum and manganese or chrome and molybdenum. Both result in frames of similar strength, but care must be taken in the case of chrome-molybdenum steel that the tubes are not over-heated during brazing. For this reason, chrome-molybdenum frames must be brazed with a silver brazing alloy which has a lower

melting point than bronze. The most common steel alloy bicycle-frame tubing is Reynolds 531 which is a manganese-molybdenum steel. Most other makers (e.g., Columbus, Falk, Vitus, Tange and Ishiwatha) use chrome-molybdenum.

Frames of a lower quality – although still quite satisfactory for most uses – are made of unalloyed steel, but preferably steel with a relatively high carbon content (known as either high-carbon or high-tensile steel). Some other frame materials include aluminium, titanium and FWRP (filament-wound reinforced plastic), all resulting in relatively light and usually prohibitively expensive frames.

BUTTED TUBES

In the case of high-quality frames, the tubes are very often 'butted'. This means that the walls of the tubes are thicker at the ends than elsewhere (as shown in fig. 11.6(b)). Most tubes have a 'butt' or thick

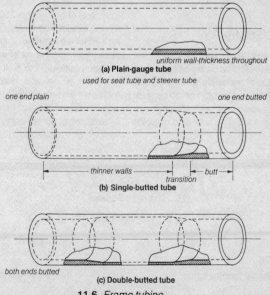

uniform wall-thickness throughout
(a) Plain-gauge tube
used for seat tube and steerer tube

one end plain   one end butted

thinner walls — | transition | — butt —
(b) Single-butted tube

both ends butted
(c) Double-butted tube

11.6 *Frame tubing*

wall-section at both ends, except for the seat tube where the top is of the same thickness so that it can hold the seat pillar. On some frames a compromise is made and only the three main tubes (the down tube, seat tube and top tube) are butted, while the other tubes are constructed of plain-gauge (i.e. non-butted) tubing. But the very best frames are butted throughout, and they will usually bear a label which says something to that effect.

The same manufacturers who make plain gauge alloy tubes also make the same tubes in butted versions, although at least two companies – Ishiwatha and Ateliers de la Rive (Durifort) – also make butted carbon-steel tubing. A frame made with butted tubing – especially if it is of steel alloy – certainly has a different 'feel' from that of a cheap frame. It is more responsive and better at absorbing road-shock, yet it is rigid enough to withstand the flexing that occurs when you press hard on the pedals. This kind of frame is certainly worth having.

FRAME GEOMETRY

The geometry according to which the frame is designed is at least as important as the choice of materials when it comes to the handling and comfort of the bicycle. The most important dimensions are shown in fig. 11.7. The left-hand drawing

shows a typical touring frame, and the right-hand one a typical racing frame of modern design. The most important dimensions are the wheelbase, the seat-tube height (also known as the frame-height) and the head-tube angle (which on most frames equals the seat-tube angle).

Touring frames have a rather long wheelbase (about 41 ins [104 cm] or more) and a rather shallow angle (72 degrees or less). This makes touring machines more springy and more comfortable than typical modern racing bicycles. They have a shorter wheelbase (40 ins [101 cm] or less) and a steeper angle (73 degrees or more). Due to the greater rigidity inherent in their steeper frame geometry, racing bicycles are slightly easier to manoeuvre, to accelerate and to ride up hills.

The height of the frame (the measurement which determines the frame-size) depends on the rider's leg length – whether the bike is used for racing or touring. Table 1 (page 253) summarizes the maximum frame-sizes recommended for certain leg lengths. Of the other dimensions, perhaps the most important is the distance between the bottom bracket and the front wheel-axle, since this determines whether there will be enough clearance between the front tyre and the toe when turning. Some racing designs are so

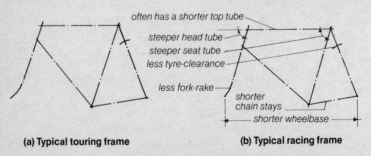

often has a shorter top tube
steeper head tube
steeper seat tube
less tyre-clearance
less fork-rake
shorter chain stays
shorter wheelbase

(a) Typical touring frame   **(b) Typical racing frame**

11.7 *Frame geometry*

short that you can't turn unless you stop pedalling, even when the bike has no mudguards. To clear the mudguards, there must be a distance of at least 23 ins (58 cm).

For structural reasons – to minimize undesirable flexing and vibration – the top-tube length will depend on the seat-tube length: from 20 ins for a 19-in frame to 24 ins for a 26-in frame. The distance between the bottom bracket and the rear wheel-axle will determine the rigidity of the bike when it comes to accelerating or hill climbing. The shorter the distance the better. But a short rear triangle has disadvantages too: it may be harder to remove the rear wheel and it will probably be impossible to use all the gears without flexing the chain too much. You will have to dispense with mudguards and the ride will be rougher if you opt for a rear triangle

shorter than, say, 17⅜ ins (44 cm).

Bottom-bracket height will determine how well you can pedal around corners. If it is high off the ground, you will get more clearance; if it is closer to the road, you will have a lower, safer and more comfortable centre of gravity. I prefer mine about 10½ ins (26 cm) high. A 'criterium' racer, who spends much of his life racing madly around in little circles, will want his at about 11 ins (28 cm). None of these dimensions is so crucial that you'll find it impossible to ride a bike that doesn't quite conform to the recommendations. You'll find you can easily adapt to almost any bicycle-frame geometry. But if you have the chance of choosing, you might as well choose wisely. My advice is not to choose too 'tight' or too steep a frame; this way, it will at least be comfortable and will add to your enjoyment in cycling.

The front forks, handlebars and head-set bearings form the bicycle's steering system. Steering has a far more important function than simply to enable the rider to turn corners, since even riding in a straight line requires constant corrections with the handlebars. Moreover, the geometry and design of the front forks largely determine the handling character-istics and riding comfort of the entire bicycle.

THE FRONT FORKS

The frame and the front forks are often regarded as a single major component, called the *frame-set*, and, like the frame, the front forks are constructed of tubular materials. They consist of two *fork-blades* and *fork-ends*, the *fork-crown* and the *steerer tube*. The steerer tube is threaded on the outside to take the head-set bearing while the inside accommodates the handlebar stem. If it is made of butted tubing, the steerer tube will be single-butted – i.e., thicker at the bottom only – since the top must provide a consistent diameter for the handlebar stem.

The fork-blades are tapered and usually oval in cross-section. They are bigger at the top, near the crown, where the greatest stresses occur, and smaller at the bottom, where the fork-ends or drop-outs which hold the front wheel are brazed on. On track-racing bicycles and cyclo-cross models the fork-blades sometimes have a round cross-section which is more rigid but less comfortable. The best fork-

blades have a tapered gauge which en-sures that after 'forming', the greatest strength is at the top (where it's most needed) not at the ends (where it's least needed).

Fork-crowns (fig. 12.2) are available in several different designs which often dif-fer more in their appeal to fashion than in their strength or quality. Improved rigidity may be expected if some form of rein-forcement is visible at the point on the inside of the forks where the fork-blade is attached.

Front fork-ends or drop-outs, like those on the rear forks, are perhaps best judged by their thickness. The thicker and slightly rounded 'drop-forged' or 'investment-

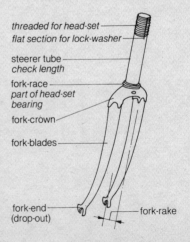

threaded for head-set
flat section for lock-washer
steerer tube
check length
fork-race
part of head-set bearing
fork-crown
fork-blades
fork-end (drop-out)
fork-rake

12.1 *Front forks*

(a) Conventional flat

(b) Semi-sloping

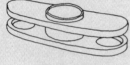

(c) Track-racing

(d) Fully sloping

blades fit over crown for flush joint

12.2 *Fork-crown types*

cast' models are more rigid than the thinner models stamped from flat plate. For the installation of mudguards it is important to check on the presence of eyelets, since nowadays these are often left off drop-outs meant for racing bicycles.

When replacing front forks, several points must be considered. Most important is probably the type of threading used on the steerer tube. Although most quality bicycles sold in the UK are built to the British BCI standards, the number of French and Italian machines sold lately

has been increasing. Some of these foreign bikes are built to metric (French) or Italian standards. You won't be able to tell the difference without accurate tools, but it is large enough to ruin a head-set or a set of forks if you try to match components with different threads. Even amongst British machines there is room for disaster. Cheaper Raleigh models, for example, are not built to the same industrial standards as lighter and fancier models. Table 10 on pages 263–4 provides a summary of the various threading systems.

The other points to consider are *blade-length* and *fork-rake*. The length of the fork-blades must match the wheel-size, allowing for mudguards which may or may not be fitted. Fork-rake is the offset which throws the front wheel-axle forward. The amount of rake is important for handling, comfort and toe-clip clearance.

THE HEAD-SET

The head-set is a double set of ball-bearings allowing the forks to turn in the head tube of the frame. It is perhaps the hardest working of all the bearings on your bicycle since it is subjected to the impact of road-shocks along its own axis. Even the highest quality head-set is barely good enough. It must be checked frequently and replaced when the bearing surfaces become pitted.

The 'cups' of the top and bottom head-set bearings are simply inserted to fit snugly into the ends of the head tube. The bottom race fits equally snugly over the fork-crown. The top race – which often looks more like a cup – is screwed on to the steerer tube and then held in place with a lock-washer and a lock-nut. The 'locking' is either provided by a flat section on the steerer tube with a matching lock-washer or else by a toothed lock-washer and a toothed cup. On bicycles with centre-pull brakes, a support for the brake

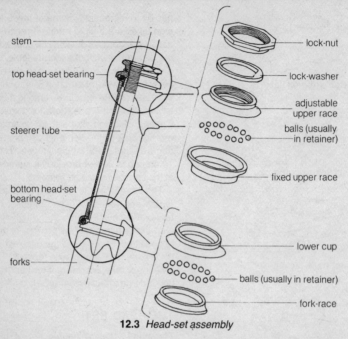

stem

top head-set bearing

steerer tube

bottom head-set
bearing

forks

lock-nut

lock-washer

adjustable
upper race

balls (usually
in retainer)

fixed upper race

lower cup

balls (usually in retainer)

fork-race

12.3 *Head-set assembly*

cable often takes the place of the lock-washer.

When replacing a head-set, it is important to note the industrial standard to which the bicycle is built. Italian and English standards (except for simple Raleigh models) are interchangeable, but French or metric components differ too much to be mixed. Both the clearance in the head tube and the threading of the steerer tube are significantly different. You should consult table 10 (pp. 263–4) and take both the old head-set and the front forks with you when buying a replacement.

THE HANDLEBARS

There are three main types of handlebar – flat, raised and dropped. Among the dropped handlebars, several different kinds are available, each one suited to a particular use. Tourers generally favour fairly wide handlebars with a relatively slight drop (for example, the French *randonneur* bar or the British North Bend). Racers will use a narrow bar with a relatively large drop for the road and an even deeper and slightly wider version for track racing. The handlebars most favoured are made of aluminium. Not only are they lighter, but their greater thickness makes them more comfortable and also slightly more resilient.

At least as important as the shape of the bars is the way in which they can be adjusted. Handlebars with a separately adjustable stem are far better than the simple versions that are welded to the stem in one piece. The only exceptions are 'roadster' bikes equipped with stirrup brakes since, in this case, an adjustable stem would interfere with the action of the brakes. Most bicycles have a binder-bolt clamped around the thicker centre section

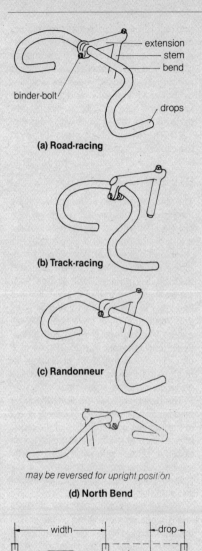

(a) Road-racing

extension
stem
bend
binder-bolt
drops

(b) Track-racing

(c) Randonneur

may be reversed for upright position

(d) North Bend

width — drop
reach

(e) Dimensional terms

12.4 *Handlebar types*

of the handlebar bend which allows the bars to be rotated or even replaced.

Upward and downward adjustments of the handlebars are possible by means of an expander-bolt which holds the stem to the steerer tube of the forks with either a cone or a wedge (fig. 12.5). To prevent the

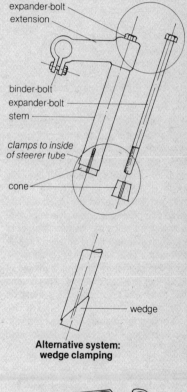

expander-bolt
extension
binder-bolt
expander-bolt
stem
clamps to inside of steerer tube
cone

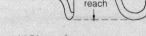

wedge

Alternative system: wedge clamping

Alternative system: recessed expander-bolt

12.5 *Handlebar stem*

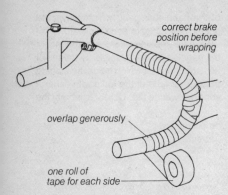

correct brake
position before
wrapping

overlap generously

one roll of
tape for each side

12.6 *Putting on handlebar-tape*

steerer tube being broken, the stem must
be inserted well beyond the end of the
threaded part of the steerer tube. Nowadays, the expander-bolt often takes the
form of a recess-headed 'Allen-bolt'
which is adjusted by means of a little
hexagonal tool called an 'Allen-key' instead of a normal spanner. It is important
to note that, since the inside diameter of
a French steerer tube is smaller, English
or Italian stems will not fit French forks.
Also, the diameters of various makes of
handlebar may be different. This means
that the stem and handlebars must be
matched.

Dropped handlebars are covered with
handlebar-tape to provide a comfortable

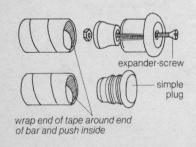

expander-screw

simple
plug

wrap end of tape around end
of bar and push inside

12.7 *Handlebar-end plugs*

grip (fig. 12.6). The tape may be of cotton,
plastic or leather. Cotton seems the best
and the price is reasonable. If you choose
plastic, you should make sure the tape is
not adhesive-backed, because if it is it
becomes very messy and sticky. The
ends of the tape are tucked into the bar-
ends and are held in place with plugs (fig.
12.7). These may help to prevent injury in
the case of an accident.

STEERING GEOMETRY

The steering geometry largely determines
the handling and the riding comfort of a
bicycle. The way in which the fork-rake
and fork-angle (or head-tube angle) are
combined is important. A shallower head-
tube angle will ensure that the front end of
the bicycle is more resilient. A bigger fork-
rake will also mean that the bike is more
springy. For this reason, touring bicycles
and 'roadsters' often have quite shallow
angles (72 degrees or less) and a relatively long fork-rake (up to 3¼ ins or 8
cm). This, together with clearance for
mudguards, results in a long wheelbase
and a comfortable, stable ride.

The disadvantages are that, on longer
bikes such as these, a lot of energy is lost
in the twisting and springing of the forks,
hills are harder to climb and handling can
become rather sluggish. This is why
modern racing bicycles (and even many
touring bikes) are built with a steeper
head-angle.

In order for a bicycle to follow a straight
line without too much effort on the part of
the rider, it must have a certain amount of
stability (called 'under-steering'). This
means that it should have a 'trail' within
certain defined limits – usually between 4
and 8 cm (1½–3¼ ins). 'Trail' is the
distance between the point where the tyre
is in contact with the road and the point
where the steering axis intersects the
road. It is the distance between points A

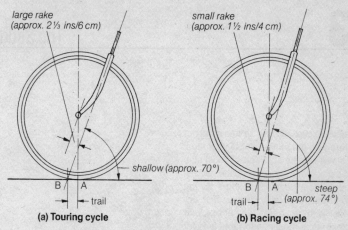

large rake
(approx. 2⅓ ins/6 cm)

small rake
(approx. 1½ ins/4 cm)

shallow (approx. 70°)

B / A

trail

(a) Touring cycle

B / A

trail

steep
(approx. 74°)

(b) Racing cycle

12.8 *Steering geometry*

and B in fig. 12.8. When the trail is nearer to 4 cm, the ride will be a little bumpy, but turning will be easy. At around 8 cm, you can ride for miles without using your hands, but the bike will be less manoeuvrable.

To achieve the right steering characteristics, head-angle and fork-rake must be considered together. To get the same handling with a steeper angle, you'll need less rake – perhaps 35 mm at 74 degrees – while a greater fork-rake will be appropriate for a cycle with a shallower angle – perhaps 65 mm at 70 degrees. When replacing forks, it is therefore important to make sure that the new one has the correct rake for the given head-angle and the kind of handling that you want.

For efficient cycling, your saddle must not interfere with the movement of your legs. It must not wobble about and it must stay in the same place in relation to the pedals. Although most people's bottoms do not respond too favourably to their first encounter with a hard leather bicycle saddle, it is the most comfortable type for cycling, and you will soon get used to it.

Sprung mattress saddles are not good. They are too wide, sloppy, wobbly and sticky, and they have a bad shape and a poor surface. So stick to leather or nylon. There's still plenty of choice – wide or narrow, single-sprung, double-sprung or non-sprung, with or without a nylon base, and men's or women's.

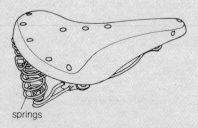

springs

13.2 *Leather touring saddle*

It is essential for the front of the saddle to be long and narrow and to provide leg guidance without interference, regardless of whether the bike is used for racing, touring or just riding in town. Besides having this long, narrow front (called the 'nose'), a racing saddle will be narrower than normal at the back, a touring saddle wider, and a women's model wider still. The wider female pelvis calls for a saddle that is wider at the back if the rider is to be at all comfortable. I'd say about 8 ins (20 cm) is adequate for most women. Some saddles do not have eyelets, so you'll have to buy a separate clamp if you want to mount a saddlebag.

Some saddles have a very thin leather cover over a stiff nylon base which may or may not be padded. These are a little lighter than leather models but, since they do not assume the contours of the rider with prolonged use, they must be comfortable from the outset or they'll never feel right. Leather does stretch and warp a little, and will keep in good condition if it is

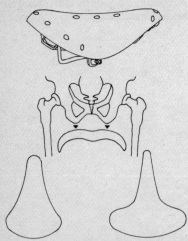

Selecting the correct width

13.1 *'Sports' or racing saddle*

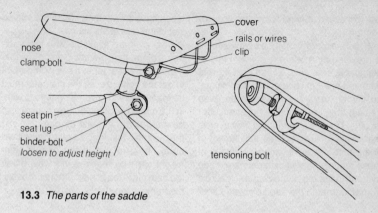

13.3 *The parts of the saddle*

occasionally treated with Proofide or neat's-foot oil underneath. More important still is to keep the leather *dry* at all times.

Fig. 13.3 shows the components of the racing saddle. The long wire rails are the only springing, apart from the leather it-self, provided in such a saddle. The nut in the nose allows you to tighten the cover.

All other adjustments are carried out with the clamp that holds the saddle to the seat pin. If the saddle is used with a conventional tubular seat pin, the clamp will have serrations which match the serrations on the bracket holding the rails. Angle-adjustment is limited by the difference in angle between these serrations (usually about ten degrees), and the distance from

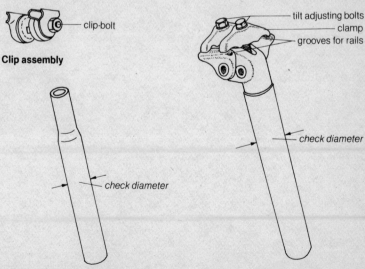

Clip assembly

13.4 *Conventional seat pin*

13.5 *Micro-adjustable seat pin*

one to the next may well prove too wide for comfort.

A more accurate method of adjustment is provided by modern aluminium micro-adjustable seat pins. These cost a great deal and are – in spite of the aluminium – no lighter. In fact, they are often even heavier than the conventional steel tubular pins. The great advantage, however, is that they provide accurate adjustment of angle and forward location. On many of these models, the adjustments are made by bolts in the top of the clamp – reached from underneath the saddle cover. Other types have a clamping bolt and a curved slot in the side of the clamp.

Seat pins are available with many different diameters, matching the inside diameter of the seat tube. It's very important to get the right size, so the diameter must be measured with a vernier gauge to within 0.2 mm. The length of the pin must also be adequate – at least 65 mm (2½ ins) must remain inside the seat tube or it will break, twist or slip. If the correct seat-height can't be reached this way, either the seat pin is too short or, more probably, the frame is too small.

Like so many other apparently simple components of a bicycle, the wheels are a minor technical miracle, a small triumph of human ingenuity. Considering their weight, they are astonishingly strong. They are flexible enough to provide an effective suspension system, they are rigid enough to transmit the driving force, and they run incredibly easily. In addition to this, the wheel consists of a number of simple and readily available components – the tyre, rim, hub and spokes – all of which may easily be replaced or repaired when worn or damaged (fig. 14.1).

THE TYRE

It is the outside diameter of the inflated tyre which determines the (nominal) size of the wheel. For sports and touring bicycles the 27-in size is common, 26 in is normal for 'roadsters', and the 700-mm metric size (often simply referred to as 27-in) is used for racing bicycles with tubular tyres. Tubulars or 'tubs' consist of a very thin rubber tube sewn up inside a cotton, silk or nylon cover with a light rubber tread; the whole thing is then glued to the (special) rim. All other tyres, referred to as 'wired-ons' (or sometimes incorrectly as 'clinchers'), comprise a separate inner tube and a cover which is held inside the edges of a conventional tyre rim by thin wires – usually of steel but sometimes of a man-made fibre – which are moulded into the sides of the cover. Fig. 14.2 shows a typical tubular tyre and fig. 14.3 a wired-on tyre, each mounted on the appropriate rim.

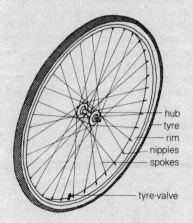

hub
tyre
rim
nipples
spokes

tyre-valve

14.1 *Parts of the wheel*

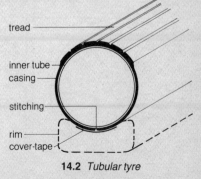

tread

inner tube
casing

stitching

rim
cover-tape

14.2 *Tubular tyre*

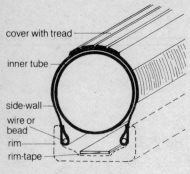

cover with tread

inner tube

side-wall

wire or
bead

rim

rim-tape

14.3 *Wired-on tyre*

Tyres differ not only in outside diameter but also in thickness or width, permissible pressure and tread pattern. Tubulars vary in width from 22 mm to 28 mm. The narrower models can be inflated to a higher pressure – which means a lowered rolling resistance but a rougher ride – and they usually have a thinner profile. They are lighter in weight and less durable. Since the inside diameter around the rim is fixed, their actual outside diameter varies with the width of the tyre – 685 mm (27 ins) is average for the heavier models.

Wired-on tyres are usually wider and heavier than tubulars, although lately high-pressure models with a narrow section and low weight have been introduced

in various sizes – most easily available to fit rims for 27-in and 700-mm tyres. A medium-weight 26 × 1⅜ in tyre with tube will weigh 700 gm, a light-weight 27-in tyre with tube 500 gm and a strong tubular around 350 gm. These different models will take pressures of 30, 80 and 100 psi (2, 5.4 and 6.8 bar) respectively and will last from 5,000 miles to as little as 1,000 miles of road-use. Since bicycle tyres are so narrow, I feel that tread-profile – needed to squeeze water out from under a wide car tyre – is unimportant. You'd probably do as well on a smooth tyre as on an intricate profile, except that you'll want a knobbly model for cyclo-cross.

In the mid-seventies, tyre and rim manufacturers finally combined to standardize the sizes of bicycle tyres so that they could be internationally interchangeable (ETRTO standards). Up to that time, you could never tell from one country to the next which tyre would fit your rim and which would not. Although we still refer to the nominal size of a tyre in inches, tyres now also bear a second series of numbers: e.g., 32–630 for a 27 × 1¼ in model. The first (two-digit) number refers to the cross-section of the inflated tyre in millimetres; the second (three-digit) number refers to the 'bed' or 'shoulder' diameter of the rim on which the tyre will

14.4 *Tyre dimensions (example 27 × 1¼ ins)*

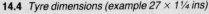

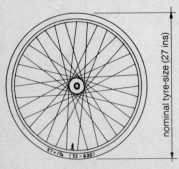

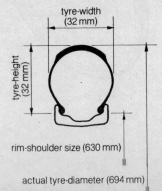

tyre-width
(32 mm)

tyre-height
(32 mm)

rim-shoulder size (630 mm)

actual tyre-diameter (694 mm)

nominal tyre-size (27 ins)

27 × 1¼ (32 - 630)

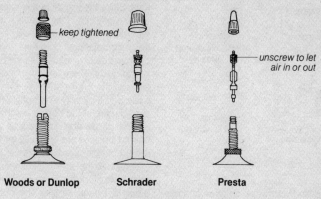

Woods or Dunlop   **Schrader**   **Presta**

keep tightened

unscrew to let air in or out

14.5 *Valve types*

fit. If you have a 630-mm rim, you now know that almost any tyre with a denomination of xx–630 should fit it. Fig. 14.4 clarifies this, and equivalent tyre-sizes are given in table 7 (p. 261).

Air is let into the inner tube by means of a valve which may be any one of three different designs (fig. 14.5). Most common on light-weight bicycles is the Presta valve; it must be unscrewed before air can be pumped in and fastened after the correct pressure has been reached. Still the most common on other bikes is the Woods or Dunlop valve which has a little rubber tube that must occasionally be checked or replaced; it is very vulnerable to vandalism since the inside can so easily be removed. The Schrader valve is the same as those found on motor tyres. Each type of valve requires its own particular pump, although adaptor-nipples will sometimes adapt a pump to a different kind of valve. The use of a tyre-gauge on Presta and Schrader valves is highly recommended to ensure the correct pressure. To establish the correct pressure, consult table 8 on page 262. Remember that high tyre-pressure is the key to reduced rolling resistance, as well as long tyre and tube life. You may have heard of

semi-solid inserts as a replacement for the conventional inner tube. They don't puncture, but they're horrible to ride. I don't recommend them.

THE RIM

The tyre rim may be one of three basic designs: Sprint, Endrick or Westwood. Tubular tyres require the Sprint rim, the Westwood rim is used with stirrup brakes and the Endrick rim is for calliper brakes in

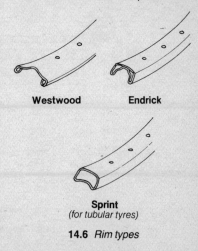

Westwood   **Endrick**

Sprint
(for tubular tyres)

14.6 *Rim types*

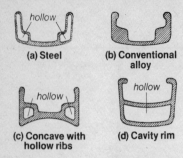

(a) Steel

(b) Conventional alloy

(c) Concave with hollow ribs

(d) Cavity rim

14.7 *Variants of the Endrick rim*

combination with wired-on tyres and has therefore become standard for sports and touring bicycles. For tubular tyres, the Sprint rim is almost invariably made of aluminium, though wooden rims do exist. The two other models are available in aluminium, chromium-plated steel or stainless-steel versions, but aluminium is advisable since it gives much better braking in wet weather. Chromium-plated steel rims are disastrous if used in the rain with almost any normal brake-block mate-

rials. Since the weight of all moving parts – especially that of the wheels – is important, aluminium rims should in any case be recommended for their lightness. Stainless steel rims are the next best.

Today there are many different versions of the Endrick rim being manufactured and they vary in weight, width and rigidity. I prefer the design which has two internal hollow ribs. The various 'double-bottom' designs are specially for the narrowest of high-pressure tyres. It is worth making sure that an aluminium rim is reinforced with 'ferrules' at the spoke-holes in order to extend its life. The number of spoke-holes and the size of the valve-hole must be noted when replacing a rim.

THE HUB

The hub forms the heart of the bicycle wheel. Although there are versions on the market with built-in three-speed gear mechanisms, brakes or light-generators, the hub always conforms to the principles shown in fig. 14.8. It is a hollow shell to

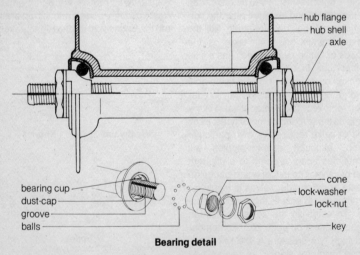

hub flange
hub shell
axle

cone
lock-washer
lock-nut

bearing cup
dust-cap
groove
balls

key

Bearing detail

14.8 *The parts of a hub*

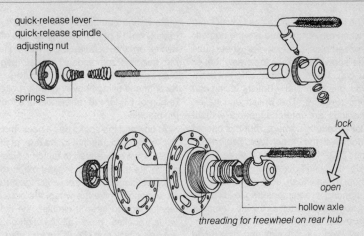

quick-release lever
quick-release spindle
adjusting nut

springs

lock

open

hollow axle
threading for freewheel on rear hub

14.9 *Quick-release hub*

which the spokes are attached and which runs on a set of ball-bearings around a central axle attached to the frame. The hub of the rear wheel accommodates either a fixed cog, a simple freewheel or a freewheel with a cluster of sprockets for derailleur gearing.

Hubs for racing or sports bicycles are usually equipped with a quick-release mechanism (fig. 14.9) and sometimes with wing nuts. I do not recommend wing nuts since they will not allow the wheel to be sufficiently tightened in the frame. Tighten the quick-release mechanism by closing the lever, not by screwing down the thumb nut! You should get a clearly recognizable locking action if the thumb nut has been correctly adjusted beforehand.

You can recognize quality by a careful inspection of the outside of the hub. The shell should be of aluminium and constructed in one piece. Inside the difference will be seen in the finish and hardness of the bearing races and cones. They should turn smoothly if they are of a satisfactory quality and if they are correctly adjusted and lubricated. Lubrication

is usually done with light grease, although oil can be used provided that it's changed after every ride – something that some 'time-trial' racers actually do!

Most manufacturers of hubs for lightweight bicycles make them in two versions – *large-flange* and *small-flange* (fig. 14.10). This does not affect the quality of

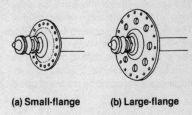

(a) Small-flange   **(b) Large-flange**

14.10 *Hub-flange types*

the hub, but it does affect the rigidity of the finished wheel. The small-flange hub allows a greater range of spoking patterns to give a more flexible, more comfortable wheel. I like to use the somewhat lighter small-flange hubs on a road-racing machine; for touring with luggage I choose the large-flange. Most track-racers also choose large-flange hubs.

The most important things to watch out for when replacing a hub are the number of spoke-holes and and – on rear-wheel hubs – the screw-thread for the freewheel or rear cog. There are three different standard types of thread – British, Italian and metric (French). The British and Italian threadings are interchangeable without causing serious damage, but this cannot be done with the French type. Table 10 on pages 263–4 gives details of thread standards. If a single fixed-cog is used (i.e., without a freewheel), the hub must have a left-handed thread measured to fit such a cog; some hubs, such as the old Campagnolo models, may have both – a freewheel thread on one side and a fixed-cog thread on the other. Finally, the width of the hub may vary. To allow the use of a freewheel with six or even seven sprockets, a greater axle length is needed than for the standard freewheel with only five sprockets.

THE SPOKES

The spokes – laced into an intricate pattern – are what keeps the wheel together. The individual spoke (fig. 14.11) may be either *plain*, that is, having a constant diameter, or *butted*, that is, thicker at the ends than in the middle. In either case, the thickness is indicated by means of one or more gauge numbers. Plain spokes are usually no. 14 (2 mm); butted spokes are thinner in the middle, e.g., 15/14 (1.8 mm middle, 2 mm ends). Table 12 (page 265) explains the gauge numbers. I recommend using heavier-gauge spokes (e.g., no. 13) for the rear wheel of a touring machine.

At one end the spoke has a hook and a thicker head to attach it to the hub; at the other end it is threaded to match a nipple which fits through the spoke-hole in the rim. The length of the spoke is measured as shown. To give the wheel the correct tension and to keep it circular, the individual spokes must all be tightened equally, a task that should be repeated at least after every five hundred miles or whenever the wheel has lost its roundness.

The pattern in which a wheel may be spoked is referred to either as a *radial*, a *one-cross*, a *two-cross*, a *three-cross*, or a *four-cross* pattern, as shown in fig. 14.12. To transmit the driving forces, the rear wheel should have a three-cross pattern at least, four-cross really being possible only on a wheel with small-flange hubs. In order to minimize weight and air resistance, the front wheel is sometimes spoked radially. For the same rather absurd reasons, the number of spokes on the front wheel is sometimes reduced to 32 or 28, the usual number nowadays

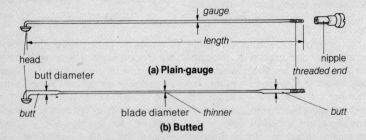

14.11 *Spokes*

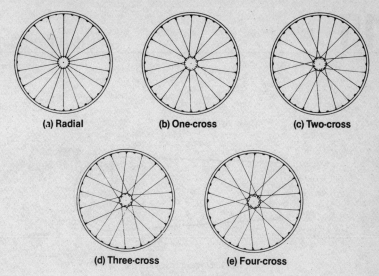

(a) Radial   (b) One-cross   (c) Two-cross

(d) Three-cross   (e) Four-cross

14.12 *Spoking patterns*

being 36. Tandems and heavily loaded bikes should have a greater number of spokes, especially on the rear wheel where either 40 or 44 are advisable.

15

The Drive-train

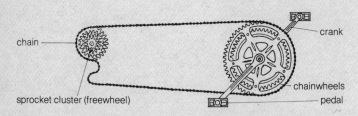

15.1 *Drive-train system*

The complex of components which transmits the power produced by the rider to the rear wheel is referred to as the drive-train. It consists of the pedals, the crankset, the chainwheels, the chain and the freewheel cluster or fixed cog on the rear wheel. These cannot be simply regarded as single components, but must be seen as a system in which each part matches the others. The derailleur, which may also be considered part of this complex, will be discussed separately in the next chapter.

THE PEDALS

There are at least four types of pedal, each one best adapted to a particular purpose. The conventional 'rubber-block pedal' is still the best choice for many simple bicycles, such as 'roadsters', 'shoppers' and children's bikes. Make sure it runs on ball bearings – many cheap versions do not – and that the pedal is wide enough not to turn under your feet. Built-in reflectors are a useful safety-feature of many of these pedals, but

(a) Rubber-block

(b) Quill

(c) Platform

(d) Rattrap

15.2 *Pedal types*

toe-clips cannot easily be installed on a rubber-block pedal.

On all other types, toe-clips can be installed. Personally, I like the flat and comfortable 'platform pedal', though it is not a very common type: Lyotard manufacture the only version I can afford. Toe-clips, if fitted, must be the right size for the foot. Fig 5.7 (page 37) shows how they should fit. Many racing pedals are available in a range of widths. Choose the narrowest that fits your shoe. For city cycling with street shoes, you may consider using short, strapless toe-clips.

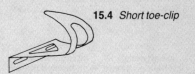

15.4 *Short toe-clip*

The interior of a pedal is shown in fig. 15.5, which also illustrates the method of adjustment. Since pedals have to resist great stress, subjected as they are to high intermittent and asymmetrical forces, their correct adjustment and lubrication is quite important. You can recognize a good quality pedal by the fact that the entire central section, including the hub, ribs and flanges, is constructed of a single piece of forged aluminium, whereas cheaper models are pieced together and will not be so precise or last so long.

There are an astonishing number of things that can be done incorrectly when installing a pedal. The first thing to do is to note which pedal goes on the left and which on the right. If they are not marked 'L' and 'R', you must hold them against the light and establish which has the left-

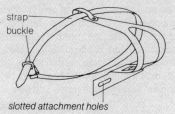

strap
buckle

slotted attachment holes

15.3 *Conventional toe-clip*

Although many experienced cyclists dislike these, I find they work very well in combination with platform pedals (fig. 15.4).

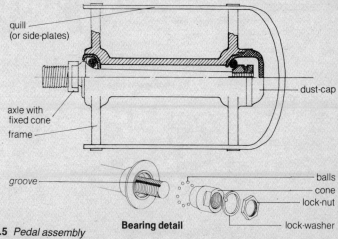

quill
(or side-plates)

axle with
fixed cone

frame

dust-cap

groove

balls
cone
lock-nut
lock-washer

Bearing detail

15.5 *Pedal assembly*

up to left   up to right

(a) Left pedal   **(b) Right pedal**
left-handed thread   right-handed thread

15.6 *Left or right pedal?*

handed thread (fig. 15.6). The one that has goes on the left crank and is screwed on by turning it to the left. To unscrew, it must be turned to the right. The other pedal goes on the right-hand side; it screws on by turning to the right and unscrews by turning to the left. In addition to this, pedals may have either French (metric) or International (British) threading. A 'W' on a French pedal may stand for Whitworth, which is British; and 'M' on a pedal may stand for metric. Table 10 (pages 263–4) gives the details.

THE CRANK-SET

The crank-set is installed at the point where the seat tube and down tube of the frame join the chain stays in the bottom bracket. It consists of the axle, the cranks and the chainwheels. The bottom-bracket bearings may be one of two designs: BSA or Thompson (there are, in fact, three but the American Ashtabula type is rarely seen in this country). Fig. 15.7 shows the two types side by side. On the conventional BSA type (which is usually better) the bearing cups are screwed into the bracket lug and are adjustable. On the Thompson bracket (found only on cheap imported machines) the cups are merely pushed inside the bracket shell and adjustment can only be made by means of an adjustable cone, similar to the one used on a wheel-hub but bigger. By comparison with the BSA, water and dust are

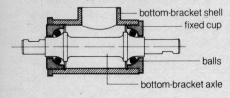

(a) BSA type (conventional)

bottom-bracket shell
fixed cup
balls
bottom-bracket axle

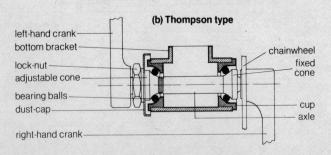

(c) Adjusting detail (BSA)

lock-ring
axle
adjustable cup
bearing balls

(b) Thompson type

left-hand crank
bottom bracket
lock-nut
adjustable cone
bearing balls
dust-cap
right-hand crank

chainwheel
fixed cone
cup
axle

15.7 *Bottom-bracket assembly*

free to enter a Thompson bottom bracket, and it must therefore be checked, cleaned and lubricated more often. It is now customary to install a plastic sleeve inside the bottom-bracket shell (around the axle) to protect the bearings against dirt entering through the frame tubes or cut-outs of the bottom-bracket shell.

The problem of different screw-thread types is also found in (BSA) bottom brackets. Bottom brackets may be threaded to one of four different standards – English, Italian, French or Swiss. In the case of English and Swiss threading, the right-hand side of the bottom bracket (the fixed-cup side) uses left-handed threading. French and Italian threading is right-handed on both sides of the bracket. English and Italian threads are also of a different size from the metric threading of the French and Swiss standards. Table 10 (pages 263–4) illustrates this.

The cranks are attached to the bottom-bracket axle either by a cotter pin or by some form of 'cotterless' system. A cotterless crank is better. It has a square, tapered hole which matches a square, tapered end on the axle. The crank is then held in place by a bolt or a nut. Fig. 15.8 shows the two systems. Cotterless cranks are usually of aluminium and are considerably lighter. During the first hundred miles or so they must be tightened at least every twenty-five miles, using a special tool that should be purchased with the bike.

Either one, two or three chainwheels are attached to the right-hand crank. On the cheapest 'roadsters' and 'shoppers' these are usually 'swaged' or moulded on and cannot be interchanged. On all good quality crank-sets, they are interchangeable. An attachment device (in one of the three designs shown in fig. 15.9) is connected to the crank and the chainwheels are attached by means of small bolts and nuts. The hallmark of quality for a cotterless crank is the integral construction of the right-hand crank and chainwheel-attachment arms. On cheaper and less rigid models, the arms are 'swaged' on to the crank.

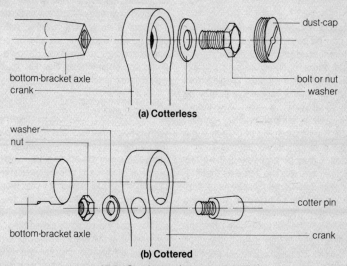

(a) Cotterless

(b) Cottered

15.8 *Crank-attachment systems*

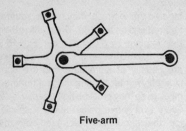

Five-arm

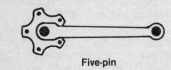

Five-pin

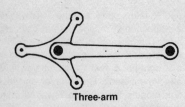

Three-arm

15.9 *Chainwheel-attachment types*

Most cranks are 170 mm (6¾ ins) long. This can be regarded as a satisfactory size for most riders but, for discriminating cyclists, some manufacturers also supply longer and shorter models, ranging from 160 to 185 mm. A longer crank may be more suitable for a rider with longer thighs, and a shorter one for smaller people. A measurement of 0.2 times the inside-leg length is sometimes recommended. It may be argued that the effect of a longer crank is the same as that of a lower gear, since it reduces the necessary pressure on the pedal while increasing the 'travel' or 'leverage'. Whatever the length, you should take care that the threading matches that on the pedal; once again, table 10 (pages 263–4) provides the details.

Chainwheels, like cranks, are nowadays made mostly of aluminium for high quality bicycles. Since aluminium versions may be made thicker without being made too heavy, and since manufacturing techniques for aluminium parts are more flexible than those used for steel, they are usually more rigid and yet lighter than steel chainwheels. On the other hand, steel chainwheels are probably tougher. Any interchangeable chainwheels must match the pattern of the 'attachment spider' on the right-hand crank, which sometimes means that they must be the same make and model.

On a double chainwheel, that is, for a ten-speed bicycle, the larger chainwheel is mounted on the outside and the smaller one inside. The sizes available vary from make to make and from type to type – they will almost all be available with between 42 and 52 teeth, but for bigger or smaller sizes your choice of chainwheels, and therefore of crank-sets as well, will be limited to a few makes and types. TA has by far the best range of differing sizes, especially for small chainwheels; these go down to wheels with as few as 26 teeth. To use a triple chainwheel (fifteen-speed), you will require a special crank and a special, longer axle. Keeping the chain and chainwheels clean is the best way to increase their life.

THE CHAIN

With its five hundred or so individual parts, the modern bicycle chain is another great achievement in the efficient transmission of power. Power and energy losses for the bicycle chain are probably lower than for any other means of transmission and the thing costs next to nothing! Fig. 15.10 shows how the chain is assembled. It is connected at the ends either with a master link, as for the slightly wider ⅛-in chains used on simple bikes which don't

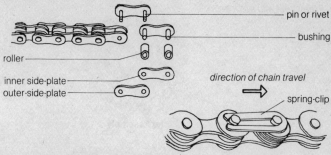

pin or rivet

bushing

roller

inner side-plate
outer-side-plate

direction of chain travel

spring-clip

15.10 *Chain*

Master link

have derailleur gearing, or simply by pushing one of the pins or rivets out and joining it to the last link in the loop, as for the narrower $^3/_{32}$-in chains used on derailleur bicycles as well as for those used on most racing machines with a fixed wheel.

The length of the chain link is always ½ in (with the exception of one very rare and expensive model) and this matches the distance between individual teeth on the chainwheel and the sprockets. The size designation is therefore ½ × ⅛ in for bicycles without derailleur and ½ × $^3/_{32}$ in for derailleur machines.

The life of a chain depends very much on the way it is cleaned and lubricated, as

does the efficiency with which it operates. Occasionally, the chain tension and length must be checked (as shown in fig. 15.11). If the chain lifts off the chainwheel more than 3 mm (⅛ in), it should be replaced. If you allow it to wear and stretch too far, the chainwheels and sprockets may also need replacing – an expensive and otherwise unnecessary process. Cleaning is done with paraffin oil and lubrication with any oil or special chain-lubricant. My best results have been with synthetic motor oil, which has incredibly high 'film-strength' and does not attract dirt.

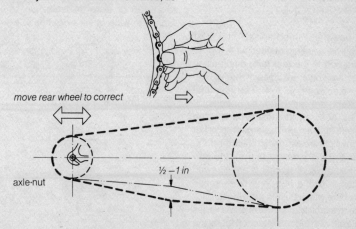

move rear wheel to correct

axle-nut

½ – 1 in

15.11 *Checking chain tension*

15.12 *Freewheel and sprockets*

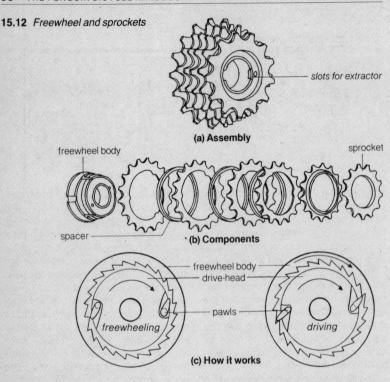

— slots for extractor

(a) Assembly

freewheel body

sprocket

spacer — '(b) Components'

freewheel body
drive-head

pawls

freewheeling

driving

(c) How it works

THE FREEWHEEL AND REAR SPROCKETS

The freewheel mechanism on most bicycles is a self-contained unit that is screwed on to the rear hub, again using one of three different types of thread (see table 10 on pages 263–4). The individual sprockets are attached by means of 'splines' or screw-threads, depending on the make and model. The largest sprocket of a multiple freewheel is placed on the inside and the smallest one on the outside. Fixed-wheel sprockets are screwed directly on to the hub, and three-speed hubs come with a built-in freewheel.

The availability of sprocket-sizes varies quite a bit, with models intended for racing usually having between 13 and 22 teeth

while touring models can have as many as 28, 30 or even 34 teeth. On some Japanese wide-range freewheels, every

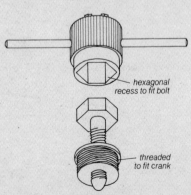

— hexagonal recess to fit bolt

— threaded to fit crank

15.13 *Crank-extractor*

other tooth is missing from the larger cogs to facilitate gear-shifting over the large differences between gears.

Some of the necessary work on the drive-train components will require a few simple specialized tools. I suggest you purchase these tools at the same time as the bicycle. A matching crank-extractor for the cotterless crank-set (fig. 15.13) is most useful and is frequently needed. Its use, as well as that of other tools, will be discussed in Part IV.

Chain Line

The correct alignment of the chain line is essential for the proper operation and efficiency of the entire drive-train and gear-change mechanism. If a single chainwheel and a single rear sprocket are installed, these two must lie directly in line with one another. This may be checked by looking along the chain from behind and by trying to line up the sprocket with the chainwheel. If multiple chainwheels and/ or sprockets are used, the chain line should be through the middle of the respective combinations (fig. 15.14). Spacers may be used on the rear hub to correct the chain line if necessary.

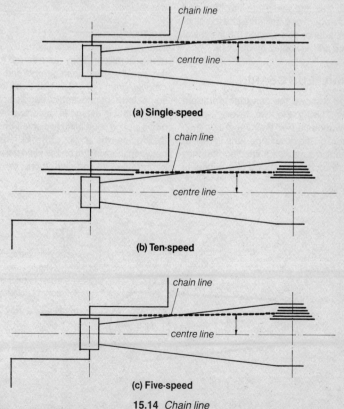

(a) Single-speed

(b) Ten-speed

(c) Five-speed

15.14 *Chain line*

Since I have already examined the advantages and disadvantages of the two gear-change systems common on bicycles – the derailleur and the hub gear – I will restrict the discussion here to the actual mechanisms involved. In the case of derailleur gearing, these are the front and rear changers or derailleurs and the shift-levers, and for hub gearing the insides of the hub and its control mechanism.

DERAILLEUR GEARING

Fig. 16.1 shows the complete derailleur system. Using the two levers – here shown mounted in their most common position, on the down tube – the derailleur mechanisms may be shifted so that they move the chain from one chainwheel to the other or from one sprocket to another. Usually, two chainwheels and five sprockets are provided, making a total in theory at least of ten different gears. Most gear-changes are made with the rear derailleur which is easier (and quicker) to shift anyway.

The Rear Derailleur

There are at least three distinct categories of rear derailleur. They are referred to as the *parallelogram*, *pantograph* and *box parallelogram* (fig. 16.2). All three have some form of moveable parallelogram linkage that is extended or contracted to move a cage containing two small wheels that guide the chain. The difference between them is that on the plain parallelogram the linkage lies more or less

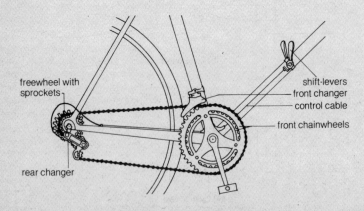

freewheel with
sprockets

rear changer

shift-levers
front changer
control cable

front chainwheels

16.1 *Derailleur gearing system*

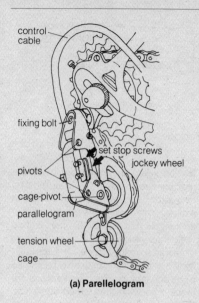

(a) Parellelogram

(c) Box parallelogram

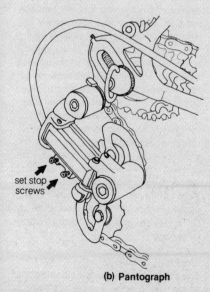

(b) Pantograph

16.2 *Rear derailleur types*

vertically, on the pantograph it lies more horizontally, and on the box parallelogram it lies inside a fixed member.

The most common type is the plain parallelogram, made by most European manufacturers. It is characterized by its very direct shifting action and it is preferred by most racers. Pantograph derailleurs are particularly popular with touring cyclists since they can handle larger gearing steps. This is because the cage which carries the two wheels and the chain travels along a path that closely follows the profile of the sprocket cluster. Pantographs are made by the major Japanese manufacturers to suit touring (for large gearing steps) and racing (small steps). European manufacturers only build these models for touring bicycles. The box parallelogram (made only by the French Huret company) has the same characteristics as the pantograph but tends to be rather flimsily constructed.

The derailleur is controlled by a Bowden cable which pulls the mechanism outwards against the tension created

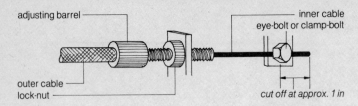

adjusting barrel

inner cable
eye-bolt or clamp-bolt

outer cable
lock-nut

cut off at approx. 1 in

16.3 *Barrel adjuster*

by a spring, built into the linkage or its container. Cable tension is adjusted by means of a *cable-adjusting barrel* or by clamping the cable at a different point, and the amount of travel in each direction is limited by a *set stop* or *limit screw*. These little screws usually have a tiny spiral spring which keeps them in the position in which they are set, even after miles of cobblestone paving. The travel of the linkage will have to be adjusted with these screws if the chain shifts past the last sprocket and lands either on the outside (between the freewheel and the frame) or on the inside (between the largest sprocket and the spokes).

The chain itself is guided through the cage and around the *tension wheel* and *jockey wheel* as shown in fig. 16.4. Spring

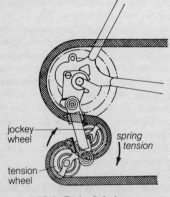

jockey
wheel

spring
tension

tension
wheel

16.4 *Path of chain*

tension keeps the chain taut when the rear wheel is installed. The chain must be the narrow $1/2 \times 3/32$ in size and be without a master link – unless the master link is of an intricate new design that makes it no wider than the other links.

As with so many bicycle parts, the quality of the derailleur can usually be judged by its appearance. The best versions are made of finely finished forged aluminium. Thin metal stampings, gaps, rough edges, etc., can all be seen as signs of an inferior product – one that will probably not shift smoothly and consistently and which may well wear out before its time.

At least as important as its quality, however, is the *range* or *capacity* of a derailleur. Most models will have no difficulty in shifting any combination of gears up to a 26-tooth sprocket and a total tooth-difference of 28 teeth. This last figure is a measure of how much chain can be taken up by the rear derailleur: the largest chain-wheel plus the largest sprocket minus the smallest chainwheel and the smallest sprocket. For mountain touring you may have to use special wide-range models, usually recognizable by letters such as GT in their designation and by their extra-large cage.

The Front Derailleur

The front derailleur is simpler than the one at the back, since it does not have a mechanism that keeps the chain tensioned. A simple guide encloses the chain

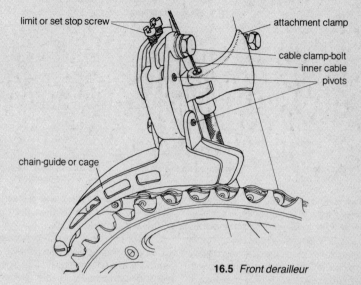

16.5 *Front derailleur*

and pushes it to the left or the right either by means of a parallelogram linkage or a simple slide. A barrel adjuster for the cable and two limiting set screws are usually provided. Except for some Japanese models, the cable action is such that you have to pull the chain out on to the larger chainwheel (for a higher gear) and release the spring action in the linkage to move it to the smaller inside chainwheel (for a lower gear).

The chain-guide must be installed at a certain distance from the chainwheel (fig. 16.6). Sometimes, shifting may be improved by bending the front ends of the sides of the guide inwards slightly, but ensuring that the chain-guide is absolutely parallel to the chainwheel is usually sufficient. Here again, range is important, if you plan to do mountain touring and want to use wide-range gearing. The *wide-range* models that can handle the difference between a really big and a really small chainwheel may be distinguished by the size of their chain-guide – it should curve down quite a long way.

Shift-levers

Shift-levers for derailleur gears may be installed at one of three points – on the down tube, at the handlebar ends or on

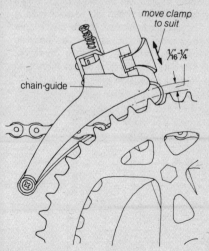

16.6 *Chain-guide clearance*

16.7 *Gear-shift levers*

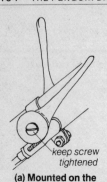

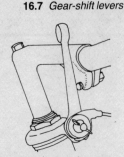

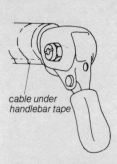

cable under
handlebar tape

keep screw
tightened

**(a) Mounted on the
down tube**

(b) Mounted on the stem

**(c) Mounted on the end
of the handlebar**

the handlebar stem. Each point requires a different type of mechanism. I consider stem shifters to be potentially dangerous – especially for male riders. Of the other two versions, more precise and usually more convenient shifting is achieved with down-tube shifters. This is because a shorter cable is required to reach from the derailleur to the position near the middle of the down tube.

The shifter for the rear derailleur is mounted on the right-hand side and the one for the front is on the left. Often the frame is equipped with bosses for the installation of the shift-levers; if not, they must be mounted with a separate clamp that is sold with the levers as a single unit. The little wing nut or screw which tightens the lever assembly must be kept tight to avoid accidental shifting when you don't mean to change gear.

Control Cables

Shifting action is transmitted from the shift-levers to the derailleurs by flexible Bowden cables. These consist of a metal-wire inner cable to take up tension and a spiral-wound metal outer cover to take up compression forces. One end of the inner cable is equipped with a nipple. Derailleur control-cable nipples are usually shaped like one of those in fig. 16.8. Other nipples are meant for brake-control cables. The nipple end of the inner cable is inserted into the shift-lever and the other, plain end is clamped at the derailleur.

The correct cable tension can be adjusted approximately by clamping the inner cable at a different point; fine adjustment to accommodate cable stretch is achieved with the barrel adjuster (see fig. 16.3 on page 102). When installing or adjusting control cables, several things should be noted. In the first place, the correct nipple and the correct thickness of inner cable must be used. But the right length is also important. To avoid leaving large loops or loose ends, cut off the inner and outer cables as short as possible without interfering with their operation. The cuts must be clean so that there is no 'burr' or protrusion left.

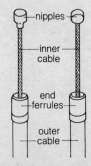

nipples

inner
cable

end
ferrules

outer
cable

16.8 *Derailleur cable*

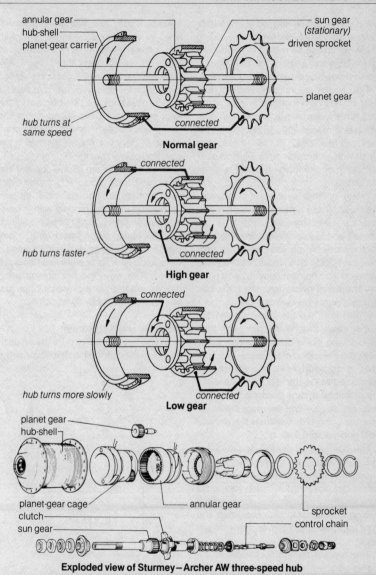

annular gear
hub-shell
planet-gear carrier

sun gear
(stationary)
driven sprocket

planet gear

hub turns at same speed

connected

Normal gear

connected

hub turns faster

connected

High gear

connected

hub turns more slowly

connected

Low gear

planet gear
hub-shell

planet-gear cage
clutch
sun gear

annular gear

sprocket
control chain

Exploded view of Sturmey–Archer AW three-speed hub

16.9 *Three-speed hub* (courtesy T I Sturmey–Archer Ltd)

HUB GEARING

I don't usually advise people to bother themselves with the construction of a three-speed hub, much less a five-speed. However, in case you are curious, here is a brief description of the way these technical miracles work (fig. 16.9). Instead of being connected directly to the wheel hub, the rear sprocket is connected to a sliding clutch which can be moved to make contact with various parts of the internal works (known as the *planetary gears*).

The *planet gears* are small-toothed gear-wheels held together in a cage. Inside, they mesh with a central *sun gear* which is immobile and which forms part of the fixed rear-axle. On the outside, they mesh with an *annular gear*, a hollow gear with teeth on the inside pointing towards the centre.

When the shift-lever is set to 'normal', the clutches are arranged in such a way that the planetary-gear system is bypassed and the sprocket drives the hub-shell directly. When you select the 'high' gear, one clutch is moved to make contact between the sprocket and the cage holding the planet gears, and the other one makes contact between the annular gear and the hub. As the cage pushes the planet gears around the sun gear, they turn, driving the annular gear at a faster rate than the speed of the cage. The 'low' gear is engaged when the sprocket is connected to the annular gear and when the planet-gear cage is connected to the hub. The cage – and therefore the hub – now turns more slowly than the annular gear and the sprocket.

The operation of the five-speed hub is too complicated to explain here. It is enough to say that it comprises two sets of planet gears and many more very small components. However, it *is* possible for a cycling enthusiast to take one apart and put it back together again so that it will still work!

The relative numbers of teeth in the planet-gear system determine the variation or 'spread' between the gears. Sturmey–Archer used to produce a whole series of different models, from versions with a wide range to those with a narrow range, which had two, three, four or five

speeds. Today, the five-speed model at least is available once more, and, with luck, other models will be re-introduced as well. On the common three-speed AW (wide range) model, the gears are spread slightly too far apart: minus 25 per cent for the low gear and plus 33$\frac{1}{3}$ per cent for the high gear. The S5 five-speed model has gears with values of minus 33$\frac{1}{3}$ per cent, minus 21 per cent, normal, plus 26$\frac{2}{3}$ per cent and plus 50 per cent.

Although Shimano, Sun-Tour and the German Fichtel & Sachs Company also manufacture three-speed hubs, as well as oddities like the models with a built-in coaster brake or automatic shifting, I would highly recommend you to buy British where hub gearing is concerned. I have seen all sorts of worn and damaged parts which were the products of other makes, while Sturmey–Archer hubs just keep on going if properly lubricated.

Controls and Adjustment
A simple lever with three marked positions mounted on the handlebars or, in the

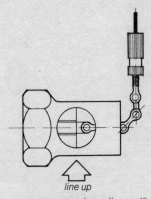

line up
engage second gear ('normal')
before adjusting

16.10 *Three-speed adjustment*

case of a five-speed, a double cable with two shift-levers, controls the rear-wheel hub. The cable usually runs over at least one little roller. This is the point to check if the gears do not shift smoothly; as a result, you may have to replace either the roller or the cable. Adjustment is illustrated in fig. 16.10. With the lever set to 'normal', the illustration shows what should be seen through the hole in the right-hand wheel nut. You must make adjustments with the adjustment barrel if yours is not the same as the picture. More details are given in Part IV.

17

A considerable amount of kinetic energy is stored in a moving bicycle – enough to crack your skull or to demolish the front of your machine should you collide with a fixed object. On the other hand, the energy is sufficient to keep the bike rolling – overcoming friction and wind resistance – for quite some time as long as there is nothing to obstruct your progress. It's the function of the brakes to dissipate this stored energy in a harmless and efficient manner, quickly but gently.

To achieve this, the brakes have to convert the stored kinetic energy to another form of energy. In the case of a bicycle brake this takes the form of heat. The heat is lost to the air, and although this may be wasteful it is better than cracking skulls. Large metal surfaces are ideal for dissipating the heat generated, so good brakes depend on good wheel rims. The second criterion necessary for good braking is the directness of the action. The closer to the point of contact with the road, the better the braking will be.

Clearly, the rim brake is the best brake possible. It is very close to the point of contact with the road and it operates on the large cooling surface of the rim. However, the rim brake has the disadvan-

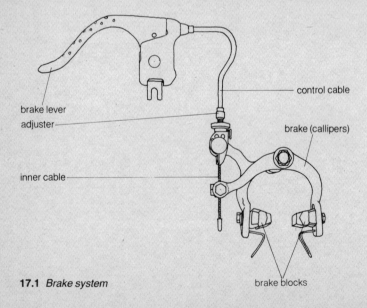

brake lever

adjuster

inner cable

control cable

brake (callipers)

brake blocks

17.1 *Brake system*

tage that it tends to become wet in the rain (or even on a wet road) and it stays wet long after it has stopped raining. The moisture on the rim acts as a lubricant which reduces friction and thus cuts braking efficiency.

Other forms of brakes have been developed which are less susceptible to the effects of moisture, but they all have their disadvantages. However, several improvements can be made to the rim brake which largely compensate for the loss of power caused by moisture on the rims. To derive the greatest benefit from your rim brake it is important to choose the right rims (aluminium is usually the best) and the right brake blocks. You must also keep the rims clean and check that they are perfectly round.

RIM BRAKES

Rim brakes either push against the sides of the rim or pull up against the inside. The latter are called *roller-lever* or *stirrup brakes* and the former are known as *callipers*. Calliper brakes come in three distinct types: *side-pull*, *centre-pull* and *cantilever*. Stirrup brakes are now only seen on some heavy 'roadster' bicycles. Of the other types, the centre-pull is usually the most satisfactory for price, weight and quality. Side-pull brakes are either very expensive (in which case they are good for racing bikes, although not necessarily any better than centre-pulls) or they are cheap and ugly. Cantilever brakes are often installed on cyclo-cross bicycles and on tandems.

The Side-pull Brake

This is the simplest and most common type of calliper brake. The side-pull brake consists of two brake arms which pivot around the mounting bolt. A spring wrapped around the mounting bolt provides the tension to keep the brake arms apart when the brake is not engaged. The brake blocks are attached through the slotted ends of the brake arms, which allows for their adjustment. Each brake arm has an extension to which in the one case the inner cable, in the other case the adjuster for the outer cable is attached. A high-quality brake will be of aluminium and of fairly rigid construction.

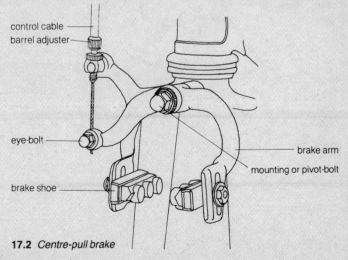

control cable
barrel adjuster
eye-bolt
brake shoe
brake arm
mounting or pivot-bolt

17.2 *Centre-pull brake*

The Centre-pull Brake

Centre-pull brakes consist of a yoke (fixed to the frame at the front fork or the rear-seat-stay bridge) and two brake arms which turn around pivot-bosses on the yoke. A spring which pushes the brake arms away from the rim is wound round each pivot-boss. A brake shoe, which holds the brake block, is attached to the lower end of each brake arm, and the upper ends are connected by a straddle cable. An anchor-plate at the end of the control cable pulls up the centre of the straddle cable when the brake levers are applied. This forces the brake shoes inwards against the sides of the rim.

When selecting a centre-pull brake, it is worth remembering that rigidity is the best way of judging reliability; the arms and the yoke should be fairly strong and solid. The brake shoes must be adjusted so that they strike the sides of the rim firmly over their

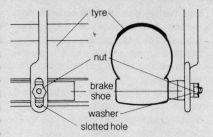

17.3 *Brake-shoe alignment*

entire length (fig. 17.3). The brake arms must be the correct length to allow this adjustment to be made within the length of the slot. Consequently, a brake made for a wide-clearance touring bicycle may not fit a tight racing frame (or *vice versa*).

The greatest advantage that a centre-pull brake has over other forms of rim brake is that it will operate quite satisfac-

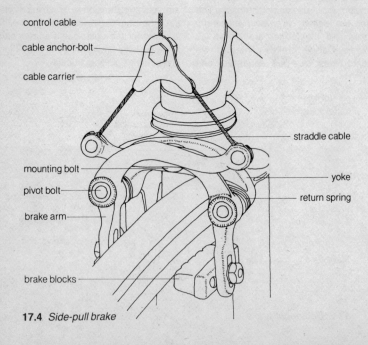

17.4 *Side-pull brake*

torily even when the wheel is slightly buckled. It will follow the wobble in the wheel when the brake is applied, yet it can usually be adjusted so that it is far enough from the rim not to drag while riding. Although riding this way is not recommended and should be corrected as soon as possible, it can happen all too often when touring with a loaded bike over rough terrain.

The Cantilever Brake

Unlike the other two types of calliper brake, the cantilever brake is not complete in itself, but must be mounted on pivot-bosses which are attached to the frame and front forks. The way it works is similar to the centre-pull brake but, since there is no separate yoke, it will not follow any wobble in the wheel. Its advantage lies in the directness of its braking. This makes the cantilever brake especially suitable for tandems and cyclo-cross bicycles where very hard braking is more necessary than braking which needs to be precisely controlled.

The Stirrup Brake

One wonders why this survival of cycling before the Second World War has not vanished like the chamber pot and the paddle-steamer. It seems in every way inferior to other kinds of rim brake. It is

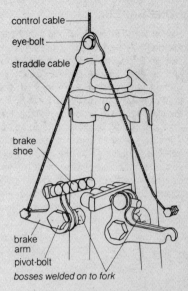

17.5 *Cantilever brake*

extremely heavy, it is difficult to adjust, its clumsy rod mechanism is very complicated, it is less efficient and it makes wheel changes and handlebar adjustment very difficult. Fig. 17.6 shows how it pulls up against the inside of the wheel rim. Stirrup brakes require Westwood rims and rather wide tyres. They are adjusted by adjustable joints in the pull-rod system.

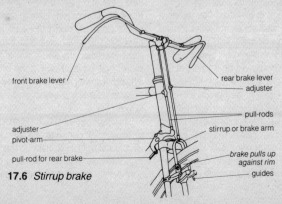

17.6 *Stirrup brake*

HUB BRAKES

Similar to the drum brake of a motor-car, the internally expanding hub brake is considered to be one of the most powerful and reliable bicycle brakes. Sturmey–Archer manufactures them for both the front wheel and the rear, and for use with the three-speed gear. Some manufacturers – chiefly the French Maillard company – make rear-wheel models for use with derailleur gearing, and these are ideally suited to tandems. The most recent Sturmey–Archer models, which are highly popular in Holland and Switzerland, are surprisingly light and effective and also allow the use of derailleur gearing.

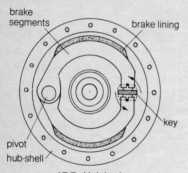

brake segments
brake lining
key
pivot
hub-shell

17.7 *Hub brake*

The greatest advantage of the internal-expansion brake is that it is, in the words of its chief manufacturer, 'self enclosed'. In other words, it is tucked away inside a widened hub and so is not affected by rain, sleet, snow or mud. This makes it an ideal brake for everyday cycling. The brake shoes should be checked once a year for wear and if necessary should be re-lined by a Raleigh dealer or any firm specializing in motorcycle or car brakes.

I doubt whether the hub brake can be as efficient as the rim brake if the latter is kept in good condition and if the brake blocks and rims are well-chosen. Firstly, the cooling surface of the drums is consider- ably smaller than that of most rims; secondly, the fact that the drums are mounted in the centre of the wheel means the braking force has to be transmitted via the spokes, which is rather indirect.

OTHER BRAKES

Four other types of brakes, although rare or unknown here, should be briefly mentioned. They are the *coaster brake*, the *disc brake*, the *plunger brake* and the *band brake*.

The coaster brake, also known as the 'back-pedalling' brake, can only be mounted on the rear wheel and is operated by pedalling backwards. It has a small cooling surface and consequently does not absorb energy efficiently, having a tendency simply to slam hard against the wheel and let the tyre take the strain. At best, this makes it suitable only for very low-speed cycling. Coaster brakes are standard for 'roadster' bicycles in Northern Europe, the USA and some underdeveloped countries where sudden but reliable braking at low speeds is more important than fast cycling and controlled braking. The coaster brake shares with the hub brake an immunity to bad weather.

The disc brake (fig. 17.8) is popular in Japan, and Shimano also offers one for sale here. It is used on the rear wheel and must be combined with a special, narrower hub. Although the disc is still exposed to the weather, it is further from the road than the rim and it therefore works better in wet weather. On the other hand, it has to transfer its braking force along the spokes, just like the hub and the coaster brake.

The plunger brake is monstrous and antiquated. It consists of a rubber plunger which is simply pushed on to the front tyre. You will see this kind of thing on cheap continental bicycles in combination with a

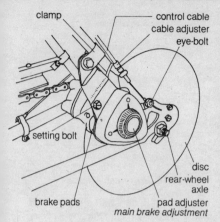

17.8 *Disc brake*

coaster brake on the rear wheel.

The band brake is a contracting brake shoe that is wrapped around an extension of the hub. It is as old as the British cycle industry, but is nowadays only seen in the Far East, where it is used like the coaster brake in most other parts of the world.

BRAKE LEVERS AND CONTROLS

The coaster brake is operated by the chain, but all other types of brake are hand-controlled by levers on the handlebars and either Bowden cables or pull-rods. The heavy pull-rod is still used for the stirrup brake and sometimes for the hub brake, but the standard method of brake operation nowadays is the Bowden cable.

The Bowden cable used for braking is similar to the one described in the preceding chapter for use with derailleurs, but it should have a thicker cross-section than the derailleur cable since it must carry stronger forces. Adjustment of the brake is necessary from time to time, to compensate for brake-block wear. It is done with the barrel adjuster as shown in fig. 17.9. When no more adjustment is pos-

17.9 *Brake adjustment*

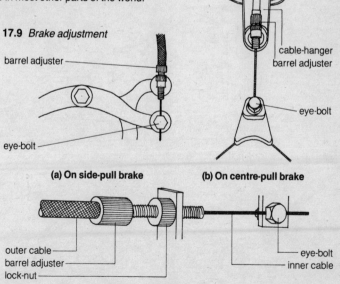

(a) On side-pull brake

(b) On centre-pull brake

Detail

sible with the barrel adjuster, the inner cable must be clamped at a different point.

Brake cables should be run in such a way that they are not forced to make excessively tight curves but must still be as short as possible in order to minimize friction. When it is first installed (and, after this, at least twice a year) the inner cable should be lubricated with light grease. It is important to make sure that no burrs have formed at the ends, especially when replacing or shortening the outer cable, since these will increase friction enormously. The inner cable will fray and eventually break at the nipple. Check this point and replace it before it is too late!

Brake levers are available in different styles intended either for dropped handlebars or for flat and upright models. Those for dropped bars should be padded with rubber hoods. Levers are usually

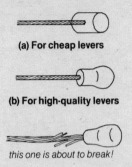

(a) For cheap levers

(b) For high-quality levers

this one is about to break!

17.10 *Brake-cable nipples*

attached to the bars with a screw-clamp which is reached through the opening formed when the brake lever is pulled. They should be installed so as to ensure a comfortable reach and adjusted so that they don't 'bottom out' when pulled. Children's levers should be smaller and closer to the bars than on adult models.

17.11 *Brake levers*

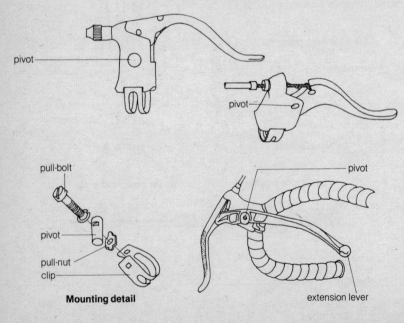

pivot

pivot

pull-bolt

pivot

pull-nut

clip

pivot

Mounting detail

extension lever

(a) On brake lever

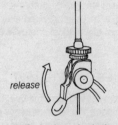

(b) On brake or brake hanger

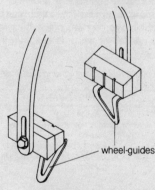

wheel-guides

(c) Wheel-guides

Some brake levers come with extensions also known as *safety levers* or *suicide levers* – the term you use depends on your point of view. They are intended to make the brakes easier to operate from the flat top of dropped handlebars. Although I do not take quite such a dim view, calling them 'suicide levers' draws attention to the fact that extensions are not rigid enough and often act too indirectly to ensure safe braking from the top position. My objection is that they make it difficult to hold the bars at the point where I hold them quite frequently – just above the brake levers in the bend of the handlebars. Fortunately, extensions can be easily removed.

To facilitate wheel removal and adjustment, a quick-release mechanism is often built into the brake lever or the hangers to which the outer cables are anchored. Modern expensive side-pull brakes often lack this feature, relying instead on a wheel-guide at the brake shoe to ease the tyre past the brake. These methods are shown in fig. 17.12. Brakes with 'automatic' adjustment use a little ratchet mechanism to keep the cable tensioned, although even these need occasional extra adjustments by hand.

17.12 *Brake-release devices*

18

'Lighting' is in fact rather a grand term for even the best of provisions made on a bicycle. The lighting capacity is severely restricted, since the source of energy is limited to what the cyclist himself provides, either in the form of energy stored in an electric battery or in the form of energy generated locally by a dynamo driven by pedal-power. The results are slight in comparison with the mass of light produced in front of a motor-car. The average car has about 100 watts of lighting power; the average bike only about 3 watts. However, it is quite possible to

achieve a satisfactory and safe level of lighting on a bicycle provided that the small amount of electrical energy is used sensibly.

BATTERIES OR DYNAMO?

The two main lighting systems both have their advantages and disadvantages (see below). The dynamo system has a single central power source – a generator or dynamo which is mounted so that it can be brought into contact with one of the tyres when needed or which is built into the

Table 18.1 *The advantages and disadvantages of the three main lighting systems*

LIGHTING SYSTEM	ADVANTAGES	DISADVANTAGES
Dynamo (tyre-driven)	1. Always available for use 2. Inexpensive to operate 3. Requires relatively little maintenance 4. More powerful than battery lights 5. Brighter when going faster 6. Less likely to be vandalized or stolen	1. Causes drag 2. May not work well in snow or rain 3. Cannot be used separately 4. Does not work when bike is not moving
Dyno-Hub (hub-driven)	1. Less drag than ordinary dynamo 2. Works well in any weather 3. Suitable for combination with rechargeable batteries 4. Other advantages same as above (except no. 4)	1. Less bright than ordinary dynamo 2. Expensive to install
Battery	1. Can be used off the bike 2. No drag 3. Works when not moving	1. Relatively expensive to operate 2. More prone to trouble 3. Easily stolen or vandalized 4. Less bright (especially headlight)

wheel so that it turns whether needed or not. Wires connect the headlight and the rear light to the dynamo.

Battery lighting usually requires two separate units, each with its own battery, reflector, lamp and switch. One is mounted in front; the other has a red lens and is mounted at the rear. Hybrid systems, in which a single central battery feeds the two separate lights or where a rechargeable battery is used in conjunction with a charging dynamo, are also possible but are rare enough to be ignored here.

The quality of both available types of lighting system has improved greatly since the two British Standards for bicycle lighting equipment were introduced in the seventies – BS 3648 for rear lights and BS AU–155 for front lights. These provide minimum standards for the shape of the light beam which combines good vision and clear visibility with the smallest possible consumption of electrical energy. I strongly advise you to make sure you only use lights that conform to these standards.

Battery Lights

The usual battery light – front or rear – has a battery, bulb and switch built in. To prevent anyone turning on the switch while you leave the bike unattended, it's advisable to take the headlight (which is usually removable) off the bike. The rear light is sometimes mounted upside down to make the switch a little less inviting. Another advantage of this position is that rain-water is less likely to get in and ruin the batteries – but first make sure that there are no holes in the bottom.

Batteries last for quite a long time if they are not exposed to water or left on for long periods. Used for half an hour a day, they last for many more hours than if switched on for several hours at a stretch. The nominal rating of a single-cell battery is

1.5 volts, so two in series will produce 3 volts. After they have been on for some time, this voltage drops rapidly, reaching an average value of about 1.2 volts.

For this reason, the correct bulb to use with two 1.5 volt single-cell batteries is one rated at 2.4 volts, not 3 volts. The amount of light will vary during the life of the battery: it will be bright at first, then dim to an average of 2.4 volts which it will hold for a long time, then finally diminish to nothing. Replace batteries when they *begin* to get dim; don't wait until they're completely dead. If you find yourself with a nearly extinguished battery and no spare, you may be able to stretch its life just a little by placing it over heat for thirty minutes or so.

Rear lights are not simply headlights with red lenses. They disperse the light much more widely. For this reason, the French 'Slim-Lite' and similar models from the Far East are a poor choice. As with headlights, the 'Ever-Ready', however maligned, remains the best available – at least at the time of writing.

Dynamo Lights

With dynamo lighting, a single, central electrical source generates the electricity which is divided between the two lights. The dynamo itself is an AC generator. This means it produces 'alternating current' that can be said to go backwards and forwards rather than in one direction, as DC, or 'direct current' (the kind of electricity stored in a battery), does. The electrical output depends basically on riding speed. The internal coils of a good generator, however, have a significant 'impedance' (that is, resistance to alternating current) at the high frequency achieved when the dynamo is driven fast. Consequently, the voltage never far exceeds that reached at about 16 km/h (10 mph) and this prevents the bulbs from burning out at higher speeds.

Due to the mechanical losses inherent in the usual design of dynamos (which run at high speeds on plain sleeve bearings), their mechanical 'drag' is high – rather like pushing a lawnmower by hand. The Sturmey–Archer Dyno-Hub is an improved generator which eliminates such mechanical losses. It is not driven by the tyre via a little roller, but is built into the wheel, thereby also eliminating the effects of foul weather. Voltage control is slightly less precise and there is rather less power at normal operating speeds than with a normal dynamo, but the advantages of having less drag and more reliability in bad weather should not be ignored.

A tyre-driven dynamo is best mounted on the rear wheel: it is safer and simplifies the wiring (fig. 18.1). So-called *block-*

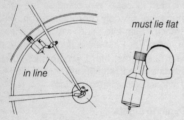

must lie flat

in line

18.1 *Dynamo alignment*

dynamos, which have a headlight attached, are usually unsatisfactory because of several factors: front-wheel mounting which is too low, a small head-

light and poor adjustability. Larger dynamos recently imported from the Far East generate more power (6 watts instead of 3 watts) at a higher voltage (12 volts instead of 6 volts) but they all seem to have poor voltage control, which often leads to the 12 volt bulb burning out (and replacements are hard to find). However, a 'heavier' 6 volt rear bulb (i.e., one with a higher wattage rating) may help.

The modern low-friction roller dynamo, which is mounted behind the bottom bracket, is very good. It runs on roller bearings, which create less drag, and it can also be used with tubular tyres since it is pushed against the profile of the tyre rather than the side, like other generators. Tyres for use with ordinary dynamos should have a kind of serration on one side (and should therefore be mounted the right way round), to prevent slip when the tyre gets wet. In general, dynamos with metal rollers seem to slip less than those with plastic rollers, although a rubber cap installed over the roller will also prevent slippage.

Wiring systems for dynamo lighting usually use the metal of the frame for one connection and wires from the generator to each of the lights for the other. The Dyno-Hub, however, requires double wiring: i.e., the frame must be insulated from the circuit. Fig. 18.2 shows which connections are to be made in either case.

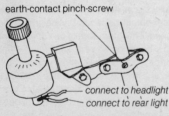

earth-contact pinch-screw

connect to headlight
connect to rear light

Tyre-driven dynamo

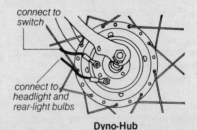

connect to switch

connect to headlight and rear-light bulbs

Dyno-Hub

18.2 *Dynamo connections*

Hybrid Systems

The Dyno-Hub, in particular, lends itself to use with rechargeable batteries to form a hybrid electrical system which will work all the time – even when the cycle stands still. A proposed diagram for such a system is given in chapter 40.

If, on the other hand, you use normal lights with rechargeable batteries, you should remember that modern NiCad batteries behave differently from conventional types. They produce a constant 1.2 volts per cell but run out very suddenly, so you should carry a fully charged spare.

HEADLIGHTS

Whether powered by a battery or a dynamo, the standard BS AU–155 for headlights specifies photometric standards to which headlight beams should conform. The light intensities at various points in the path of the beam are measured in lumens. These minimum requirements ensure that a path will be adequately illuminated which is long enough and wide enough (measured at some distance from the bicycle) for safe cycling at night – provided of course that the right batteries and bulbs are used and that the beam is correctly adjusted.

The shape of the beam itself varies. The conventional round source gives a conical beam and throws an elliptical or parabolic spot on the road. Other beams are in the shape of a cross and throw a spot of light shaped like the one shown in fig. 18.3 on to the road. To achieve such an intricate beam, the lens on the head-

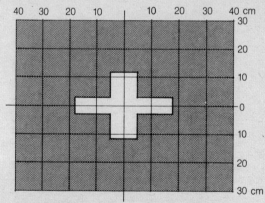

18.3 *'Ideal' beam for a bicycle headlight*

Cross-shaped (BS AU-155) beam projected on to wall from distance of 100cm (40 ins)

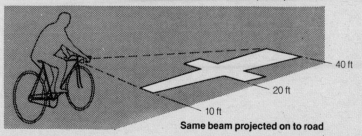

Same beam projected on to road

light is designed in a complex pattern of grooves and ridges. This treatment ensures the best possible lighting. In other words, the maximum amount of light will fall in the most important area and the minimum amount of light will be wasted in other directions. With a good lens, a relatively weak source of power (requiring little dynamo drag or ensuring a long battery-life) will be adequate to give a reasonable quality of lighting. In general,

it can be said that a good headlight will have a relatively large diameter (or, if it has a rectangular shape, a relatively large diagonal width).

Lastly, the headlight should be mounted as high as possible – on the handlebars is a better position than the front forks – and, when mounted, it should be adjusted as in fig. 18.4 or 18.5, depending on the beam-shape.

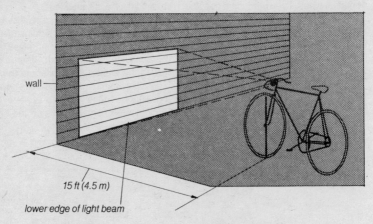

18.4 *Adjusting headlight with rectangular or round beam*

18.5 *Adjusting headlight with cross-shaped beam*

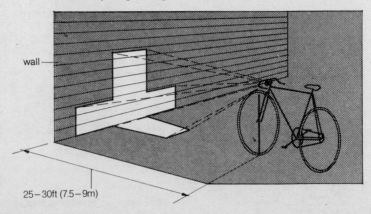

REAR LIGHTS

Good rear lighting means that the cyclist is clearly visible to others. The standard BS 3648 is therefore primarily a standard which specifies the size, colour, spread and reflectivity of the rear light, although it also specifies the maximum allowable battery-drain for battery versions (similar to the requirements for headlights). In general, a good rear light must be large, red and reflective. It should also be mounted high up on the bicycle, and great care must be taken that it does not become obscured to the rear or sides by luggage.

REFLECTORS

With reflectors it is possible to achieve a level of visibility far in excess of the powers of most bicycle lighting systems themselves – provided that two conditions are met:

(a) the reflective surface is facing directly towards the path of a strong source of light; for example, a car head-light;

(b) the paths of the bicycle and the other vehicle are either directly in line or converge beyond the faster vehicle's braking distance.

The second condition is often badly misunderstood. It means that lateral reflectivity, such as that provided by reflective tyre side-walls or spoke reflectors, is of no use whatever. The only useful reflector is one mounted on the rear facing backwards. A brief look at a full moon will clarify another condition. The effectiveness of a reflector is directly related to its surface area – the bigger it is, the brighter it will be. I consider a surface

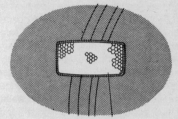

18.6 *Reflector*

area of 60 cm² (10 sq in) to be adequate. Mounting the reflector as low as possible will improve its effectiveness when cars use dipped headlights.

In any direction not covered by the reflector, the electric lights of the bicycle must make the cyclist visible. For this reason, it is of paramount importance for these lights to be large, high and un-obscured.

19

My definition of an accessory is anything that may usefully be attached to a bicycle and which is directly related to the operation of the machine but which is not essential to it. Consequently, I'll ignore radios and heart-rate monitors, as well as purely decorative items. What we will consider are mudguards, chainguards, luggage carriers, locks, prop stands, pumps, water bottles, cyclometers, speedometers and bells.

MUDGUARDS

Although the 'roadster' comes equipped with mudguards, many lighter machines do not. If you intend to fit them, I would recommend the lightest models available. Plastic 'Bluemels' mudguards are good but rather fragile, especially in winter when they crack easily at freezing temperatures. German 'ESGE' guards are more durable. They are built from a fibre-reinforced plastic and are made to look like metal. They come in two widths; get the wider one.

Metal mudguards are all right, but they are heavier and have a tendency to rattle and rust if the wrong materials are selected. Choose only aluminium or stainless steel, and take any sign of rattling as a message that something is wrong. Fasten mudguards as soon as they come loose. Long-distance tourists tend to favour metal mudguards, especially the aluminium versions, which are light and

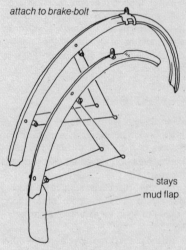

attach to brake-bolt

stays
mud flap

19.1 *Mudguards*

very strong. Unlike the plastic versions, they will not crumple if a branch gets caught between the front wheel and the mudguard.

In some countries, the rear mudguard has to be partially white to increase visibility. Although there is no such law in Britain, it isn't a bad idea. For this reason I would not suggest selecting dark colours, but choose either the bright reflective metal ones or a white plastic model, preferably with a good-sized reflector installed.

CHAINGUARDS

Here, I would suggest that either you go all the way or don't bother at all. The very sturdy, fully enclosed chainguards that come on luxury 'roadster' bikes – old-time favourites in the export market – perform very well. They protect not only flapping trouser legs and long skirts but also the chain itself. An exposed chain becomes dirty and wet and looses its lubrication very rapidly, but, when fully enclosed, it may travel five thousand miles without additional lubrication, cleaning or even adjustment.

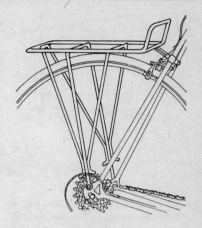

19.3 *Rear carrier*

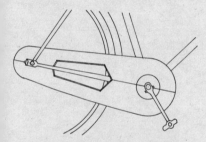

19.2 *Fully enclosed chainguard*

The Dutch de Woerd company manufactures a chainguard of this kind, using light but strong plastic. It can be easily installed on any bike provided that it does not have derailleur gearing. If you use derailleur gearing, you'd be best advised to forget about a chainguard altogether. The customary narrow strip, inaccurately described as a chainguard, that can be installed on a derailleur bicycle only means there is more to rattle and come loose; in fact, the main advantage of this device seems to be that it can be easily removed. The 'chain ring' often installed over the top of a chainwheel is equally useless – it rubs either against the chain or against the front derailleur, and it gets in the way when the chain accidentally runs off the chainwheel.

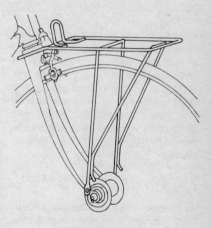

19.4 *Front carrier*

LUGGAGE CARRIERS

These were discussed earlier in chapter 9. I wouldn't be without one, certainly not for everyday cycling. Do get a safe device for attaching things to the rack – preferably a leather belt rather than the popular elastic cords. These have a tendency to get caught in your spokes when they come loose – a very unpleasant experi-

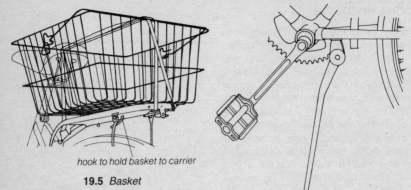

hook to hold basket to carrier

19.5 *Basket*

ence. There are also wire baskets that fit on the rack; the best ones are made of plastic-coated metal.

LOCKS

In addition to locks that have separate chains or cables (see chapter 9), there are locks that can be mounted and left on the bike. These don't usually provide the security of a chain lock but are handy if you leave the bike for a few minutes in an area where a professionally equipped bicycle thief would be easily noticed – in front of the library or on a busy shopping street.

PROP STANDS

As a general rule, these objects are ridiculous. They are supposed to support the bicycle from one side – providing nobody breathes (fig. 19.6). There are, however, two models on the market that are not quite so useless. The first is mounted much closer to the rear wheel than normal (fig. 19.7); the other, which originated on the continent, has two legs instead of one. This will even support a loaded bicycle (but not one loaded with a child!) and can also be used as a repair stand (fig. 19.8).

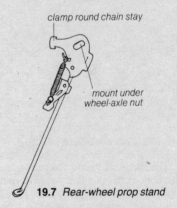

19.6 *Conventional prop stand*

clamp round chain stay

mount under wheel-axle nut

19.7 *Rear-wheel prop stand*

19.8 *Double stand*

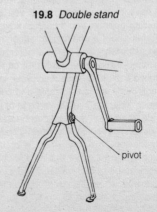

pivot

19.9 *Pump*

mushroom clip
attach to frame tube

thumb lock

PUMPS

The message is brief: don't get one with a flexible tube-connector, since it will not allow you to pump up the tyres to a sufficiently high pressure. Ask any physicist if you don't believe me. Modern, high-pressure tyres − even wired-ons − take pressures of up to 115 psi (8 bar), and that calls for a very powerful pump. The best make at the time of writing is 'Zefal'.

Nowadays, 'frame-fit' pumps are popular; they fit directly between the tubes of a (men's) frame. Elegant though these are, they have a handle that seems designed to make pumping impossible. So you may prefer the kind that are held at the top by a mushroom clamp on the frame tube and at the bottom by being clamped between the frame tubes at the bottom bracket. For those with more money than sense, there are carbon-dioxide (CO_2) cartridges for 'automatic' tyre-inflation!

WATER BOTTLES

And that's what you put in it: water, without soda or alcohol − although fruit juice or tea are all right. Buy the most expensive bottle-cage (because it will be light and won't rattle, rust or break) and the cheapest bottle (because that will be stolen). Once it has been stolen, you can replace it with a washing-up liquid bottle, which is bigger anyway. Since vigorous cycling causes a loss of water at a rate that exceeds the body's capacity to absorb it, the best thing to do is to drink

frequently, beginning well before you leave home. Two water bottles on the bike, each holding one pint, are no luxury − and I suggest you refill the bottles well before they are empty.

To store hot drinks, or to keep cold ones cool, you can buy 'thermobottles' insulated with styrofoam. These have a slightly smaller capacity but may be useful. You can keep an ordinary bottle cool by wrapping it in a wet cloth, keeping it wet by occasionally squirting some water out of the bottle − although I don't recommend this with fruit juice.

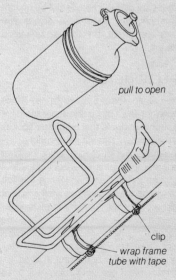

pull to open

clip

wrap frame tube with tape

19.10 *Water bottle and cage*

CYCLOMETERS

This gadget counts the miles you've ridden. There are two types: those that go
'tick . . . tick . . .' and those that don't. I like
the ones that don't. Although they're more
expensive they are silent and accurate,

19.11 *Belt-driven cyclometer*

rubber belt

need no adjustment and stay on the wheel
when you take it off. Huret is the only
manufacturer of this type (at least at
present). If you do choose the other
variety, you may consider placing a piece
of valve-tube over the little nipple that's
mounted on a spoke to deaden the sound.
Either type of cyclometer must be bought
to match your wheel-size, unless you
intend to cheat on the accumulated
mileage.

SPEEDOMETERS

Once again, there are two types – if we
ignore for the time being the expensive
electronic gadgets that count the spokes
as they go by. The simplest variety runs
off a little roller pushed against the tyre;
the other kind runs off a toothed wheel
attached to the front hub. Since the first
type is cheaper, easier to install and is at
least as accurate (since it is even independent of tyre-size), I'd suggest you
choose that one, especially if you have a
machine with quick-release wheels. They
are made by I K U and Huret. It is advisable to make the little roller run on a
treaded part of a tubular tyre since it will

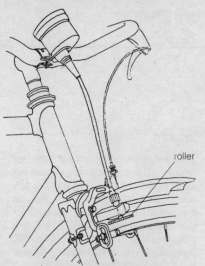

roller

19.12 *Tyre-driven speedometer*

slip on the smooth side-wall when wet. If
you buy a speedometer you will not have
to buy a cyclometer, since the mileage is
recorded as well.

BELLS

Bells are anti-pedestrian devices and, if
the political cyclists don't grow up and
accept the fact that cycles are vehicles
and belong on the road, we may soon
need them as much as they do on the
continent. The simplest bell is one that
has no rotating mechanism inside but
which relies simply on a spring-activated
hammer at the end of the finger-lever.
This type is light and doesn't rust, break or
rattle. If it fails to work, it can be adjusted
by bending the lever. A drop of oil on the
pivot-point will also be well rewarded.

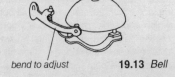

bend to adjust   19.13 *Bell*

20

There's a lot more than just iron to today's version of the 'iron horse' and, although it is the manufacturer of the bicycle who usually selects the materials for the various components he installs, it's useful for the cyclist himself to have some idea of the materials used. Not only the materials but also the finish applied to the bicycle and its many components determines to a large extent the quality and life-span of the entire machine.

STEEL AND STEEL ALLOYS

Steel is nothing but iron with a little carbon added to make it stronger. The more carbon, the stronger the steel – up to a maximum of about 0.3 per cent. Steel bicycle frames made of normal-diameter welded tubes (fig. 20.1) should have a

wall-thickness of about 1.4 mm; those made of cold-drawn tubes (fig. 20.2) about 1.2 mm. Cold-drawn tubes are drawn out of the solid metal, resulting in a seamless tube; cheaper welded tubes can be distinguished by feeling for the internal seam on the inside of the lugs (this is most easily done at the bottom bracket). The weight saved by using seamless tubing is about twenty per cent of the frame-weight.

Not only will a lighter frame weigh less, it will also ride better and have a more responsive 'feel'. Selecting even stronger materials results in frames that are even lighter and better to ride. To achieve the greater strength which allows the tube walls to be even thinner, the steel must be 'alloyed' – which means that other metals are mixed with the 'smelt'. The first metal

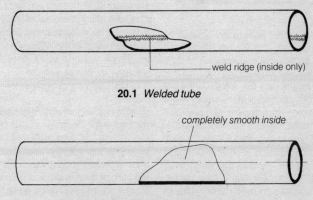

weld ridge (inside only)

20.1 *Welded tube*

completely smooth inside

20.2 *Seamless tube (plain gauge)*

used is manganese, and even the better grades of carbon steel have up to 0.9 per cent manganese content. Other metals used for alloying are chromium, molybdenum, nickel and vanadium – always used in very small percentages.

The resulting alloys are variously called chrome-moly steel, manganese-molybdenum steel, etc., and are usually so much stronger that the same tube-strength may be achieved with tubes as thin as 0.9–1.0 mm. The best known of these materials is of course Reynolds 531 (a manganese-molybdenum alloy), but there are several other types, including the even stronger Reynolds 753 and foreign makes like Columbus, Ishiwatha, Vitus and Tange. Only Reynolds 531 has the advantage that it may be brazed at higher temperatures (up to 850° C or 1,560° F) without any significant loss of strength; the other alloys all seem to be limited to brazing at lower temperatures. This is only possible with the more expensive silver brazing rods, and these are difficult to use.

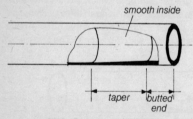

smooth inside

taper   *butted end*

20.3 *Butted end of tube*

More weight may be saved if the walls of the tubes are thicker at the ends – at the points where the highest stresses are concentrated – than they are in the middle. This results in 'butted' tubing, already mentioned in chapter 11. A label on one of the frame tubes usually explains this. If the label is unintelligible, it may be because it's written in French. This will mean that the dimensions of the tubes will have been made to French standards and will be slightly smaller in diameter. Cable clamps and other attachments made to fit a British bike may therefore be impossible to tighten. Worse than this, though: the frame will not be quite as rigid.

Parts of the bicycle which may also be made of some form of steel include non-structural members (e.g., mudguards), minor structural parts (e.g. spokes and luggage carriers), ball-bearing parts, axles and fasteners. For some of these components, relatively cheap steel may be strong enough, but axles and ball-bearing parts require special steels with special treatments if they are to be satisfactory.

These parts must all be extremely tough, resisting deformation even when considerable forces are exerted on them, and – the ball-bearing parts at least – must have very hard, smooth and accurate surfaces. Ordinary carbon steel is often suitable for bearing parts provided that they are 'case-hardened' (i.e., packed with glowing carbon for some time) in order to create a very hard layer on the surface without making the inside of the component too brittle. Special steel alloys with higher percentages of chrome are even more suitable. Sometimes, stainless steel is used for parts like the spokes and the chain. I don't recommend it, despite its attractiveness, since it is not as tough as other materials.

ALUMINIUM AND ALUMINIUM ALLOYS

Weight is a very important consideration, especially for the moving parts of a bicycle. Where the possibilities of making a component with light tubular steel or steel alloy is limited (due to the complexity of the part), it is often made of aluminium or an aluminium alloy. Once again, alloying other metals with the aluminium base

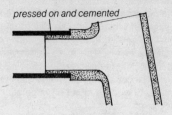

pressed on and cemented

(a) Internal lug

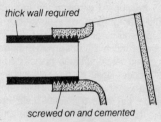

thick wall required

screwed on and cemented

(b) External lug

20.4 *Aluminium lugging*

material creates a greater strength and hardness which is important, for example, in chainwheels.

Aluminium and its alloys are usually about sixty per cent lighter than identical steel components. However, often they would not be strong enough if they were made to the same dimensions. Consequently, they are made slightly thicker. Even so, they are still considerably lighter than their steel counterparts. Sometimes aluminium is used even for frames – for example, the portable Bickerton and the German Kettler, as well as several light and expensive racing frames, built by Alan or Bador.

When used for frame tubes, aluminium must have different dimensions to those of steel. Either the wall-thickness or the tube-diameter must be greater, or an entirely different frame design must be used (for example, one with thinner parallel double tubes). Most aluminium frames currently available are rather conventional. The Kettler frames – used mainly for rather simple bicycles – are welded from tubes of a larger diameter. Most of the other models have thicker tube-walls and conventional outside diameters, cemented to the lugs.

TITANIUM AND TITANIUM ALLOYS

The modern, rare and expensive metal, titanium, has also found its way into the bicycle industry. It is sometimes used for frames and sometimes for small items like axles and bolts. It is about 40 per cent lighter than steel and is about as strong. Moreover, alloys can be made which combine the same light weight with a strength that exceeds that of most steel alloys.

The main problem – besides the expense – is that titanium is hard to machine and join. The result is that small parts, offering weight-savings which are hardly worthwhile, are highly expensive and offer an increase in quality that does not seem to justify the price. Titanium is slightly less rigid than steel and must therefore be made either with thicker tubes or with additional reinforcements. The Speedwell company makes a very fine titanium-alloy frame, and several component manufacturers make their most expensive models with little pieces of titanium to save a small amount of weight here and there.

PLASTICS

Every few years another manufacturer introduces an all-plastic frame. Not one of them has been even remotely satisfactory. The problem is obvious: there isn't a plastic that combines most (let alone *all*) of the qualities of steel with the same weight when built into a conventional bicycle frame; plastic simply isn't tough enough to withstand the many stresses to which a bicycle frame is exposed.

The closest we have come so far to a plastic frame are the FWRP (filament-wound reinforced plastic) frames made as an experiment primarily in the States. These usually comprise aluminium tubes wrapped with resin-embedded carbon or boron fibres – very rigid, light and prohibitively expensive. Until further notice you may expect to find plastics on bicycles within your price-range used only for non-weight-bearing parts such as mudguards, lamp housings and so on.

FINISHES

To protect corrodable metals from the effects of the elements, some surface finish is applied to your bike – as it is to the Menai Bridge. Such finishes are divided into several categories: surface enhancement, non-metallic coating, metallic coating and chemical conversion. Or, to use English words and slight generalizations: polishing, painting, plating and chemical oxidizing or anodizing.

At least as important as the quality of the finish is the preparation of the part prior to the application of the finish. Whether the subsequent process is to be painting or plating, the part to be finished must first be very carefully cleaned, derusted, de-scaled and de-greased.

Painting

A good paint surface will consist of several layers: first, a phosphate layer to fill the finest pores in the metal and to improve adherence, next a primer and, finally, several finishing coats, which may be either of enamel (which consists of a lot of pigment mixed with a little solvent) or lacquer (consisting of a lot of thinner with a little pigment). Lacquer gives a slightly translucent finish and is less durable than enamel. It does not require such rigorous drying and hardening conditions and must be applied in a greater number of separate layers. The more flamboyant, often slightly metallic finishes are usually of lacquer. A good enamel finish is usually only to be found on large-series bicycles.

Some modern finishes look very much like enamel but are actually resin or thermo-setting plastic. These finishes may be applied either in the form of a liquid (epoxy paint) or a powder, to be melted and cured in an infra-red drying chamber much like the drying area used for curing baked-enamel finishes (though the process does not take as long). An example of an epoxy finish which can be applied by relatively small-scale operators is Du Pont's 'Imron'. The Dutch Batavus-Intercycle company uses the powder process in its 'Durolon' finish.

Plating

Chromed surfaces are quite common on bicycles. Like finishing, it is essential that the surfaces be meticulously prepared before the chrome is applied. After this, several coats of metal are applied in a galvanic process – copper, nickel and, finally, the hard chrome layer. You will soon find out what happens if one of these has been omitted when you buy cheap chrome-plated components – the chrome will very quickly start to peel off.

There are several other plating finishes used on bicycle components, and they are usually done by galvanizing or nickel-plating. Spokes and other minor parts with a rather dull, grey finish are usually galvanized, while items like nuts, bolts, and spoke nipples are often nickel-plated. Nickel is softer than chrome and will not peel off if the part is deformed. Galvanized surfaces soon look shabby but are very durable.

Anodizing

Anodizing is a process used to treat aluminium. A thin surface-layer of aluminium oxide is formed to protect the underlying metal. Aluminium – contrary to popular belief – *does* corrode if unprotected, especially if subjected to a salty atmosphere. Anodized surfaces have a satin-like, grey finish, although for a while it was popular to mix a dye into the anodizing bath, resulting in components that looked black or gold – rather poor taste, if you ask me. Since aluminium oxide is considerably harder than bare aluminium, parts which have been anodized may well be more durable than they would be if left untreated.

Chemical Oxidization

This is the conventional way to treat sprockets, since it is an operation that may be combined with the hardening process used to make them so durable. It gives a matt-black finish. Titanium parts are often similarly treated because titanium seems to resist most other finishing processes, including painting. If this is the case, the result will be matt-grey.

Part 3
THE BICYCLE EXTRAORDINARY

21

There are several different historical records that can be, and often have been, used to mark the beginning of bicycling history – a stained-glass window in a church at Stoke Poges in Buckinghamshire, a faked Leonardo da Vinci drawing discovered on the back of an original manuscript, and even a relief on an obelisk thirty-three centuries old, now adorning the Place de la Concorde in Paris. These and several others all show a figure – either a man, a god or an angel – and an object with two wheels looking to all the world like an early form of today's bicycle. Then there are the various muscle-powered vehicles with more than two wheels, or sometimes less. These range from the monocycles shown on an Etruscan illustration dating back to about 1,300 BC, to four-wheeled contraptions attributed to men as diverse as the English-man John Vevers and the Bavarian craftsman Stephan Farfler in the seventeenth century.

All this is very interesting, but I hold that the history of the bicycle started only when a continuous and inter-related process of development began. Concerning the date – and the man responsible – there can be little argument. It was either in 1816 or 1817 that the German Baron, Carl Friedrich Drais zu Sauerbronn, invented and built the first in a continuous line of manoeuvrable, two-wheeled, man-powered vehicles of which my own light-weight Colnago as well as my mother-in-law's Dawes Kingpin are direct descendants.

Drais's machine (fig. 21.1) was a wooden structure with two wheels in line. The rider straddled the frame across a slightly padded seat and propelled the

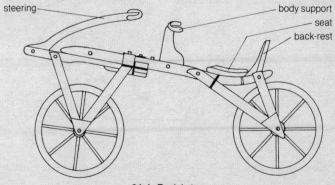

21.1 Draisienne

bike forwards by pushing off from the ground, first with one leg and then with the other, balancing chiefly with the steering mechanism. Similar vehicles – later called *hobby horses*, *dandy horses* or *draisines* (also spelled *draisiennes*) – were still built in most Western European countries until the 1860s, though they never dominated the street-scene as did later versions of the bicycle, in some countries at least. Though the device was light-weight and fast by the standards of the day, it was still too clumsy, too expensive and too much of an oddity to become a popular means of transport. It needed improvements and, above all, it needed methods of mass production.

These improvements – both in design and in production techniques – followed slowly, introduced variously by small-time experimenters, ingenious craftsmen and enterprising industrialists. Knight, in England, built a steel version of the *draisine*; others like Philipp Moritz Fischer in Germany, improved it by attaching pedals to the front wheel. But perhaps the most ingenious design was that of the Scottish blacksmith, Kirkpatrick Macmillan: he drove the (enlarged) rear wheel by means of treadles (fig. 21.2). His bicycle, which was probably first built in 1839, has not survived, but copies constructed in later years by Gavin Dalzell and Thomas

McCall remain to this day in both the London Science Museum and the Scottish National Gallery.

Macmillan's bicycle, described in contemporary literature as a *vélocipède*, had long been unmentioned by cycling historians, even in Britain, and instead the Frenchmen Pierre and Ernest Michaux were regarded as the first to follow Drais. Perhaps this is because Macmillan was not enough of a businessman to capitalize on his inventive skills, but it is more likely due to the fact that Macmillan was several steps ahead of everybody else. Not only did his bicycle have a larger rear wheel that was driven by the cyclist, it also had indirect transmission. Bicycle technology had a lot to catch up on!

This was to take a long time. The various direct and indirect drive-mechanisms designed by Gompertz and Fischer never reached the scale production stage: the first was of no practical use because it was hand-driven and so very tiring; the second was a good piece of handiwork but was completely overlooked. The bicycle seemed to be waiting for an invention that would combine both technical and commercial innovation. Clearly the Michaux company's *vélocipède* was this, even though it is still uncertain whether they themselves actually were the technical geniuses behind the invention or

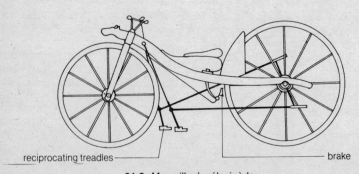

reciprocating treadles ————————   ———————— brake

21.2 *Macmillan's* vélocipède

21.3 *Michaux* vélocipède *or 'boneshaker'*

whether it was their employee, Pierre Lallement. He certainly allowed no opportunity to pass without advertising his contribution and he even saw fit to patent the *vélocipède* in the USA.

The first Michaux bicycle (fig. 21.3) was better than most of the earlier experimental pedal-driven devices built by people like Fischer because it was not simply a *draisine* with a pair of pedals attached to the front axle, but was a lighter, more elegant vehicle. It was also much more innovatory. It had a short frame consisting of a kind of backbone that ran from the steering head to the rear-wheel axle and that carried a long 'leaf-spring' which supported the saddle, and it had two relatively light wooden wheels. It came out in 1861, and was highly promoted a few years later, being without doubt the greatest sensation at the Paris World Exhibition.

Pierre Michaux, a well-known carriage-maker by trade, and his son Ernest, who was evidently a first-rate technical and commercial entrepreneur, soon established the *vélocipède* business as an industry. Production figures for the first ten years of operation show a startling increase and, what was equally important, each new model incorporated more tech-

nical innovations and refinements. The biggest milestone was probably the introduction of ball-bearings in 1869. Racers sponsored and equipped by the Michaux firm tested and publicized the outstanding qualities of the engineered bicycles being produced by the Paris-based company.

The English racer, James Moore, was perhaps the best known and by far the most successful among the men and women who raced for Michaux. He won the first track race on record in 1868, covering a distance of 1,200 m (about three-quarters of a mile) at the St Cloud race track. The year after this, the Michaux riders, led by Moore as the winner, took all the prizes in the first long-distance road race – a distance of 123 km (76.4 miles) from Paris to Rouen. There were 198 participants, including five women.

The outbreak of the Franco-Prussian War in 1871 marked the end of the French cycling boom and the beginning of an incredibly rapid and fruitful development of the bicycle industry in Great Britain. Several French *vélos* had at various times come across the Channel to England where industrial technology and engineering science had come into full swing during the 1850s and 1860s. The bicycle became one of the products of the industrial revolution.

The manufacturers of another unique product of modern mass-technology, the sewing-machine, assumed responsibility for the bicycle, lending the new product the use of the technical and commercial talents of such men as James Starley, Henry Lawson and William Hillman. From the simple French *vélocipède*, known as the 'boneshaker' in Britain, evolved the extraordinary vehicle which characterizes the second half of the nineteenth century possibly more than any other single product – the 'high wheel' or 'ordinary' (fig. 21.4).

that evolved during those years of exciting technological progress; there were advances in materials, construction methods and structural and mechanical design which were at least as significant. Tubular steel frames, tension-spoked wheels, hollow metal rims and solid rubber tyres (an American contribution) were but a few of the many improvements that allowed the manufacturers each year to build a lighter, stronger, cheaper, faster and more comfortable bicycle than had ever before been thought possible.

There was one inevitable problem with the basic 'ordinary' design, however. With the rider sitting almost directly above the

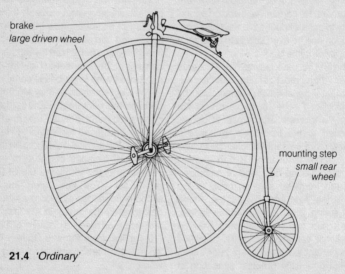

21.4 *'Ordinary'*

The principle of the 'ordinary' was simple enough. Using a directly driven wheel, the greatest size possible will permit the highest speed; the bigger wheel amounts in fact to a higher gear. Even the length of the rider's legs did not limit the increase in wheel-size since the pedals could be built up and operated by treadles, as with one model which had a 7 ft front wheel.

However, it was not the shape alone

big front wheel, equilibrium was easily disturbed. Many a bicycle trip ended by falling head-first and, although the fear of being ground under the wheels of a lorry following behind was not yet present, as it often is today, cycling could not be considered an entirely safe pastime.

To increase the safety of the bicycle, a different design was needed – one that placed the rider's weight further back.

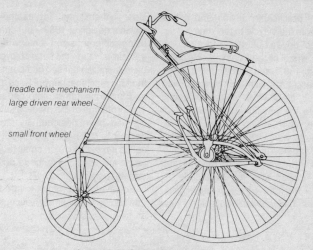

treadle drive-mechanism
large driven rear wheel

small front wheel

21.5 *Star safety bicycle*

Several solutions were soon provided, one of which was simply to turn the whole design back to front. The American A. B. Smith Machine Co. did just this with its famous Star bicycle, first introduced in 1882 and then improved in 1885. No longer would a pebble or a pothole be likely to send the rider over the handle-bars (fig. 21.5).

An alternative way of achieving a safer design was to use indirect gearing to drive a smaller wheel at a higher rate, still reaching the same speed as a much larger wheel driven directly. Chain-drive, planet gearing and lever-ratchet devices were all used in the construction of these designs, but the chain, which was then being rapidly developed, was ultimately

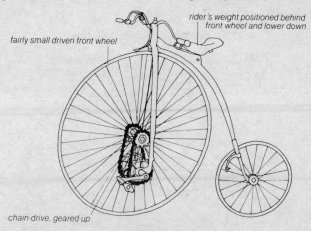

rider's weight positioned behind
front wheel and lower down

fairly small driven front wheel

chain-drive, geared up

21.6 *Kangaroo*

the only practicable device and it has stayed with the bicycle to this day.

Indirect drive could be used either on the rear wheel or the front wheel. Briefly, between 1883 and 1884, there were some successes with front-wheel-driven machines, all of which looked extremely similar to the traditional 'ordinary' – for example, John Kemp Starley's Facile, Singer's Xtraordinary Safety and Hillman's Kangaroo (fig. 21.6).

Soon, however, a more rational and original design was to supersede all others – the rear-wheel-driven bicycle. Rear-wheel drive wasn't an entirely new idea – there was, for example, Macmillan's design of 1839 – but chain-drive, using different-sized chainwheels and sprockets, made the safety bicycle possible (Macmillan himself had been no safer than his machine; he was twice locked up and fined for running into pedestrians!). The prototype of the modern safety bicycle had been designed by Lawson as early as 1879. He had appropriately called it a *bicyclette* or 'small bicycle', the name still used in France to describe all (safety) bicycles (fig. 21.7).

However, the prototype introduced by Lawson wasn't finally accepted until

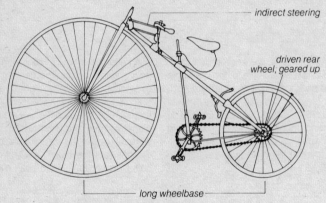

indirect steering

driven rear wheel, geared up

long wheelbase

21.7 *Lawson's chain-driven* bicyclette

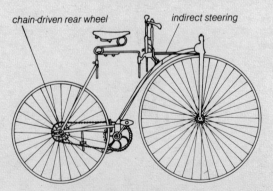

chain-driven rear wheel

indirect steering

21.8 *Early Rover safety bicycle*

1885, when it was incorporated into the design of John Kemp Starley's Rover safety bicycle (fig. 21.8). This unlikely looking design was quickly developed until it clearly held all the characteristics of a modern bicycle. By 1887 it had reached a stage where it could hardly be distinguished from much more recent designs. It had equal-sized wheels, a diamond-shaped frame, direct steering with a sloped and curved front fork – in other words, everything except pneumatic tyres (fig. 21.9).

The pneumatic tyre was the final stage in the evolution of bicycle technology and was first introduced by John Boyd Dunlop of Belfast in 1887. It was later perfected by the French Michelin brothers who invented the removable pneumatic tyre. By the turn of the century, almost every aspect and component of the modern bicycle had been introduced in an elementary form. Of course, much of this technology has since been applied with success to other fields of engineering, ranging from the aircraft and the automobile industry to space-craft construction. The bicycle has long been regarded as being of lesser importance, but it may still prove to have been the most important development of the industrial revolution. We must wait and see!

21.9 *Later Rover (c. 1887)*

If I were stranded alone on a desert island, I would not want to be stuck with nothing to read but bicycle books. The present selection is not a description of my choice of reading under such circumstances. It is just a list of what is available and useful. Though an astonishing amount of verbiage has been devoted to the subject, little of it has any great literary or entertainment value. All the same, most of these books contain valuable advice on some (often limited) aspect of cycling and they are worth reading, if not buying. For further details about these books and for a wider selection, you should refer to the bibliography on pages 273–5.

Bicycles and Tricycles
Archibald Sharp

This book is the exception to the rule and deserves to be taken into exile on a desert island as very stimulating reading. It should be bought, read and read again. Yet it was written a long time ago – and is now reprinted from the 1896 edition originally published in London. It includes a full introduction to physics and mechanics and is the definitive scientific reference book for all technical aspects both of cycling as an activity and of the design and construction of bicycles and their components. It is also easy to read – Sharp was as good at explaining as he was at analysing his subject.

DeLong's Guide to Bicycles and Bicycling
Fred DeLong

Call this the 'Compleat Cyclist'; the author, America's leading authority on cycling, who again is a knowledgeable engineer, discusses just about every aspect of the bicycle in this book. The amount of information contained in this one volume is overwhelming; it is, however, poorly organized and abominably written. DeLong acquaints you with such hidden secrets as how to lubricate your chain with a hypodermic needle and gives descriptions of unavailable gear-change devices, but there is also much more and the book is well worth the price.

Glenn's Complete Bicycle Repair Manual
Clarence W. Coles and Harold T. Glenn

Consider this the companion to DeLong's book. However, don't read the first forty pages, which are stultifying. Use it as it was intended to be used: as an excellent and thorough repair manual. The approach is step-by-step and fully illustrated but, like all repair manuals, it neglects to warn the reader of the enormous pitfalls that result from the different national standards for threading (on, for example, the bottom bracket, rear hub and head-set). In spite of this, there isn't a better repair manual on the market.

Sutherland's Handbook for Bicycle Mechanics
Howard Sutherland and John P. Hart

This book covers the areas neglected by other writers – it tells you what to look out for, what may vary, and how to find your way through the labyrinth of bicycle components. It even contains relatively accurate tables to determine correct spoke-lengths and alternative tyre-sizes, which are often a source of confusion. But you can also discover from this book which tools fit which parts and which components can be combined with the products of other manufacturers. Very useful information!

The Raleigh Book of Cycling
(ed.) Reg Shaw

A collection of sixteen essays on different aspects of cycling and the bicycle: some very informative, some not so outstanding, others quite mediocre. Not altogether a bad book, although it gives insufficient factual advice and contains few clarifying illustrations. It does at least cover some of the subjects otherwise ignored, such as traffic regulations and road sense, and has a comprehensive list of organizations – both national and international – in the appendix. It is also moderately priced.

Richard's Bicycle Book
Richard Ballantine

A beautifully illustrated and amusing paperback. The book originated in America but was extensively reworked and updated for sale in Britain. This book excels in its very clear, sympathetically written and well-illustrated introduction and its descriptions of repair and maintenance of the many parts of the ten-speed bicycle. A comparison of the fine line-drawings by John Batchelor with the photographs in the Coles and Glenn book will enable you to appreciate the superiority of this form of illustration.

The Penguin Book of the Bicycle
Roderick Watson and Martin Gray

This book is fun to read and would be perhaps another candidate for my desert island, although it is in no way a manual from which to obtain useful information. Instead, this book gives you an insight into the social and literary aspects of the bicycle. It also contains extremely readable chapters on racing and technical development. For those already 'into cycling', it is highly recommended.

King of the Road
Andrew Ritchie

Ritchie covers the history of the bicycle and of cycling as an activity. He does a good job, with a great deal of background information, plenty of old illustrations and a delightfully personal prose-style. Ritchie quotes generously from period literature and so succeeds in conveying to the reader the fact that the bicycle was indeed taken seriously by both the engineering industry and by society as a whole in the nineteenth century. It is a delightful and fascinating book.

Cycling
Italian Cycling Federation's Central Sports School (CON–FIAC)

This book is a comprehensive guide to cycling as a sport. The pomposity and clumsiness of the translation should not discourage anyone interested in the physical aspects of cycling – whether they are interested in racing or not – from reading this authoritative manual.

The Physiology and Biomechanics of Cycling
Irvin E. Faria and Peter R. Cavanagh

Although poorly written, this book is interesting and is probably the best layman's guide to biomechanics and physiology, as well as many of the physical aspects which will be covered in chapters 24 and 25 of this book. I recommend it to anyone curious about the scientific and medical aspects of cycling.

Bicycling Science
Frank R. Whitt and David G. Wilson
Here, two renowned professors of engineering and acknowledged cycling experts have written a work similar to the one written by Archibald Sharp at the close of the nineteenth century – a summary of the state of the art in the field of bicycle science. It is a fascinating study, though hardly suitable bedtime reading, and it is crammed full with facts, graphs and tables. An excellent reference manual for anyone wanting factual information about the physical aspects of cycling and bicycle design.

The Bicycle Planning Book
Mike Hudson
This is a nice little book, with lots of pictures and facts. But it is also a dangerous one – it is the work of a zealous enthusiast. I have already quoted one of the gems from this Friends of the Earth publication, namely the statement that 'bicycle accidents occur because of the mixing of cycles with motor traffic'. The author's aim is quite clear – he wants cycle paths to be provided and he wants bicycles off the roads. He has gathered all the material that he thinks will support his case, and he has interpreted other information to fit it. I would suggest that you also consider the other side's arguments, which are backed by much more reliable scientific data concerning the behaviour of traffic and the physical characteristics of vehicles – bicycles and motor cars.

Cycling Transportation Engineering
John Forester
This presents the arguments for the other side. It is perhaps a little verbose, and is not as attractively presented as Hudson's easily quotable pseudo-factual summary, but it is scientific and thoroughly researched. Though written in America, everything discussed also applies to Britain. Order this book if you want to understand the subject of cycling as a means of transport. Even if you are more inclined to argue on Hudson's side, you will at least know what you're talking about if you've read Forester's book.

Effective Cycling
John Forester
Unlike his other book, this is only available by post directly from the publisher (details in the bibliography). But if you want to learn to handle yourself safely in traffic, there isn't a better source of information available. Forester has a slight tendency to get over-involved with details, but if you are able to see the wood for the trees you will certainly learn to be a safe and effective cyclist.

The Young Cyclist's Handbook
Ken Evans
Not aimed at us perhaps, but this is certainly an excellent book for anyone up to the age of sixteen. Evans, a *Cycling* magazine editor of long standing, presents his subject skilfully, authoritatively yet readably in this well-illustrated and comprehensive book. It should be enough to whet any young person's appetite for cycling – and it is very reasonably priced.

The C T C Route Guide to Cycling in Britain and Ireland
Christa Gausden and Nicholas Crane
How to travel anywhere on your bike! Gausden and Crane, both cyclists with many years' experience in the Touring

1. German long-distance touring bicycle, built about 1910. *(Photo courtesy Batavus Intercycle, Netherlands.)*

2. *right* The Bike Hod offers large-capacity haulage with a minimum of interference. The coupling to the saddle pin is just flexible enough to keep it steady without disrupting the handling of the bicycle. *(Photo courtesy Bike-Hod Products.)*

3. *below right* A tandem with cross-over drive, viewed from the right. Note the use of an oval bottom tube to gain rigidity.

4 and 5. Folding bicycles have fascinated designers ever since they were
first used in the First World War. Although none has ever been as comfortable
(or fast!) as the original Moulton of the early sixties, the most compact and
lightest model must be the Bickerton. It weighs a ridiculous 18lb and fits in its
own handlebar bag. It can also be obtained with three- or five-speed gearing.
(Photo courtesy Morris Vulcan Ltd.)

6. David Gordon Wilson of the Massachusetts Institute of Technology designed this reclining bicycle and called it Avatar 2000. Wilson considers this design to be safer than any other bicycle.

7. Suspension bridge engineering is here applied to the bicycle. This experimental design from the Dutch Union company uses a tension-braced cantilever structure for its frame. The design is unbeatable for lightness and rigidity.

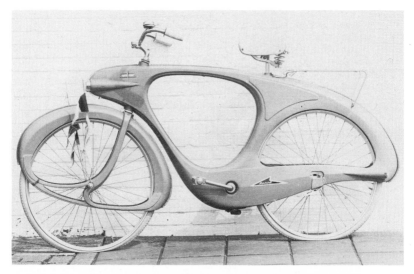

8. Plastic frames have been shown from time to time. Usually they were a scheme to make a 'quick buck', as they say in the States – you send in your money and that's it. This design, like many others, never reached the street. *(Photo courtesy Batavus Intercycle, Netherlands.)*

9. Aerodynamics is the latest craze. This 'streamlined' track-racing bicycle uses all the tricks of the trade – oval tubing, built-up rims and minimal numbers of spokes of flattened cross-section.

10. The aristocrats of the cycling world – including the Royal Family – always seemed to prefer more than two wheels. This Royal Salvo was designed by James Starley and so impressed Queen Victoria that she ordered one. *(Photo courtesy Batavus Intercycle, Netherlands.)*

11. Professor Schöndorf of the Cologne Technical University has attempted quite successfully to design tricycles that will be acceptable to those who can't or don't want to cycle like you and I.

12. The Japanese Shimano
company markets this very
'slick' crank-set. At least one
French manufacturer has
followed suit.

13. T. W. Holdsworth's
beautifully built lugless frame.
It has a unique binder-bolt detail.
*(Photo courtesy T. W. Holdsworth
[Norman Fay Cycles Ltd].)*

14. Detail of an Alan aluminium frame. The frame tubes are not painted but anodized.

15. The French Bador aluminium frame – sold under many names – uses internal lugging and an integrally forged aluminium head tube.

16. In recent years there has been a trend towards the manufacture of bottom bracket bearings with non-adjustable sealed ball bearings, such as this very fine unit by EDCO. *(Photo courtesy Edouard Dubied et Cie SA, Switzerland.)*

17. *below left* Very light precision head-set bearing from EDCO, Switzerland. Most parts are of anodized aluminium except for the bearing races, which are of hardened and precision-ground steel. *(Photo courtesy Edouard Dubied et Cie SA, Switzerland.)*

18. *below right* When you change gear with a derailleur, the chain is simply 'derailed' from one sprocket on to another.

19. Sturmey–Archer S5 five-speed hub. This little masterpiece has the versatility of derailleur gearing with the reliability and ruggedness of fully enclosed hub gearing. It requires two controls similar to those for a ten-speed derailleur. *(Photo courtesy TI Sturmey–Archer Ltd.)*

20. Huret's Duopar wide-range derailleur has two link mechanisms to enable it to handle the most unusual combinations of wide-range gears.

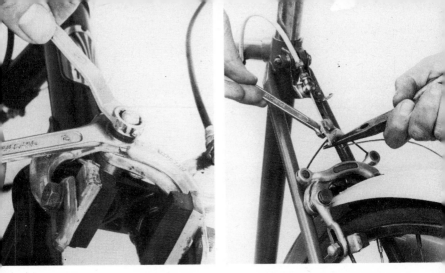

21. *above left* To centre the side-pull brake, the lock nut must be held with the brake fixed in the correct position while the second nut is tightened. Although some manufacturers now offer simpler centring tools, this method must still be used to adjust the tightness of the pivot bolt.

22. *above right* Even centre-pull brakes can be adjusted quite simply – wrap the cable round the nose of your pliers while tightening the eye bolt with the spanner.

23. Lightweight hub brake from Sturmey–Archer. It has the same dimensions as standard large-flange hubs and has a light alloy shell. *(Photo courtesy TI Sturmey–Archer Ltd.)*

24. *above left* Quick chain lubrication. It is still advisable to remove and clean the chain in paraffin oil before lubricating.

25. *above right* Though less convenient than electric lights, the old acetylene lanterns outshine most modern bicycle lamps.

26. The Sanyo Dynapower tyre-driven dynamo also has the advantage of ball bearings, virtually eliminating drag. It is mounted under the bottom bracket.

27. Not necessarily bad, but a sign of lesser quality – a swaged-on chainwheel. It will flex or even come loose under high pedalling forces.

28. High-quality crank-sets have separate chainwheels bolted to an attachment spider which forms one unit with the right-hand crank.

Department of the Cyclists' Touring Club (CTC) give an all-embracing network of cycling connections covering Great Britain and Ireland. Unlike conventional route descriptions, the emphasis has been placed on the idea of a *network*, with all routes connected in several ways to other routes. This gives the cyclist the freedom to choose the length of his trip and will help him actually get somewhere. My only criticism is that it lacks information regarding the nature of the terrain – a few brief hints such as 'fifty miles of high mountains' or 'thirty easy miles with the prevailing wind' would have made the book even more useful.

German Books

I cannot resist recommending two German books of historical value. The first is *Mit dem Rad durch zwei Jahrhunderte* by Max J. B. Rauch, Gerd Volke and Felix R. Paturi, a beautifully illustrated Swiss publication. Even for those who do not read German, this expensive and impressive volume makes a splendid present.

The second German book is completely different – *Fahrrad-Technik* by Siegfried Rauch and Fritz Winkler. 'Bicycle Technology' is what the title means and it is written for engineers and manufacturers. It is the world's only comprehensive summary of bicycle manufacturing techniques and criteria for design. It may be interesting to the out-and-out bicycle enthusiast with a little engineering knowledge.

Bicycle Magazines

The major British publication is the weekly *Cycling*, which is primarily of interest to racers but also contains a lot of technical and touring advice. Then there is *Cycletouring*, the monthly magazine published by the CTC. This is perhaps the most 'relaxing' cycling publication I know. Not as slick as some of the foreign publications, *Cycletouring* is always enjoyable and I've never read anything in it to irritate me – as I have in almost every other publication I receive. A relatively new publication is *Bicycle*, which is the first really comprehensive bicycle magazine to appear in Britain since before the Second World War. Let's hope it can survive!

Perhaps the world's most comprehensive cycling magazine is the American monthly, *Bicycling*. It covers just about all aspects of cycling and looks very attractive; the ads alone are worth the price of the subscription! *Bike-Tech* is an interesting bi-monthly from the same publisher. It features detailed reviews of the technical and scientific work being done in the field of bicycle design. Another American magazine is the quarterly *Bicycle Forum*, directed at traffic planners, bicycle safety-programme instructors, bicycle activists and all others concerned with the bicycle as a vehicle.

23   Cycling as a Means of Transport

The bicycle's function as a means of transport is much more important than its use as a piece of sports equipment, a health device or a protest symbol for the ecologically minded. To get you from A to B quickly and conveniently is the primary task of the bicycle; all other advantages for rider, society and environment are fringe benefits – nice, but not essential. With the recent upsurge of interest in the bicycle as an 'alternative' means of transport, large numbers of well-meaning and vocal but often naïve and inexperienced cyclists have taken to the streets and have caught the public's attention. They seem to be concerned chiefly with the fringe benefits and see the task of handling a bicycle in traffic as difficult and risky.

These people have looked briefly and fearfully at the position of the cyclist in city traffic and have evidently concluded that the risks are too many and too great. Something needs to be changed – either themselves or the environment of today's urban traffic – and they appear to have come to the conclusion that it's the *environment* which will have to be changed to accommodate *them*. So, with understandable and often admirable energy, they campaign to achieve just that. Their arguments are appealing and their conclusions simplistic – the answer to their prayer is the provision of cycle paths. Even the CTC – long opposed to separate facilities for cyclists – now supports them under certain circumstances. Others point to Holland or Stevenage,

thinking that what was done there can and should be done elsewhere and will be to the benefit of cyclists everywhere. They see the road to Utopia as a great cycle path, and believe that *any* cycle path is better than riding in the road.

Unfortunately for them, things are not that simple. Even the best cycle path is rarely as safe, fast or convenient as the existing road network and most are far worse. I speak as one who has made a very close study of traffic behaviour, accident patterns and the physical characteristics of the bicycle. But I also speak as one who has experienced riding in every conceivable physical and social environment, ranging from the separate facilities provided in Stevenage to the California freeways, from the cycle paths of Holland to the dense traffic of the city streets of London and New York, from Italian mountain roads to the urban jungle in Germany. Finally, I speak as one who has gone through all this before. I witnessed the growing call for 'bikeways' in the States and the disillusionment that followed, when it emerged that safety and convenience were both *decreased* rather than *increased* with the additional separation of bicycles.

The failure of cycle-path construction in an existing environment was perhaps best expressed by the highly regarded American transport engineer, Harold E. Munn, who made the ironic comment that 'the problem with bikeways is that there is no room for them where they are needed, and where there is room, they are not needed'. Of course, this argument need not apply to a new town planned from scratch and I'd be the last to claim that the cycle paths in some of the planned communities like Stevenage, Milton Keynes or the Dutch town of Lelystad restrict either the safety or the convenience of cyclists. But I also maintain the following:

(a) In those countries where cyclists are separated from other traffic – that is where cycle paths are the norm – the rate of accidents involving cyclists is no lower than in countries such as the UK and the USA where cyclists and motorists share the same roads.

(b) There is very convincing evidence – both behavioural and physiological – to suggest that accidents are in fact *more* likely to occur in an environment where cyclists are separated on cycle paths only to reappear at crossroads and junctions.

(c) There is substantial scientific data and overwhelming direct evidence proving that both the travel speed and the range of the cyclist is considerably poorer in a separated environment than when the cyclist shares the roads with others.

(d) Sooner or later, whatever the extent of separation, the cyclist must return to the shared road, and the cyclist used only to cycle paths will be ill-prepared in comparison with the cyclist who has 'grown up in traffic'.

(e) Pedestrians and cyclists alone make a disastrously frustrating and inhibiting mixture.

(f) It is most important to defend the cyclist's right to use all roads. Wherever cycle paths have been built abroad, the cyclist's right to the road has been restricted.

CHARACTERISTIC NEEDS OF THE BICYCLE

In order to design and create the right kind of facilities for bicycles, shared or separate, the particular needs of the bicycle must be considered. These are very modest but, surprisingly, they are often completely overlooked by those most concerned with bicycle facilities. To appreciate these requirements, all that is needed is a modest understanding of the laws of physics and mechanics. To apply them correctly, a training in engineering is of more use than social awareness, environmental concern or even good intentions. Here is a brief summary of some of the points to consider:

(a) *Speed.* All facilities should be designed to allow a speed of at least 40 km/h (25 mph) on the level and considerably more on downhill stretches. As we will see in chapter 25, this is a speed that any cyclist with a modern light-weight bicycle can maintain for some time.

(b) *Curves.* The bicycle's ability to handle sharp curves is limited by lateral traction of the tyres and pedal scrape when banking in a level curve. It has been found that, to be safe at reasonable cycling speeds, facilities must be designed with the same curve-radii as those customary for motor vehicles travelling at the same speed (fig. 23.1 overleaf).

(c) *Hill-climbing.* Every difference of a metre in height corresponds to an additional horizontal distance of eighty metres in terms of energy consumed by the cyclist. Consequently, it is extremely important never to force the cyclist to climb any more than is absolutely necessary – this includes 'bumps' up and down separated cycle paths and any multi-level crossings (see fig. 25.3 on page 162).

(d) *Width.* Even though a bicycle is relatively narrow (about 60 cm or 2ft), it requires a minimum width at the *narrow-*

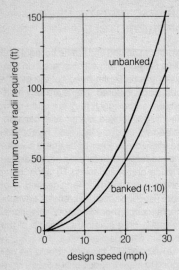

23.1 *Necessary curve-radii for bicycle facilities*

crossed safely at right angles. Whenever the angle between the road and the ridge is less than seventy degrees, special provisions must be made to allow the cyclist to take a safe path. Parallel cracks and ridges in the road surface must be eliminated.

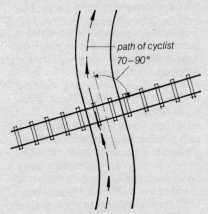

23.2 *Cycle-proof railway crossing*

est point between two obstacles of 1.5 m (5 ft). This includes 25 cm either side for necessary steering corrections and a 20-cm additional margin as well. All separate cycle paths longer than about 25–50 m (depending on the density of cycle traffic) must be wide enough to allow cyclists to overtake one another, since their speeds vary much more than is often assumed: from 10 km/h (6 mph) for a young child or an elderly person riding at a slow pace, to 50 km/h (30 mph) for a healthy adult trying to keep up with traffic.

(e) *Surface.* A light-weight bicycle with high-pressure tyres has only limited suspension, and unevennesses in the road lead to a very substantial energy loss. For this reason, the road surface must be free from all bumps, ridges, pot holes and 'rumble-strips'.

(f) *Ridges and railway crossings.* Due to the narrow width of the bicycle tyre and the sensitivity of the steering, ridges and rails of almost any size can only be

(g) *Continuity.* As is explained in the next chapter, changes in riding speed mean that the cyclist has to use a disproportionately high amount of energy. It is therefore essential to allow the cyclist a clear path – one at least as direct as that for the motorist – with all curves, crossings and bottlenecks designed to allow a speed of 40 kph (25 mph) or more, depending on the terrain.

(h) *Overhead clearance.* Although even the tallest cyclist is not likely to exceed a height of 2 m (6 ft 6 ins) when cycling upright, an overhead clearance of less than 2.4 m (8 ft) is too low because the rider will not feel certain of clearing it.

(i) *Debris.* Debris and in particular glass is not only a nuisance to the cyclist but often highly dangerous. Whereas the normal road surface is to a great extent 'automatically' cleared by the wheels of passing cars, all separate cycle paths, as well as the inside curves of all roads, must be constantly swept clear.

(j) *Snow and ice.* On major roads, bicycles are not usually too difficult to handle on ice or snow as long as particularly tight or sudden manoeuvres are avoided. Wherever separate cycle paths are provided they must be kept free from snow or ice, since motorized traffic does not create a cleared track on them and because tight manoeuvres are often necessary – especially when the cyclist leaves or joins the path.

BICYCLES AND PEDESTRIANS

Contrary to what you may have been told elsewhere, bicycles and pedestrians do not mix well. Pedestrians can do many things a cyclist cannot do – like taking a sudden step to one side, stopping and starting without restriction or mounting steps. Since a bicycle cannot be heard by a pedestrian, he has no adequate warning of the cyclist's approach, unlike motorized traffic. Although the bicycle, even at speed, does not have the same amount of energy as a moving car (and therefore there is less danger of serious injury in the event of an accident), pedestrians and cyclists do get in one another's way.

More significantly, the manoeuvres required of the cyclist in order to avoid collision with pedestrians are so complex and so unpredictable, that he himself runs a very great risk of falling and being seriously injured. The only practical way to decrease this risk is to reduce the speed of the bicycle to a walking pace, which may be possible for very short stretches in pedestrian precincts and other pedestrian zones but is totally unacceptable if the bike is to be seriously used as a means of transport.

In recent years, efforts have been made to relieve traffic in built-up areas. The aim is to restrict the speed of motorized traffic

to a point where it is relatively safe for pedestrians and causes such inconvenience to through-traffic that the latter will eventually be diverted from city streets to the main roads. I am very much in favour of this kind of development – as long as bicycles are not then barred from main roads.

Unfortunately, some advocates of traffic relief are trying to use the bicycle as a weapon in their struggle and want to divert all cycle traffic to residential streets with a low traffic density. Their argument sounds convincing – the bicycle does not kill. But the fact remains that cyclists themselves are killed, and this is more likely to happen in residential streets than on busy main roads. Although the number of accidents per mile of road is lower on such streets, the number of accidents per vehicle-mile is anything from five to twenty times as high as it is on main thoroughfares. And bicycles are vehicles! To compel cyclists to use streets relieved of traffic is to expose them to much *greater* risk and also means drastically reducing the cycle's potential as a viable means of transport by reducing its speed to the walking pace necessary for survival in this kind of 'humanized' environment.

BICYCLES AND MOTOR TRANSPORT

Bicycles have no difficulty in using the facilities designed for cars. These offer the smoothest surfaces, the right curve-radii and sight-distances, direct connections, freedom from excessive gradients and the absence of the unexpected – 'predictability' being the keyword to safe traffic behaviour. Separate bicycle facilities often mean that the cyclist appears where he is unexpected and this exposes him to unnecessary risks. With separate cycle paths, even the safest and simplest

23.3 *Conflicts at cycle-path crossroads*

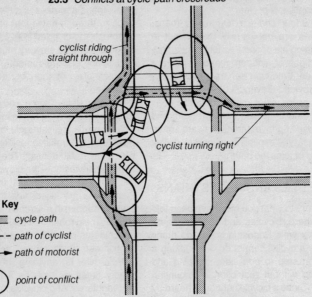

cyclist riding
straight through

cyclist turning right

Key

cycle path

path of cyclist

path of motorist

point of conflict

23.4 *Conflict-free cycling: the Highway Code method*

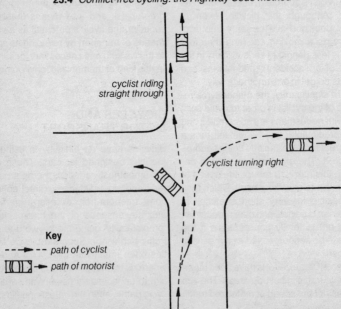

cyclist riding
straight through

cyclist turning right

Key

path of cyclist

path of motorist

manoeuvres may become dangerous and complex.

Crossing a junction on a major road does not sound difficult, and in normal traffic it isn't. But on roadside cycle paths, this becomes a complicated and hazardous manoeuvre. The cyclist finds himself out of line with the other through-traffic and is forced to cycle to the left of motor vehicles turning left. If he overtakes them, or even if he merely travels alongside them, he is likely to get run over or may be cut off at the junction. Turning to the right on a bicycle becomes a perfect nightmare under such circumstances.

Though cycle paths are not the answer, there is still plenty which can be done to improve the environment for cycling. Motorways (especially their entrance and exit roads), one-way traffic systems, poorly paved roads, narrow traffic lanes and excessive motoring speeds are all factors that inhibit cycling. These are the hazards that we ought to attack. But, generally speaking, the existing road network is by far the most suitable environment for both motor traffic and cycling. Cyclists and motorists *can* exist side by side!

Be prepared for a shock – I maintain that the bicycle was the most important technical invention of the nineteenth century. With the possible exception of the wheel itself, no other invention has ever led to a more extensive range of research, experiment, inventiveness, development and social change than that of the bicycle.

The fruits of this can still be seen ubiquitously. The Vietnamese mobilized and supplied an entire army by bicycle for twenty years during what eventually became a major war. In China, roads and cities are alive with people on cycles. But less obvious offshoots of the bicycle industry are in evidence everywhere in the fields of science and technology and are of equal importance. In fact, without the inventions and developments made by bicycle engineers in the second half of the nineteenth century, neither the motor nor the aerospace industries would ever have been possible.

This fact is often forgotten or ignored by those easily impressed by the achievements of technology in the twentieth century. But the fact is that the bicycle is based on sound physical principles, with a design and application as calculable and scientifically verifiable as any other technology, however great its pretensions.

Considering this, it is obvious that I can't do justice to the subject of bicycle technology in a two-thousand-word essay. But what can be done here is give you an idea of some of the principles of physics and engineering as they are applied to the bicycle. I will look at two aspects – the forces that must be overcome by the cyclist in order to move forward and the engineering criteria involved in bicycle construction.

WHAT SLOWS YOU DOWN?

Without an opposing force, the bicycle would go on indefinitely once it started – there would be continuous motion, the ultimate in energy efficiency. Although the bicycle is efficient when compared with other forms of transport, energy is not free and, to make the bicycle move, you have to overcome several forces of resistance. These include the effects of gravity, friction, wind resistance, rolling resistance and changes of momentum. I will examine these one at a time.

Gravity

Although gravity by itself is only a minor form of resistance under most cycling conditions, it is the easiest to explain and it can be used to clarify the other forms of resistance. Imagine participating in the slightly unusual annual event of cycling to the top of Mount Snowdon. Imagine also that you are thoroughly conversant with the metric system and know Snowdon's height (which is 1,000 m or 3,500 ft) and that you and your machine together weigh 75 kg (160 lb) – all of which is very convenient for our purposes.

The road is steep and, ignoring all other forces of resistance except for Newton's law, you will climb this gradient by pulling on your rear wheel. When you reach the top, you'll have done an amount of work that can be measured – you will have carried a weight of 75 kg over a vertical distance of 1,000 m, very much like the man in fig. 24.1. This amount of work may

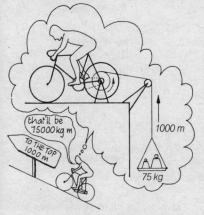

24.1 *Overcoming gravity*

be expressed by simply multiplying weight by distance:

work = weight × distance
     = 75 kg × 1,000 m
     = 75,000 kgm ('kilogrammeters')

That work may be completed quickly or slowly, depending on your strength, but the same total amount of work is always necessary. At a faster pace, the same work is completed in less time, which requires more 'power'. If you take one hour (3,600 seconds), then the formula below will tell us how much power you need:

$$power = \frac{work}{time}$$

$$= \frac{75,000 \text{ kgm}}{3,600 \text{ sec}}$$

$$= 20.8 \text{ kgm/sec}$$

This figure can be expressed in more familiar terms by converting it into kilowatts:

$$power \text{ (kW)} = \frac{power \text{ (kgm/sec)}}{100}$$

$$= \frac{20.8}{100}$$

$$= 0.2 \text{ kW}$$

This is a performance which few cyclists can maintain for long, as we will see in the next chapter. At a slower pace less power would have been required but the climb would have taken longer – for example, 0.1 kW in two hours.

The effects of gravity are difficult to avoid. Even drilling holes all over the bicycle results only in very minor weight reductions. The benefits of a diminished food intake also reach a limit somewhere and you can't avoid every hill. So your rewards are the pride of achievement and the joy of downhill riding. Sensible gearing is the best way to make the endeavour relatively painless.

Wind Resistance

Have you ever noticed that, on a bicycle, the statistical law of probability does not hold? Almost every wind is a headwind! This is not quite as unrealistic as you might think because the effect of riding at speed is to create something that feels just like a headwind. To calculate the effective wind resistance, you need to find the relative air speed, which is the resultant of the two arrows (officially called 'vectors') representing the direction and speed of riding and the direction and speed of the wind (as shown in fig. 24.2 overleaf).

The work required to overcome wind resistance can be calculated, but what is more useful is the determination of the required power as a function of (relative) wind velocity – think of it as the power

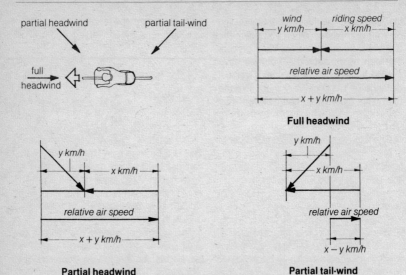

24.2 *Effects of wind and riding speed*

needed to ride a bicycle without friction on a level, windless road. The power required is dependent on the following factors: drag coefficient, frontal area and speed. The effect of speed is enormous; to go twice as fast, for example, requires eight times the power!

Estimates for the drag coefficient and the frontal area have long been established by the pioneers of bicycle science. Even the most recent information obtained from wind-tunnel tests confirm that the drag coefficient of a cyclist is about 0.9 (two to three times that of a

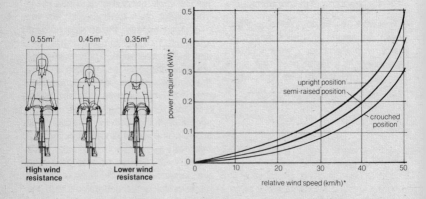

24.3 *Power required to overcome wind resistance only*

motor car). The frontal area depends very much on the rider's profile (see fig. 24.3 on page 154). It is less for a crouched position (about 0.35 m²/3.3 sq ft) and higher for an upright position (0.55 m²/ 5 sq ft). Drag can be determined from a formula, which is quite difficult to calculate, or from a graph, which may be easier (fig. 24.3).

The thing to remember is that the frontal area can be minimized by holding the drops of the handlebars and by not wearing loose clothing. For time-trial racing, it is sometimes worth reducing the width and the number of protrusions of the bicycle, thus cutting down the frontal area and also improving the drag coefficient. The ultimate in this field of bicycle engineering is demonstrated annually in Brighton and in the Californian town of Ontario, in contests organized by the International Human-Powered Vehicle Association. At the time of writing the US highway speed-limit of 55 mph (88.5 km/h) had been broken by several entrants using numerous tricks of airfoil design and ingenuity but powered only by human muscles, of course.

Rolling Resistance

The term 'rolling resistance' covers several different aspects of physics as applied to a wheeled vehicle. The rolling resistance of a bicycle is primarily determined by the angle shown in fig. 24.4 and the area of contact between the tyres and the road. The latter is easy to calculate using the formula: *weight divided by tyre pressure*. This is, of course, much more for a balloon-tyred tank than for a racing bicycle. A racing bicycle with high-pressure tyres inflated to 105 psi (7.5 bar) and weighing 75 kg (165 lb), rider included, will offer a rolling resistance which is only one third that of an equally heavy bike with low-pressure tyres!

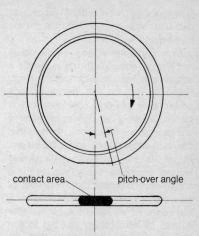

contact area   pitch-over angle

24.4 *Factors determining tyre rolling resistance*

Friction

Friction losses are those which occur on the contact surfaces of bearings, gears and chain-links. Estimates of friction-loss factors have been made for the various components of the bicycle. They are essentially a function of the load upon that component, and of its accuracy, surface finish and lubrication. For the entire bicycle, the losses are quite low – between ten and fifteen per cent of the total power developed.

There are ways to limit friction losses; they include selecting the highest-quality components, good adjustment, and thorough cleaning and lubrication of all moving parts. The most significant losses will inevitably be in the drive-train, and, for this reason, there has been a long-standing dispute between the advocates of derailleur gearing and those favouring hub gearing ever since the introduction of derailleurs. The planet gears in a hub gear do not (so far) run on ball-bearings or roller-bearings, and this can mean losses of up to six per cent for a three-speed in a high or low gear. On the other hand, the flexing of the chain with derailleur gearing can also result in more friction in the extreme gears.

Even minor items like the little jockey and tension wheels of the derailleur are a subject of controversy. On the one hand, because they do not transmit much power, they can only contribute friction losses that are a very minor proportion of the total; on the other hand, the fact that they turn rather fast increases the losses. Roger Durham, a well-known Californian bicycle engineer, finally resolved the controversy between the opponents of sleeve-bearings and those satisfied with the conventional solution for those little wheels by establishing that the friction losses amount to approximately 400 kgm of work per 100 miles. I would say that's negligible but you are quite free to disagree. Roger himself uses the argument to sell his very fine ball-bearing jockey and tension wheels.

All Together Now

To give you an idea of the way in which these resistances combine, the following graphs summarize the approximate totals for two different kinds of bicycle: the first when riding on level ground without wind (fig. 24.5); the second when climbing hills (fig. 24.6). Note: each graph shows conditions for two different bicycles. As you will notice, at lower speeds the rolling resistance plays a major role. When riding faster than, say, 16 km/h (10 mph), your main problem is wind resistance. This is, of course, a significant force of resistance whenever there is a headwind, even at lower riding speeds. The message is simple – whether travelling at a low speed or a high speed, the modern ten-speed bicycle with dropped handlebars and high-pressure tyres is clearly superior to the balloon-tyred 'sit-up-and-beg' model, since it offers the advantages of gearing on hills, as well as lower rolling resistance (espe-cially important at low speeds) and lower wind resistance (especially important at high speeds). You may also be interested to note that climbing an incline of 100 m (325 ft) takes as much work as riding an additional 4 km (2.5 miles) at 30 km/h (19 mph).

MASS, MOMENTUM AND ACCELERATION

In city riding, especially in heavy traffic but even more so in the kind of environment where the bicycle is treated as a separate being and is forced to follow a roadside cycle path, the cyclist cannot ride at a constant speed; he continually has to accelerate and decelerate, stop and start. The power required to do this depends on the total weight (if we use 'weight' as meaning 'mass', though this is not strictly correct) of bike and rider and the rate of each acceleration. (The deceleration is carried out by the brakes.)

To conserve your energy, you must try to make your speed as steady as possible – look ahead and judge how best to maintain as much momentum as possible, speeding up and slowing down gently and reducing the number of stops to a minimum. Here, too, the kind of bicycle largely determines the difficulty of this. In the first place, gearing allows you to accelerate more easily and, in the second place, less weight accelerates with less difficulty. The weight of the moving parts is particularly important, since they must be accelerated to move round as well as forward – the faster a bicycle part moves, the more important is its weight. This means that it is better to save weight on the tyres and rims than to save the same weight on the cranks, not to mention the frame. It can be said that each gram taken away from the tyre or the rim is worth about two grams taken from the frame; other moving parts fall somewhere in between the two.

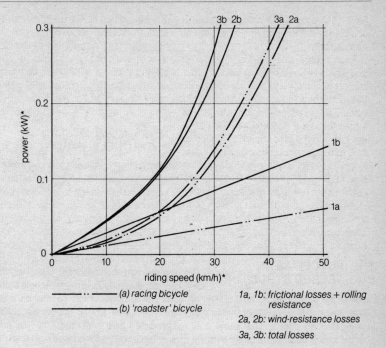

(a) racing bicycle
(b) 'roadster' bicycle

1a, 1b: frictional losses + rolling resistance
2a, 2b: wind-resistance losses
3a, 3b: total losses

24.5 *Power required to overcome combined energy losses*

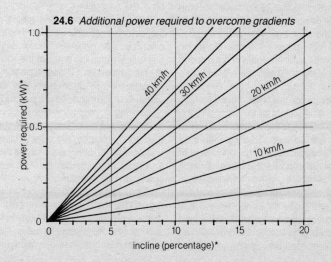

24.6 *Additional power required to overcome gradients*

24.7 *Main stress points*

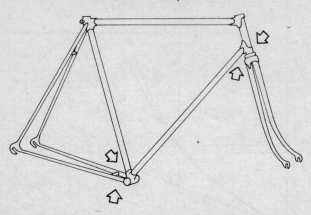

THE BICYCLE AS AN ENGINEERED STRUCTURE

Think of the bicycle frame as a cluster of points in space fixed together by more or less rigid connections. The same may also be said of other parts of the bike, for example, the wheels. The art of building such a structure is to make it rigid, yet as light as possible. For this reason, bicycle engineers over the years have become expert at designing just within the limits of the strength of the materials they use, without over-stressing them. Both the static forces, which remain constant, and varying forces must be taken into account.

To design for the static forces is easy enough. The weight of the rider and the force he applies to the various parts of the bicycle can be calculated by means of simple physics. The main principles of engineering involved are those showing that a structure – like any individual member of that structure – will have the maximum rigidity for its weight if it has its greatest cross-sectional dimension perpendicular to the bending or twisting force. Translated into cycling terms, this

means that the strongest tube has the greater diameter, and the most rigid frame will have tubes which lie further apart (provided that all the tubes are rigidly connected and braced). This explains why the *mixte* frame is more rigid than the traditional women's frame and why the 'shopper's' single frame-tube has to be of such a great diameter for the bike to stand up at all.

The constantly changing forces on a bicycle are more difficult to deal with precisely because engineers design bicycles so closely within the limits of the strength of the materials. These stresses are associated with a phenomenon called 'fatigue', which may lead to a part suddenly breaking at the point where it is closest to its strength-limit. Such points can be defined in advance, since they have two characteristics – they are highly stressed and they occur at points of a sudden change in cross-section.

Highly stressed points occur at every lug, but particularly at the lower head-lug, at the chain-stay-to-bottom-bracket joints and at the fork-blade-to-crown joints. Sudden changes in cross-section also

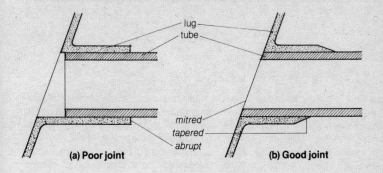

lug
tube

mitred
tapered
abrupt

(a) Poor joint

(b) Good joint

24.8 *Lugged joints*

occur at every lug (fig. 24.8). That's why a good frame-builder will taper down the lugs, making the transition less abrupt. A potential danger-point can occur when a poor frame-builder has cut off the butted tube at the wrong end, shortening the butt to coincide with the transition of lug-to-tube (fig. 24.9). Your best protection against blunders of this nature is the security provided by the reputation of an established frame-builder or manufacturer. But, as you see, there's more to bicycles than meets the eye!

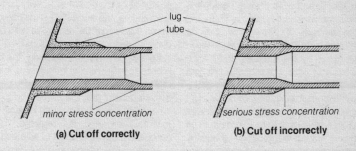

lug
tube

minor stress concentration

serious stress concentration

(a) Cut off correctly

(b) Cut off incorrectly

24.9 *Lugged joints on butted tubing*

25

Bio-mechanics: Your Body at Work

Riding a bicycle is a matter of equilibrium – the equilibrium between gravity and momentum which keeps the cycle from falling over, and the equilibrium between resistant forces and driving force which determines the speed of travel. Having looked at the nature and magnitude of the forces of resistance in the last chapter, I shall now deal with the second half of the equation and consider how much power the human body has to offer.

This is the field covered by the fairly new science of bio-mechanics, related closely to physiology and ergonomics. Bio-mechanics is concerned with the physical ability of the human body. It attempts to answer questions about the amount of power that may be generated by the human body: how efficiently and for how long this may be done, which muscles are most appropriate for particular motions, and what are the best forms of movement.

The amount of power that can be generated by the human body is limited in two ways – by the muscles and by the circulatory system. The essential problem here is to determine which occurs first – breathlessness, or aching muscles. The very strong muscles used in the conventional motion of cycling have proved to be so powerful that, in the case of a healthy person, they will not suffer excessive fatigue until after the circulatory system has reached the limit of its capacity. For this reason, the 'bicycle ergometer', which may be familiar to you from ECG heart-

tests, has become the standard instrument for all bio-mechanical research into physiological output, whether related specifically to the bicycle or not.

The amount of power produced may be measured, for example, by an electric generator driven via the cranks. It has been shown that a trained athlete usually has a capacity which exceeds that of the average cyclist by between twenty and eighty per cent, depending on the length of the exercise. A distinction is made between very brief bursts of power lasting only for a few seconds and longer activity lasting for more than a few minutes.

During longer activity, the oxygen required by the circulatory system to convert the food or stored body tissue into muscle energy must all be supplied by the process of respiration. Such energy is referred to as 'aerobic', meaning 'in the presence of oxygen'. For activity lasting ten minutes, the aerobic limit may lie between 0.23 and 0.34 kW (0.3 to 0.45 hp), diminishing for longer periods.

For very short bursts of activity, the fast process of using up the limited supplies of stored energy in the form of blood sugar is activated. This process is referred to as 'anaerobic' ('without oxygen') since no external oxygen is required. Anaerobically, power outputs of as much as 0.9 and 1.3 kW (1.3 and 1.8 hp) have been recorded for regular cyclists and top athletes respectively. Fig. 25.1 summarizes the results gained by one author (D. R. Wilkie, 'Man as a Source of Mecha-

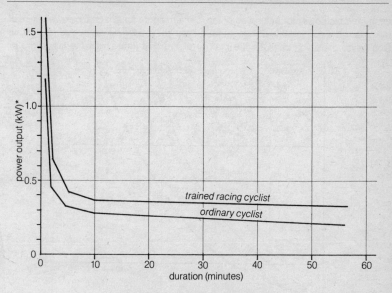

25.1 *Maximum power output of cyclist*

nical Power', *Ergonomics*, vol. 3, no. 1 [1960] with two different cyclists working for various lengths of time. What should be kept in mind is that, at each point along the graphs, the power shown can be maintained only for the corresponding period of time and is followed not by a diminishing power output but by total rest.

Furthermore, it should be noted that these are maximum figures, achieved perhaps during a race and not the kind of thing you'd do for fun. To illustrate this, it may be interesting to note that the power required of Bryan Allen during his three-hour bicycle-powered flight across the English Channel in 1979 was calculated to have been 0.18 kW (0.24 hp), which is slightly more than the power output required during a six-minute ECG. The average cyclist, it seems, will usually be limited to not more than 0.11 kW (0.15 hp) for anything other than strictly competitive cycling or perhaps for hill-climbing.

With these figures we can get some interesting results. We can plot them on the same graphs, illustrated in the last chapter, which show the total power outputs required at different speeds and gradients. This way we have a little more insight into what is possible on a bicycle and what isn't. Eddy Merckx, when he established his 1972 record of nearly 50 km (30 miles) in one hour, probably produced over 0.4 kW (even taking into consideration the fact that wind resistance at the height of Mexico City is lower than at sea-level and that his bicycle and his riding position were more streamlined than that of the average cyclist). But the graph also shows that any trained cyclist can achieve 40 km/h for an almost indefinite length of time, while at a comfortable pace he should be able to ride well in excess of 30 km/h (18.5 mph).

Fig. 25.3 shows the power output required for different gradients and the power available for three different conditions – very short anaerobic activity, maximum aerobic power for a duration of ten minutes and a comfortable power output. Don't ever think you can use the max-

imum figure for anaerobic power since, if you do, you will be exhausted for the rest of the day (unless it's the last climb or

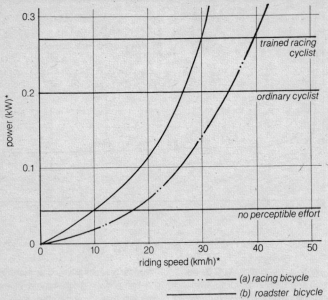

25.2 *Required and available power during a one-hour ride on a level road*

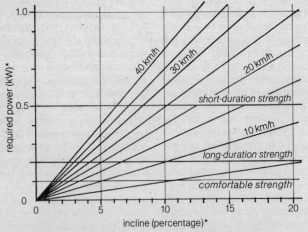

25.3 *Required and available power during hill-climbing*

sprint in a race, when you may have no further need of energy). If you realize that the recent practice in motorway building has been to limit inclines to no more than 4 per cent, you will appreciate that there can be scarcely a road that cars can use which bicycles can't.

EFFICIENCY

The 'efficiency' of an activity is the ratio of power output to power input and it is represented by a figure between 0 (a total waste of activity) and 1 (a total conversion of energy without losses). To calculate the efficiency of the human body, it is possible to use oxygen intake as a measure of the energy expended by comparing it with the mechanical energy measured at the output.

It has been shown that to generate 0.1 kW (0.13 hp) of output on a bicycle requires an oxygen intake of 1.3 litres per minute. This can be shown to correspond to an overall efficiency for the bio-mechanical process of 0.25, a figure that is more impressive than it appears – it compares very favourably with all but the most advanced thermo-dynamic engines. It should of course be noted that we are talking here of 'marginal' energy – i.e., energy that uses more than the approximate 0.3 litres of oxygen per minute required to maintain the functions of the human body when at rest.

Perhaps the most useful aspect of 'efficiency' as a measuring tool is that it allows bio-mechanics researchers to compare the relative advantages of different forms of movement. This has had its uses in such tests as those carried out in Loughborough and other places to determine the optimal saddle-height. In that case, several test subjects (the scientific term for 'people') had their efficiency measures compared at different seat-height positions. Similar tests have at

times been conducted to establish the relative efficiency levels of cycling with different crank-lengths, gears, handlebar positions, etc.

You should be warned at this point, though, not to be taken in too easily by the pseudo-scientific value attached to every piece of data that can be expressed as a formula. Unless there is a convincing theory to explain the logical origin of the formula given, you may be buying the modern equivalent of the sun-spot theory, which was popular during the early days of economic research and claimed that the fluctuations and trends of the business cycle were caused by flares on the sun's surface. So, for example, it should be kept in mind that the frequently quoted '109 per cent rule' to determine the height of the saddle (page 34) is just one of various possible expressions of an average value for several different riders and lacks any definitive basis in theory. It's all right to use such rules as a starting point, but the fine tuning will be up to you!

A NOTE ABOUT 'ANKLING'

Bio-mechanical research – even without a convincing theory to confirm it – can, however, be very useful in destroying some of the myths surrounding cycling. Perhaps the most commonly accepted myth which has been copied from one cycling book to the next is the one surrounding 'ankling'. It was for a long time claimed that, while pedalling, the ankles should be flexed to vary the aspect of the foot as illustrated in fig. 25.4a (overleaf). The benefit of this movement was thought to be an extended power-stroke, allowing the rider to push the pedal forward near the top and back near the bottom of the stroke.

What in fact occurred – if this trick was ever mastered – was an effect corresponding to that produced by a shorter crank and a rather awkward stretching of muscles that would have been better avoided. With the aid of high-speed photography and strain-gauge technology, bio-mechanics workers at Penn State University soon settled the issue. The photographs showed that experienced and trained racing cyclists, far from making the movements prescribed for 'ankling', actually moved their feet much as shown in illustration 25.4b. Next,

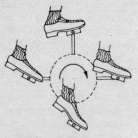

(a) As it used to be taught

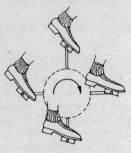

(b) As it is in reality

25.4 *'Ankling'*

efficiency tests revealed that both power output and efficiency were higher with this 'natural' pedalling motion than when 'ankling' according to textbook instructions, even after repeated practice.

It was shown that it probably does help to attempt to push the pedal forward at the top and backwards at the bottom of the stroke but that this movement was obviously not improved by the unnatural

inclination of the foot used in 'ankling'. Toe-clips narrowly escaped being redesigned in accordance with the false 'ankling' concept before forces working on the pedal were measured in connection with these same tests.

Authors of bicycle books have in the past often made the most bizarre claims concerning the effects of wearing toe-clips – some going so far as to claim that they can double pedalling efficiency. The assumption was that toe-clips made it possible to exert an upward force on the pedal during the up-stroke in addition to the downward force exerted during the down-stroke. Measured pedal-forces, with toe-clips installed, have since shown that, except when moving off from a standstill, they tend to be orientated and distributed approximately as shown in fig. 25.5 (varying along the revolution as well

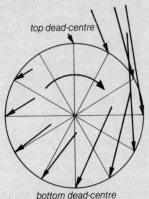

top dead-centre

bottom dead-centre

25.5 *Relative magnitude and direction of pedal-force*

as from one revolution to the next) but that the forces are never directed upwards. The value of the toe-clip, it seems, lies primarily in the aid it provides in locating the foot correctly over the pedal and in assuring contact with the shoe-plates or cleats. As for doubling pedalling efficiency, that is a myth!

INCREASING THE POWER-STROKE

Although we've seen that cycling is relatively efficient, it may still be possible to increase the total power developed, regardless of the efficiency of such an increase. The proponents of 'ankling' were perhaps on the right track in thinking that when pedalling the answer lay in an increased power-stroke in relation to the part of the movement during which no useful work is done. Several variants on the conventional pedalling motion with direct circular-to-linear (i.e., round chainwheel to chain) transmissions have at times been proposed and sometimes even marketed.

The treadle-driven bicycles, such as the Macmillan design of 1839, require a

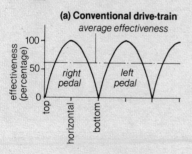

↓ top: zero power output

↓ horizontal: 100 per cent power output

↓ bottom: zero power output

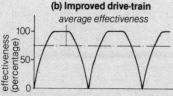

(a) Conventional drive-train
average effectiveness

right pedal   left pedal

(b) Improved drive-train
average effectiveness

25.6 *Power output over pedal-stroke*

different kind of motion from that of the conventional pedal bicycle, as do certain other drive-mechanisms. The approximate power output curve for a conventional bicycle is shown in fig. 25.6a and is explained by the fact that very little or no power is transmitted when the pedals are in the top and bottom dead-centre positions. An improved design could have a power output curve as shown in fig. 25.6b, in which relatively high power values are maintained throughout a larger part of the down-stroke.

One possible solution, dating back to the nineteenth century, but re-introduced from time to time as a novelty, is the application of elliptical chainwheels and round or differently orientated elliptical sprockets. Although one manufacturer in the late seventies advertised this device as giving an increase in power of fourteen per cent, I have not yet seen any reliable bio-mechanical data to substantiate his claim. The effect of the elliptical chainwheel (fig. 25.7) is that the part of the

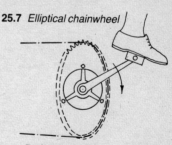

25.7 *Elliptical chainwheel*

During powerful part of stroke: 'high gear'

Near dead-centre of stroke: 'low gear'

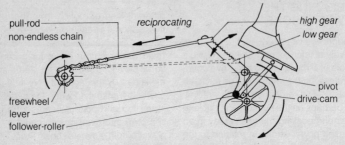

25.8 *'Bio-Cam' drive*

stroke with a relatively high power output is transferred in the equivalent of a high gear, while the less powerful part is covered quickly in a low gear. Oddly enough, some manufacturers have orientated their elliptical chainwheels in the opposite direction and yet claim similar gains!

Perhaps more promising and supported at least by some performance data is the revolutionary transmission developed by the well-known American bicycle engineer Larry Brown. His 'Bio-Cam' drive is shown in fig. 25.8. The cranks drive cams which in turn guide follower-rollers, each one connected to a length of (non-endless) chain which drives a freewheel placed on either side of the wheel. By an intelligent choice of cam shape, the movement may be improved to suit the rider, while the point of engagement between the follower-roller and the chain can be varied to select the equivalent of a higher or lower gear.

We saw in the last chapter that the trained cyclist generally has more power than the average rider, not to mention the man weened on the motor car. Fitness is one of the attributes of the active sportsman most eagerly sought by those in favour of cycling – the most quoted example of this is probably Paul Dudley White's advice to his patient, Dwight Eisenhower, to take up cycling in order to keep his heart pumping.

Although he lived to the age of seventy-eight (which isn't bad for anyone residing for any length of time at the White House), and ignored his physician's advice, Eisenhower might well have lived longer and been fitter if he had taken to cycling and continued the habit. Possibly his opinion of cycling was much like my view of another trend of recent years – jogging. It may well be very healthy, but it is a deadly bore and is totally impractical. Perhaps his attitude is understandable if you consider that, until recently, nobody in the USA except a few eccentrics like myself seemed to believe that a bicycle could actually be used to get somewhere. Yet I used to commute daily by bicycle to my San Francisco office, oblivious to the incredulous frowns of the doorman, my boss and my colleagues.

Anyone who does not use his bicycle for going to work or to do errands quickly, and who does not participate in organized cycling as a sport, might be well advised to do as White and other reputable doctors recommend – cycle for fitness. For anyone apart from a masochist, it is far more enjoyable and practical than most other forms of exercise – it is certainly better than jogging, roller-skating or skipping. During a thirty-minute cycle ride you may cover 15–20 km (9–12 miles) and, besides taking exercise, you can vary your route exactly as you wish – something that is one of the obvious shortcomings of skipping and which is not much better satisfied by other forms of exercise.

The effects of a regular training programme for fitness, using the bicycle in particular, were first described by another American heart-specialist (you'd be forgiven for thinking the Americans had invented the bicycle!) called Kenneth Cooper, in his book *Aerobics*. 'Aerobics' – we've encountered the term before – means the activity within the range of the body's capacity to absorb oxygen. The idea of it is that, with regular exercise at a level not too far below the maximum limit of this aerobic capacity, the heart – being much like any other muscle in the body – will be trained and strengthened.

It has been demonstrated that a stronger heart is a healthier heart which will last longer, if only because it will pump more slowly when the body is at rest and may become less excited when more is being demanded of it. Increased heart-capacity – which was once dreaded and referred to as a 'sports heart' but has since been proved to be perfectly healthy – allows more blood to be pumped around the circulatory system with every heart-beat.

Thus the amount of oxygen needed to perform a task can be absorbed at a slower pulse-rate and more can be achieved without the pulse-rate rising.

A normal pulse-rate while resting is about 70 beats per minute; less if you are fit, more if you're not. You can easily establish your rate with the aid of a wrist-watch with a second-hand or digital device. This pulse-rate corresponds to an intake of about 0.3 litres of pure oxygen per minute under standard conditions and this is what is necessary to keep the normal bodily functions in operation. When more work is being done – climbing stairs, skipping or riding a bicycle – more oxygen will be needed to allow the combustion of food or body tissue. This oxygen is carried by the red blood corpuscles; a greater amount of work per unit of time means that a greater amount of blood is needed to circulate round the body in that time, and this requires the heart to pump it faster. From 70, the pulse-rate may increase to 100, 150 or even 200 beats per minute, depending on the intensity of the work.

When the heart-beat is greatly increased over a long enough period, the heart muscles will tend to get stronger. The general rule by which to gauge your rate is a pulse of 180 minus your age. If this is maintained for at least ten minutes, it will affect the training of the heart. So, if you're forty, you should reach a pulse-rate of at least 140 and maintain this for ten minutes or more. That, in a nutshell, is the message given by dozens of expensive books and manuals which claim to show you how to live to be a hundred on a bicycle.

What the other books do that I don't is tell you how to go about it. Cooper, for instance, provides a series of time-tables and performance tests to be carried out before and during the training programme. Of course, there is nothing wrong with the cook-book approach, but it is not necessary, especially if you become convinced that training has to be done in a certain way and can be done no differently – either Cooper's way or no way at all. On the contrary, there are many ways to crack an egg and you will be much better doing it your way at your own pleasure and convenience than following a method that doesn't agree with your schedule or your inclination.

Here, briefly summarized, are the major points to keep in mind when cycling for health and fitness:

1. Warm up by cycling at a normal pace before increasing your speed.
2. Cycle fast enough to reach your training pulse-rate: 180 minus your age in years.
3. Maintain this pulse-rate (though not necessarily that riding speed) for at least ten minutes.
4. Decrease the riding speed and heart-beat, and ride at a more relaxed pace for several minutes before you get off the bike.
5. If you are still perspiring after completing the exercise, it's advisable not to try to cool off too suddenly with a cold shower or by drinking a cold liquid immediately.

LOSING WEIGHT ON THE BICYCLE

Among the many advocates of cycling, there are those who recommend such activity as a cure for the most common symptom of affluence – being overweight. It's true that cycling can burn off some of the calories contained and stored in the form of excess fat tissue on the human body. But I don't think you should fool yourself into believing that this alone will solve the problem. The best solution is to practise the simple exercise, recom-

mended by our final American representative, bicycle-book author Eugene A.
Sloane: 'Place palms of the hands against
the edge of the dining-room table and
push back!'

The human body will itself select the
most convenient metabolism for the production of energy, the easiest of which is
to convert the sugars obtained from the
food you have most recently eaten. As
long as there is food in your stomach, your
'spare tyre' will remain unaltered, since to
reduce that requires a much slower and
less efficient metabolism. Finally, when all
else has been used (which occurs only
after cycling the length of the country
without a proper meal to keep you going),
the body will even attack its own proteins
and muscle tissue – a kind of cannibalism.

Even when you get to the stage where
the accumulated body fats are broken
down, the process does not happen over-
night. It has been estimated that a kilo-
gramme of body fat can be converted into
the equivalent of 29,000 kJ. (This is the
modern scientific terminology: kJ means
kilo-Joules and it has been introduced to
express what were previously measured
in Calories and British thermal units; the
equivalent statement would be that 1 oz of
fat equals 780 Btu or 200 Calories.) That
energy is enough to keep you cycling for
almost fifty hours at a relaxed pace, since
one hour's level cycling will use only about
600 kJ in addition to the 600 kJ required
when at rest. Cycling faster will accelerate
the process, as will hill-climbing, but you
will be unlikely to maintain either of these
activities for as long a period of time –
perhaps a ramp to the moon, inclined at a
gentle gradient of 10 per cent, might help.

So, to conclude the argument, cycling is
healthy; you may even lose weight doing
it, but only if you eat less and cycle fast
and far. The regular cyclist, in fact, has a
very good chance of never reaching the
stage where he has to worry about losing

weight. Exercising regularly – whether
this is intentional or incidental to cycling
for other purposes – he will probably use
up any excess food well before it has a
chance to accumulate in the form of body
fat.

MORE ON HEALTH

There is more to be said on the subject of
health and cycling. Perhaps the most important point is that however good vigorous exercise may be for helping to avoid
problems in an otherwise healthy heart, it
may be dangerous with a heart that is not
healthy in the first place. If there is any
reason to doubt the condition of your heart
– due to hereditary symptoms in past
generations or personal symptoms now
present – it would be a good idea to get
the advice of a doctor, explaining what
kind of exercise you have in mind and the
nature of your suspicion. The doctor may
well assure you that there is no need to
worry or you may be advised how to limit
your exercise to something that will not
jeopardize your health. On the other
hand, you may be told to abandon the
whole idea, advice which I would take if it
were given to me – even if it ruined my
fitness plan!

There has long been speculation about
the negative effects on health caused by
cycling. For many years, it was believed
that cycling in city traffic, where there
were high levels of air pollution, was particularly harmful, but it now transpires that
there is less cause for alarm than was
formerly believed.

One British experimenter, Ronald Williams, is reported in the *British Medical
Journal* (December 1979) to have found
that after ten miles of city cycling in London on densely trafficked roads, blood
analyses showed that the cyclist had very
low concentrations of harmful substances
in the blood. The primary measure is the

COHb level – COHb being the deadly carbonmonoxide attached to the blood's haemoglobin. For a heavy smoker this value may rise to between 14 and 20 per cent, while even a non-smoker in a smoke-filled room may acquire a level of 3 per cent. Dr Williams found that the cyclist had a level of 0.3 per cent – an astonishingly low figure – which he says is typical for an inhabitant of the Outer Hebrides and is much lower than that of a motorist in the same kind of traffic conditions as those to which the cyclist was exposed. Even the counts of other pollutants proved to be lower for the cyclist than the average values for motorists. This was probably due to the increased activity of the circulatory system which may act to flush these harmful substances out of the blood-stream.

27

If, as I said in the last chapter, the essential content of many unnecessary volumes about cycling and health could be reduced to a few paragraphs, the opposite must be said of bicycle racing; a dozen books could easily be written without any danger of being repetitive. In this brief chapter all that can be done is to touch the surface of this fascinating subject. I'll consider the major differences between the various forms of bicycle racing, take a brief look at the equipment and training needs, and leave the rest to you. Clearly, you will not learn to race by reading – only by doing it.

This means you must join a cycling club. There are hundreds in this country – some of which cater only for tourers; some of which do racing; and many of which provide for both. British cycle racing has long been separate from the international scene, since it is organized by several national bodies independent of the international sanctioning organization for bicycle racing, UCI (*Union Cycliste Internationale*). In Britain there are several different organizations: the British Cycling Federation, affiliated to the UCI; the Road Time Trials Council, which supervises a uniquely British form of racing – the race against the clock or 'time trial'; the Road Records Association; the Scottish Cyclists' Union; the Women's Cycle Racing Association; the Women's Road Records Association; and several others.

All these organizations, despite their past record of antagonism, now work together without much friction. Several act together in the coordinating Cycling Council of Great Britain; the others each have their own closely defined functions, unchallenged by splinter groups. One advantage of the British scene which is envied world-wide, is the fact that racers and tourers can move freely from one activity to the other. This creates a large pool of potential racers and means that there is great experience and expertise at all levels and in all forms of bicycle sport.

Although the customary breakdown of cycling as a sport creates two categories – road racing and track racing – I would make a distinction between five separate activities: *track racing, time trialling, long-distance trials, road racing* and *cyclo-cross*. Each of these forms of cycle racing requires its own type of facilities, equipment and a particular attitude on the part of the participants. In the following sections they will each be briefly described.

TRACK RACING

The secret of track racing is tactics, although physical and technical ability are necessary too. The track consists of a narrow, banked oval which usually measures no more than one third of a kilometre (about a fifth of a mile) in all – although indoor tracks are often smaller still. The surface of the best tracks consists of smooth wooden boards, although outdoor tracks (this in fact means all

permanent British tracks) may be sur-
faced with less expensive materials.

Many different disciplines may be held
on a track – sprints, pursuit, paced racing,
team pursuit and Madison racing are
some of the better known. In each case, a
bicycle with no gearing or brakes is used.
Track bicycles have very steep frame-
angles and a fixed gear and are built to be
extremely stiff and strong, unless they are
to be used for time-trial track events,
where extremely light machines are also
fashionable. Light-weight bikes are not
really necessary, as we have seen in
chapter 24, since weight is only important
for accelerating and hill-climbing, which
are both insignificant in time trialling.

The most spectacular form of track racing is perhaps the *sprint* – once you get
used to the fact that it's quite unlike any
other sport. Only the last 200 metres are
timed, but even this time is insignificant
because the sprint is a race between two
or more people and not one against the
clock. The riders may take several minutes to find the position in which they can
best complete the last 200 m – taking
shelter in their opponent's slipstream and
making the most use of the effects of
gravity if the track is steeply banked (that
is, small).

Pursuit racing places the riders at opposite sides of the track; they cannot pace
one another as this is essentially a time
trial. The race is completed when the
prescribed distance is covered or when
one racer has caught up with his opponent. In *team pursuit* there is pacing. Two
or four racers combine to form a team
which makes the best use of their ability to
pace one another and in which individual
members take turns in leading. In the
case of a four-man team, only the time of
the third rider is recorded.

The *Madison* is also a team event, but
here the teams rarely ride together; only
one rider races at any one time. Mean-

while his team-mate may be 'warming up',
cycling slowly high up on the track, or he
may be resting. Hours, sometimes days,
can pass with little happening apart from
the regular change of position. But then,
one team may develop a plan of action
and a sudden chase begins; the pace is
increased and the riders take turns at
every other lap. A team which has begun
such a chase when the opponents are
unprepared can gain a significant lead in
this way. The opponent will then wait for
an opportunity to regain the lost laps in the
same fashion. Finally, at the completion of
two thousand miles, or more in a six-day
race, the whole thing may be decided by
points, awarded for special events.

Motor-paced racing is to my mind very
boring; it is also very noisy. However,
some people love it. The benefits of pacing are used to the full in this discipline,
where cyclists often use gears as high as
140 ins (development 11.2 m) for speeds
in excess of 50 mph. It is also a race of
tactics but the pace-setter on the motorcycle does all the brainwork while the
cyclist simply pedals and follows. In races
behind 'big' motors, the distance between
the pacer and the cyclist is maintained by
a roller mounted on the pacing machine
and the bicycle is equipped with a smaller
front wheel (24 ins) and a fork that is raked
in instead of out. Races behind 'Derny' or
'Joco-machines', which are quite popular
on the continent, are ridden at lower
speeds behind motorized bicycles and
use an ordinary track bicycle.

The correct preparation for all track
events can only be done on a track,
though you should still do many miles of
riding on the road to train your heart, your
lungs and your legs. Those forms of racing which require team-work – whether
the team consists of several cyclists or of
a cyclist and a pace-setter – must of
course be practised as a team; to race
together, you must train together.

TIME TRIALLING

If the keyword for track racing was often 'tactics', the secret of time trialling could well be wind resistance. But there is also a human factor – the ability to assess your own capacity and to keep a constant pace which is just within the limits of pain and is calculated to create exhaustion only when the finish line is reached. Time trialling as it is practised in Britain is a road event, but it is one in which every man is on his own. The rider is often racing not to beat an opponent, or even to beat the time set by an opponent, but is very often merely attempting to improve upon his own time.

Time trials may be held over almost any distance, preferably riding along a level road, once 'out' and once 'back', thus compensating for any possible wind and terrain advantages. The most frequently contested distances are of 10, 25, 30, 50 and 100 miles. The big stage races also contain one or more time trials, often of irregular distances, simply in order to get some form of time difference between the riders, most of whom stay so close together in the normal stages that the same times would otherwise be recorded.

To ride a good time trial, several things are necessary:

(a) a combination of bike and rider which minimizes wind resistance and has the best possible 'streamlining' (low drag coefficient and frontal area);

(b) a knowledge of the terrain, which allows the rider to select the correct gearing and pedalling rate for every section of the route;

(c) the rider's knowledge of his own abilities when applied to the distance involved;

(d) plenty of practice in riding for the distance required;

(e) possibly most influential of all, just plain luck; for example, a passing motorcar which the rider can surreptitiously follow for long enough to gain a second or two, or a change of the wind in his favour. Every time triallist needs this kind of luck if only to keep up his morale. It is how he can improve on a time that is optimal for the conditions; it isn't cheating, it's Fortune smiling!

However, there is not much to be gained through luck once you become involved in 'real' international time trialling ridden on an outdoor track. The most prestigious of these is the 'World Hour Record' – riding at an exhausting pace for 3,600 seconds. In 1972 Eddy Merckx established a world hour record at 49.431 km (30.72 miles). At the time of writing, there has been no news of anyone having broken the 50 km/h barrier. There may be another rider as strong as the Belgian, but to break the record he will probably need an improvement in aerodynamic characteristics – which is hard to achieve within the UCI rules.

LONG-DISTANCE TRIALS

This is another typically British phenomenon and is the province of the Road Records Association. In the nineteenth century unofficial records were often set – and were claimed still more often – for distances such as those from London to Brighton and even from Land's End to John o' Groats. Today the procedures are a little more formalized; the cyclist is closely followed by an (expensive) support team and the times and distances are checked closely. To do this kind of thing you need time and money as well as everything else involved in road time trialling. Some say you also need a masochistic personality.

ROAD RACING

This kind of racing – banned in Britain for many years as constituting 'vicious driving' – is no longer a sport restricted purely to the continent. Among amateur events, the British 'Milk Race' rates very highly in the international world of cycling and British professionals regularly compete in all the major international events. In the stage races, in particular, which take anything from days to weeks, the keys to success are tactics and team-work. The teams may be formed of riders with some regional or national affinity but are more likely to be mixed teams sponsored by some company which, in most cases, is not even a bicycle manufacturer.

Even though such a stage race may go on for hours without any great *racing* skills being apparent, the pace is quite fast and normally averages well over 35 km/h (22 mph) even during amateur races. An even higher pace is often maintained during the other varieties of road races, such as the 'criterium', a race consisting of many laps round a relatively compact circuit measuring perhaps a few miles per lap. Finally, there is the one-day distance road race, a tough test of cycling skill and strength as well as of team-work.

For almost all road racing the best training is to ride alone often in order to build up strength and endurance and to practise handling skills – an art best mastered through participation in a great number of races or by riding fast in groups. The bicycle should be light and strong, with a relatively narrow handlebar bend and gearing to suit the terrain encountered – usually of a much narrower range and higher in absolute terms than one might otherwise have chosen; you become accustomed to standing up and pushing your way up to the top of a hill if the compensation is having the choice of plenty of good, high gears for use on level roads and downhill sections.

CYCLO-CROSS

'Mudplugging' is another word for this; it is the art of cycling through the most unsuitable terrain, a game that has greatly increased in popularity with the advent of televised contests – at least, it is popular among the spectators. The bikes are highly reinforced versions of road machines, usually equipped with cantilever brakes. The bicycles are carried as often as they are ridden, so it is important to minimize the weight and the number of protrusions. It's thought to be good 'clean' (though muddy) fun.

28

Since any civilized account of tandem riding will inevitably include some reference to 'Daisy, Daisy' and since I'm as sensitive to such traditions as the next man, we can begin straight away by dispelling one of the more romantic notions of British folklore – Daisy never rode a tandem! Even if you've never heard the second, usually forgotten verse in which the fair maiden declines the modest offer, you should learn now that the vehicle in question was not a tandem but a rather archaic product of the wheeled-goods industry known as a 'sociable'.

Whereas riders on a 'sociable' sit side by side, making it very difficult to ride without a Daisy to balance your weight, tandem riders sit *tandem*, which is Latin for 'at length'. You may have a hard time finding a 'sociable' these days – although I did find a manufacturer of these vehicles in California recently – but tandems are regaining their popularity. This is not entirely due to a nostalgic wave of interest in the impractical, but is partly because of a change in riding habits and partly because of the undoubted advantages of the tandem as an enjoyable and energy-efficient vehicle.

The secret of the efficiency of tandem riding is wind resistance – more commonly though inaccurately known as 'head-wind' – the ever-present enemy of all cycling at speeds in excess of 10 mph. As was explained in detail in chapter 24, wind resistance is due to several factors. The easiest one to control is profile – the area

of the bike and of your body which faces forwards. For two separate bicycles, the profile is twice that of a single machine; but a tandem, although it has two motors just like the two singles, has a profile which is almost as small as a single bicycle. There is therefore considerably less total wind resistance than with two separate bikes.

The result is that on a tandem you can ride considerably faster than if each person were to ride alone. Alternatively, if you ride at a normal speed, you'll have less work to do. This makes the tandem an excellent machine for long, fast touring – better indeed than for everyday cycling, although I still think that to ride a tandem to work is far more sensible than to commute by car.

Like a car, the tandem can only be used to the greatest efficiency if two people have the same goal and starting point, work to the same time-schedule and enjoy the same interests along the way. Besides this, tandem riding requires team-work. But once the two riders, referred to as 'captain' and 'stoker', are attuned to each other and have developed a shared riding style, the team can move with an ease and pleasure that never ceases to astonish those who ride separately – it's a marvel of cooperation and coordination.

However, there are certain hitches in riding a tandem. Keeping it on the road can present a problem, since such a heavily loaded and 'over-powered' device seems to operate near the upper limits of many of the components for much of the time. In fact, I have never known a tandem rider who didn't sooner or later hope to find a hacksaw in his tool kit which would put an end to the whole venture once and for all. In the following sections, I'll take a close look at the design of the various components of the tandem and try to establish some sensible standards for the selection and maintenance of such a machine.

TANDEM FRAMES

If a fishing-net can be described as 'a bunch of holes held together with pieces of twine', I'd like to think of a bicycle frame as a cluster of fixed points in space held together with pieces of tubing. The trick is to fix those points rigidly in relation to one another, and on a tandem frame this is no mean achievement. You have a lot of points to think about – two saddles, two bottom brackets, two wheel-axles and the head-set bearings. And then, in addition to this, you have to carry twice the weight and twice the motive force on a longer (and therefore more easily flexed) structure.

To obtain the rigidity required of a good tandem frame, several different methods may be applied, either singly or in combination with each other:

(a) Use tubing of a greater diameter.

(b) Use tubing with a greater wall-thickness.

(c) Reinforce the lugged and non-lugged joints.

(d) Install additional bracing tubes.

(e) Replace single tubes with sets of double parallel tubes.

(f) Replace some round tubes with elliptical (oval) ones and arrange these to take greater stresses in a particular direction.

A good tandem frame may incorporate every one of these different engineering solutions. It will cost a small fortune but will be worth every penny. In fig. 28.1 you will find the points to watch on a tandem frame; these are the parts which undergo the greatest stress and which certainly need reinforcement. Fig. 28.2 shows several possible shapes for tandem frames.

The one thing that is quite unacceptable is the conventional ladies' frame, even for the back seat of a tandem. There is just no way of making a machine designed in that way rigid enough without its weighing too much. Of particular interest, perhaps, is the tandem with the bent rear-seat tube. This gives it a very tight frame with a small wheelbase and is considered better for racing and hill-climbing, but it gives a ride which is less than luxurious. In fact, to be at all comfortable for a longer ride, a tandem frame should be built on

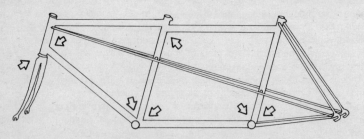

28.1 *Main stress points on a tandem frame*

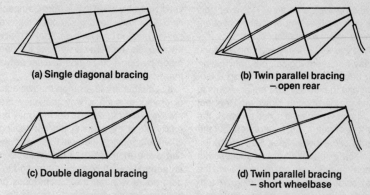

(a) Single diagonal bracing

**(b) Twin parallel bracing
– open rear**

(c) Double diagonal bracing

**(d) Twin parallel bracing
– short wheelbase**

28.2 *Examples of well-braced tandem frames*

the long side so there is plenty of room for the 'stoker' to move with ease and without wiping his brow on the 'captain's' jersey.

THE DRIVE-TRAIN

Connecting two sets of cranks to a single rear wheel presents another problem.

There are several different ways of doing this and the two necessary chains are arranged differently according to the method used (fig. 28.3). The one which is easier to handle mechanically and which results in the lowest stresses upon frame and drive-train components is the one shown in fig. 28.3c which places both

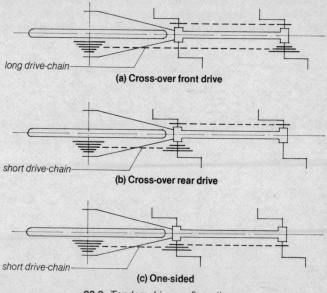

long drive-chain
(a) Cross-over front drive

short drive-chain
(b) Cross-over rear drive

short drive-chain
(c) One-sided

28.3 *Tandem drive configurations*

chains on the same side. However, this design limits the number of different gears available with a derailleur system.

And you will certainly need those gears! It may not seem logical, but uphill riding can become extremely painful on a tandem and the lowest gear never seems to be nearly low enough. However, I feel that for mountain riding it's not so much the *number* of gears that is important but the 'depth' of the lowest gear. So perhaps the increase in popularity of machines with fifteen-speeds does not really provide the best solution for tandem riding. A ten-speed, or even a five-speed, provided it offers a wide range between the gears, may do just as well and will at the same time offer the additional benefit of less elaborate components which are easier to maintain and more readily available.

For any configuration other than the one in fig. 28.3c, you'll find the machine needs special tandem components, even if you're content with five gears or less. These are rare and expensive. The French TA company probably offers the widest range at the lowest cost; for racing,

you'll probably need to buy from Campagnolo. The freewheel, which often takes a severe beating on a tandem, should really be a special tandem version like the one made by Sun-Tour; it has heavier pawls than standard freewheels.

It is customary to arrange the two sets of cranks in such a way that they are always in line (fig. 28.4a), but they may be easily offset by undoing the connecting chain and moving the crank-sets in relation to one another (fig. 28.4b). It has been an age-old cause of dispute among tandem riders whether the synchronous or the offset configuration is the more effective. 'Offsetters' claim their way gives a more constant power output (which is true) and that it will therefore be more efficient (which is debatable). Races have been won and lost using both methods and the best thing to do is to try for yourself so that you can decide which gives you the best result.

To adapt a standard tandem for a child 'stoker', you can install a crank-set-raising device known as 'kiddy-cranks' (fig. 28.5). The firm which supplies these

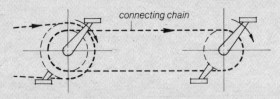

(a) Conventional crank alignment

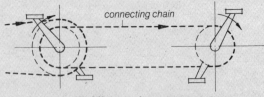

(b) Offset crank arrangement

28.4 *Tandem crank arrangements*

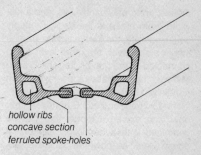

hollow ribs
concave section
ferruled spoke-holes

28.6 *Concave-section rim*

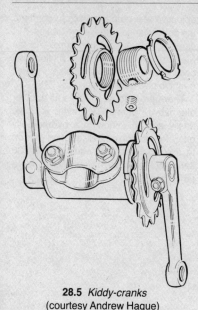

28.5 *Kiddy-cranks*
(courtesy Andrew Hague)

and many other tandem specialities is
Andrew Hague, whose address can be
found on page 271. The tandem is an
ideal bicycle on which to introduce children and handicapped people (from the
blind to light epileptics) to the fun, adventure and exercise provided by cycle touring. Many frame-builders and specialists
can provide modifications to the standard
tandem which will make this possible.

TANDEM WHEELS

Since you are carrying twice the load on
the same two wheels, you'd better use
strong wheels. Unless you want to go in
for tandem racing, I think that 27-in light-
weight wheels are disastrous for tandem
riding – they are too flimsy. Use 26 × 1⅜
in tyres or the French 650B tyres; mount
them on a strong aluminium rim such as
the concave-section 'Weinmann' model
(fig. 28.6) and use at least forty spokes of
straight 13-gauge thickness to lace them.

Use three-cross on large-flange hubs with
special tandem axles and don't attempt to
use quick-release hubs. In short, you
must pay far less attention to weight and
rolling resistance than you pay to strength
and reliability on a tandem wheel. After all,
you've still got the advantage of having
twice the power with a machine that only
has two wheels. Surely, the time it takes to
straighten out a wheel that has been over-
stressed and has buckled can never be
repaid by the minor advantages gained
from lighter, narrower wheels.

TANDEM BRAKES

Remember how a brake functions? It
safely converts excess kinetic energy
stored in the moving bicycle and rider(s)
into heat before an accident occurs. The
tandem brake has to handle the energy
stored in a body of twice the mass, probably travelling at a considerably faster
pace than usual – when riding downhill,
tandem speeds in excess of 80 mph (130
km/h) have been recorded. That's far
more energy than can reasonably be expected to be absorbed by two ordinary
bicycle brakes.

So either you need to have stronger
brakes or more brakes. Ideally, you
should have both. The standard for tandem design has become a set of calliper

brakes, preferably cantilevers, and a full-width drum brake at the back. Probably you'd operate the two callipers from a single brake-lever, the other lever being connected to the hub brake. The French Mafac company makes a lever which can handle two brakes simultaneously.

As for hub brakes, Sturmey–Archer now also makes a model that can be combined with a derailleur, although it doesn't look as powerful as the established French Maillard hub brake. Don't take my word for it, however; I have no objective test data by which to compare the performance of these two brakes. All I can say is that a full hub brake like the Maillard will have a larger friction and cooling surface which, if all else is equal, ought to give better braking.

There are also disc brakes as another alternative. Shimano's model is quite easily available, now in a hydraulically operated version as well, but it only fits on to a special rear hub equipped with 36 spoke-holes (which is insufficient for a tandem wheel).

29 The Custom-built Bicycle

What extravagance – a tailor-made bicycle! But hundreds of cyclists every year decide it's worth the extra expense, time and trouble to have their bicycle custom-built – their own personal machine which fits them and nobody else. It costs a great deal, but, when you consider that there are off-the-peg bicycles on the market costing the same as a small car ten years ago, you may begin to see a method in this madness. Once you have begun to pay such large amounts of money, you may as well buy the ultimate: a bicycle that is perfectly matched to its rider and to the purpose for which he wants to use it.

Ideally, the custom-built bicycle is based on a tailor-made frame designed to fit the discriminating rider's measurements and personal needs and equipped with individually selected components. But a second option should not be overlooked. Although it isn't cheap either, you can equip a standard frame with components, the types and sizes of which you select yourself. This way you may well achieve an effect similar to that of the real tailor-made cycle: a unique machine – your very own individual bicycle.

Whichever way it is made, the custom-built bicycle is not for everyone and is not suitable for every purpose. Before you consider an investment of time and money of this nature, you must be an experienced cyclist – one who completely understands what it is he wants that a standard machine can't provide. You won't qualify for this unless you've ridden for many thousands of miles on different bicycles in a variety of different and demanding circumstances and unless you've made up your mind precisely how and for what purposes the new machine will be used.

Even then, it may turn out that a custom frame is not really what you need. I had this experience myself many years ago when I wanted to become involved in racing. A two-hour session at the frame-builder's which involved much measuring, head-scratching and calculating, was at last rewarded with a geometric sketch of the proposed frame. It was a nice sketch, impressively dimensioned, and I would have ordered the frame at once had I not thought to compare it with the dimensions of my existing off-the-peg quality frame. As it turned out, the proposed geometry was essentially the same as what I already had and since my frame-builder – like most of his colleagues – had too much business anyway he soon persuaded me to stick with what I was riding. The money I had saved financed a cycling holiday in Ireland and I never did take up racing – I went back and ordered a touring frame, which was quite different.

Indeed, the use to which you intend to put a bicycle is of prime importance when selecting the frame or components. A quick look back at chapters 11 and 12 will remind you of the various elements of frame geometry that establish a bicycle's suitability for one use or another, and other components have been similarly described in the subsequent chapters. Clearly, however, the frame is where the fun starts, and quality frames – custom-built or ready-made – don't come from mass-assembly lines but from the work-shop of a craftsman – the frame-builder. Let's take a brief look at what goes on there.

THE FRAME-BUILDER

Most frame-builders are like cyclists – they work best alone. So most of the best frame-building shops are small with one craftsman and possibly a few helpers each working on his own product or doing specialized tasks like cutting, brazing or painting. Your frame may well be the work of only one man who has worked on it from the conceptual design to the comple-tion of the last brazed joint, perhaps even preparing the finish and painting it himself as well.

Although some frame-builders have no alternative but to conduct their business transactions by mail, the personal touch is probably more valuable than the prestige associated with a frame made in Stock-ton-on-Tees or Paris. You can do worse than to find a frame-builder near home. The frame-builder will ask you to explain what you want the bicycle for: time trialling, 'criterium' racing or perhaps long-distance touring, loaded or unloaded, on rough roads or tarmac-covered highways. He may even want to know whether you cycle by pushing in a high gear or prefer to spin fast and easily. After all, he wants to make a tool that matches the user and the use it will receive.

He will measure every limb on your body and may even suggest a solution for a rider with arms or legs of unequal length. He will use either a fairly standardized table such as the popular one assembled by the Italian Cycling Federation's Central

29.1 *One of several methods of determining frame dimensions*

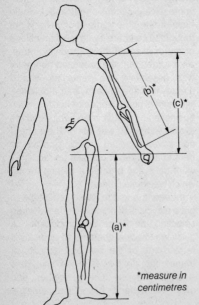

Frame-sizing table			
Lower limb (a) (cm)	Seat tube (cm)	Arm + chest (b + c) (cm)	Top tube (cm)
80	51	100	53
81	51.7	101	53.4
82	52.4	102	53.8
83	43.1	103	54.1
84	53.7	104	54.4
85	54.3	105	54.7
86	54.9	106	55
87	55.5	107	55.3
88	56.1	108	55.6
89	65.7	109	55.9
90	57.5	110	56.2
91	57.9	111	56.5
92	58.5	112	56.8
93	59	113	57.1
94	59.5	114	57.4
95	60	115	57.7
96	60.5	116	58
97	60.9	117	58.3
98	61.3	118	58.6
99	61.7	119	58.8
100	62.1	120	59
		121	59.2
		122	59.4
		123	59.6
		124	59.8
		125	60

*measure in centimetres

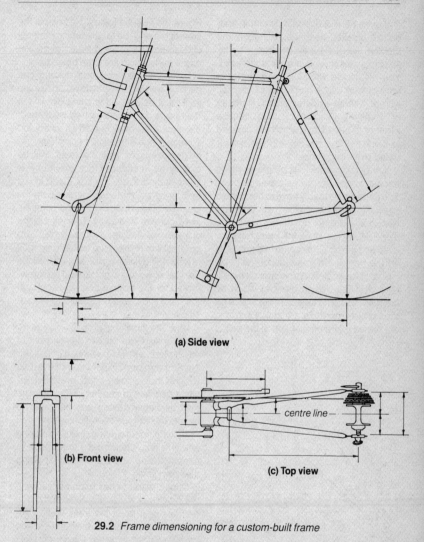

(a) Side view

(b) Front view

centre line

(c) Top view

29.2 *Frame dimensioning for a custom-built frame*

Sports School or one based on his own experience. Essentially, he will determine all the dozens of dimensions and angles that are shown in fig. 29.2, and maybe even more if he advises you on the selection of other components too.

Together you will decide what kind of lugs will be used, or perhaps he'll suggest building a lugless frame which is lighter and is not necessarily weaker if built correctly. You may decide, if you really want, to have the bottom-bracket shell slotted (this is a rather foolish thing to do since it saves very little weight and gives water and grit a perfect opportunity to ruin your bottom-bracket bearings – though the problem can be partly overcome by installing a plastic sleeve around the axle). You will decide what kind and quality of drop-outs to use – horizontal or vertical, with or without eyelets, forged, stamped or investment-cast. You can choose whether to have stays which are dimpled to clear the chainwheel and the tyre or round-oval-round ones.

It may take some time before anything happens once you've paid your deposit. The parts will probably have to be ordered specially and the builder will probably have far more to do than your frame alone. However, once the parts have arrived and the time has come to begin work on the frame, the frame-builder sets his jigs to the angles and dimensions recorded in the design drawing which he made for you. The tubes are cut to size (at the correct end if it's a butted tube) and are mitred to the right shape at the points where they will be joined. He selects the correct brazing rod for the tubing material chosen and cleans and clears of grease all the parts which are to be brazed.

Next, the assembly and brazing can begin. It will take several days, since each joint must be allowed to cool slowly if the material is not to be seriously weakened; each sub-assembly is also checked and corrected and sometimes completely remade to ensure that the result is exactly as intended. Once the frame is completely brazed, the flux (used to aid the brazing material penetration) is cleaned off and all beads and splutters are ground or filed away. To minimize the chances of fatigue failure, which are greatest where there are sudden changes of total wall-thickness, the ends of the lugs are filed down to a slight taper. The screw-thread for the bottom bracket is cut and the head tube reamed to take the head-set bearing cups.

Now the finishing process can start. This consists not only of painting but of much more, as was described in chapter 20. Some frame-builders do not even do this job in their own shop, preferring instead to give it to another craftsman who may be better trained and equipped to handle the various operations associated with cleaning, preparing, painting, curing and finishing. Others take great pride in demonstrating their skill and applying their own finish.

Once the frame has been painted and the paint has hardened sufficiently, it is perhaps best to let the frame-builder install the bottom bracket, the head-set and the seat pin, since he has the correct tools for the job and can make any of the corrections that are sometimes needed even on the most carefully built frame. The rest you can do yourself, unless you'd rather have the other components on your untouched frame installed by an experienced bicycle mechanic.

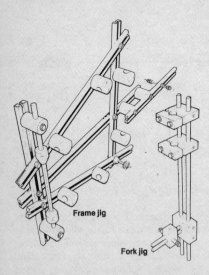

Frame jig

Fork jig

29.3 *Frame and fork-building jigs* (courtesy Andrew Hague)

FROM THE FRAME TO THE CUSTOM-BUILT CYCLE

A custom-built bicycle is not just a bicycle with a custom-built frame – individual selection of the remaining components can be as important as the geometry of the frame itself. This is a field reserved entirely to yourself, even if you haven't a tailor-made frame. You can select the right crank-length, the best handlebar extension and the ideal bar design, the pedals, saddle, chainwheels and derailleurs – all to match your own individual riding habits. Here again, there are different makes and qualities to select from.

If you want the best regardless of cost (or simply want others to know you have the best) you can make the selection process relatively easy where makes and types of components are concerned – just learn to pronounce the word 'Campagnolo' and practise saying 'Cinelli' a few times. The Italian former bicycle racer, Tullio Campagnolo, is the owner of a reputable aluminium forging and casting works. In his racing days he invented the first practical quick-release mechanism for use with bicycle hubs and, having bought out the Fratelli Brevio firm of bicycle-component manufacturers in the 1950s, he soon became the unchallenged leader in the manufacture and design of superb light-weight equipment for racing bicycles. Almost anything not made by Campagnolo can be obtained with the finely engraved Cinelli name and symbol; these come from more than a dozen different smaller workshops in and around Milan.

Although there is no doubt about the excellence of these products, one may well ask how good need a component actually be. Indeed, I feel that for most uses – including racing – other components, which are often cheaper, will serve our needs just as well as many of the items produced by Campagnolo. Even within the Campagnolo catalogue there are enough different series of components listed to keep you reading, checking and comparing for a long time. Do you want the 'Super Record' line, which has the lightest parts, often held together with titanium screws and liberally drilled out, grooved, recessed and engraved? Or do you need the similar but slightly heavier 'Nuovo Record' group? There are also 'Gran Sport' and 'Nuovo Sport' – more suitable for touring. The choice is yours.

In recent years, some other manufacturers have followed Campagnolo's example, producing components with a similar price-tag which have the same silky finish and aesthetic appeal and are usually of a similar quality. Such items come from Japan, France or Italy, with names like Ofmega, Shimano Dura-Ace, Sun-Tour Superbe, OMAS, Stronglight, Mavic or Maillard. Not to mention the wide variety of unique designs produced in small series or even made individually and found primarily in the USA: Avocet, Phil Wood, Roger Durham, etc.

Clearly, there are enough quality components to choose from and, with the recent worldwide gain in popularity of the lightweight bicycle, even the availability of quality equipment which is reasonably priced has expanded dramatically. Although the quality of the individual components is important, what matters even more is that the right sizes, kinds and types are selected and carefully and intelligently installed. For a mountain-touring cycle, it is more important that the crankset and derailleur can handle the kind of gearing you need than whether it has aerodynamically shaped crank-arms or a titanium spindle. And if you forget my warnings about interchangeability and correct fitting in the preceding chapters, your custom-built bicycle may never work. If a custom-built bicycle is what you want, then it will be an extension of your personality – it will reflect your love of cycling.

Even if what you own and ride is something less splendid than a custom-built bicycle, it is still likely to be unique. The number of options and modifications possible with a basic bicycle are so great that hardly two machines are ever identical. In order to maintain your bike in the most intelligent manner possible, it is good to keep track of the peculiarities of your machine in a systematic manner.

Perhaps the best way to do this is with a chart or catalogue, listing the sizes and type of all the components installed on your bicycle. A suggested format for such a catalogue is given on the following pages. You may either complete the form in the book itself or you may prefer to make a photocopy. Enter the information at the head of the form at least, since it will help you to identify your bicycle should it ever get lost or stolen (though it is still necessary to keep the receipt of purchase).

The remaining information can be entered in part or in full as the exact details become available. These facts are an enormous help in avoiding sometimes disastrous mistakes when replacing or overhauling parts of the bike. To give but one example, if you try to screw a French freewheel on an English-threaded rear hub you will ruin the hub at least and possibly also the freewheel. Clearly, it will save you time, money and frustration if you know from the table what will fit and what will not.

Another use of the table is as a 'dream sheet' where you can list intended modifications of your present bike, or specifications for a future one. Having as a starting point the essential data of the frame (in ink) you can dream up the remaining entries (in pencil) and use the form as an aid when shopping for components.

BICYCLE DATA

Make: ....
Type: ....
Year: ....
Frame no.: ....
Size: ....
Colour: ....

Frame
Make: ....
Height: ....
Length/wheelbase: ....
Head-tube angle: ....
Seat-tube angle: ....
Tubing: ....
Weight: ....
Remarks: ....

Steering
Head-set: ....
Thread type: ....
Head-tube length: ....
Fork-rake: ....
Bar-extension size: ....
Bar diameter: ....
Bar type: ....
Remarks: ....

Saddle
Make: ....
Type: ....
Seat-pin make: ....
Seat-pin diameter: ....
Remarks: ....

Brakes
Type: ....
Make: ....
Model: ....
Size F/R: ....
Brake blocks: ....
Cables: ....
Remarks: ....

Lighting
Type: ....
Make F/R: ....
Bulbs F/R: ....
Batteries F/R: ....
Remarks: ....

Gear Table

Sprocket sizes

No. of teeth on chain wheels

Wheels
Tyre type: ....
Tyre size: ....
Valve type: ....
Rim type: ....
Rim size: ....
Rim material: ....
Spoke size F/R: ....
No. of spokes F/R: ....
Hub make F/R: ....
Threading rear hub: ....
Remarks: ....

Crank-set
Bottom-bracket make: ....
Thread type: ....
Axle length: ....
Crank length: ....
Cotter-pin size: ....
Remarks: ....

Pedals
Make: ....
Type: ....
Threading: ....
Toe-clips: ....
Remarks: ....

Front derailleur
Make: ....
Type: ....
Capacity: ....
Remarks: ....

Rear derailleur
Make: ....
Type: ....
Capacity: ....
Remarks: ....

Chainwheels
Make: ....
Sizes: ....
Hole pattern: ....
Material: ....
Remarks: ....

Freewheel/sprockets
Make: ....
Threading: ....
Sprocket sizes: ....
Remarks: ....

Part 4
MAINTENANCE AND REPAIRS

The bits and pieces – approximately one thousand of them – that make up the modern bicycle endure remarkably well for most of the time. However, the inevitable does occasionally happen and sooner or later you will be confronted with the task of getting home with a sick or ailing bicycle. More often than not, the problem can be solved on the spot with the help of a few simple tools, a little common sense and the instructions contained in the following pages.

In subsequent chapters, we will investigate more deeply the groundwork of bicycle maintenance and repairs and look at most of the things which are encountered. But such detailed knowledge – and interest – is not required of every cyclist; if you'd rather put the book back on the shelf, feel free to do so. However, what follows in the present chapter deserves to be read by even the most diehard non-mechanic since it will prevent little things from ruining your cycling. The tools listed should be bought at once and the instructions can be photocopied and carried in the saddle-bag.

THE ESSENTIAL TOOLS

Only a few tools need to be taken on most trips. The side pocket of your saddlebag will hold them easily and still leave room to spare, although more could be carried on longer trips. Here are the basics:

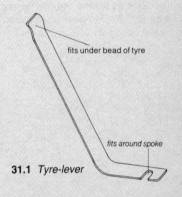

fits under bead of tyre

fits around spoke

31.1 *Tyre-lever*

(a) *Three tyre-levers* (fig. 31.1). These are not required if you have tubulars rather than wired-on tyres – if that is the case you'll want to carry at least one spare tub instead.

(b) *Puncture-repair kit.* Again this is only useful if you use wired-ons, although

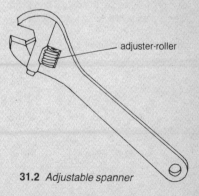

adjuster-roller

31.2 *Adjustable spanner*

on a longer trip you'll have to be prepared to patch tubulars, since there is a limit to the number of spares you can carry.

(c) *Small adjustable spanner*, preferably of the kind illustrated in fig. 31.2, which is precise and can get into tight corners.

(d) *Small screwdriver* with a 4-mm-wide blade ($^5/_{32}$ in). This size has the advantage that it will give a reasonable fit for most ordinary screws and also for any cross-shaped Phillips-head screws used on the bicycle (fig. 31.3).

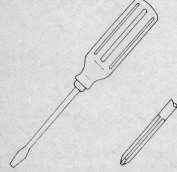

(a) Standard blade   (b) Phillips-head blade

31.3 *Screwdriver*

(e) *Allen-keys* to fit Allen-bolts (those with hexagonal recesses in the bolt-head) used on the bicycle; the 4, 5, 6 and 7 mm sizes are usually all you need (fig. 31.4).

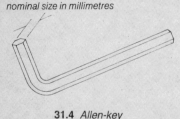

nominal size in millimetres

31.4 *Allen-key*

(f) *Crank-extractor*, only for a cotterless crank – make sure it's the correct make and model (fig. 31.5).

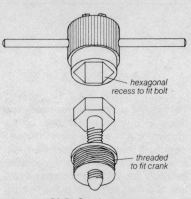

hexagonal recess to fit bolt

threaded to fit crank

31.5 *Crank-extractor*

(g) *Small pliers*, preferably needle-nose pliers (fig. 31.6).

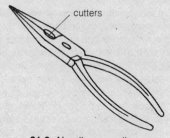

cutters

31.6 *Needle-nose pliers*

(h) *A pocket-knife* or small penknife.

(i) *Spare parts:* tyre-valve parts, brake cable, chain master-link, lightbulbs, battery, etc.

All these items should be wrapped in a piece of cloth that will also serve to wipe your hands and the bike. In addition, it is absolutely essential to carry a pump and it is advisable to take a water bottle, a small first-aid kit, something with which to clean your hands, and some change to make a phone-call home when all else fails.

MENDING A PUNCTURE

This is without a doubt the most frequently encountered roadside repair. If you use tubular tyres you won't need to do any repairs; instead you should take the old tyre off the rim, pushing sideways in a rolling motion, and put the spare on. If it is a new spare it may be a very tight fit, but don't give up – it will eventually stretch over the rim.

If you use ordinary wired-on tyres proceed as follows:

1. Check the valve and tighten or replace it if necessary. Pump up. If the tyre still leaks, proceed.

2. Turn the bike upside-down to rest on its saddle and handlebars, but make sure that protruding items will not get damaged.

3. Remove the wheel by loosening the axle-nuts or the quick-release lever. On the rear wheel of a derailleur bike the chain and the derailleur cage will have to be held back (fig. 31.7). On a bike with a hub brake, coaster brake or stirrup brake, the brake must first be loosened. On a hub gear, the gear-control cable or chain must be unscrewed.

4. Check the outside of the tyre-cover for embedded sharp protrusions. Remove any such items and mark their location.

5. Remove the valve lock-nut and the interior if necessary and push the valve through the valve hole.

6. Push the valve body in and work the tyre into the centre of the rim (fig. 31.8) along its entire circumference.

31.8 *Work tyre into centre of rim*

7. Put a tyre-lever under the bead of the tyre as shown in fig. 31.9, and then hook the other end on to a spoke.

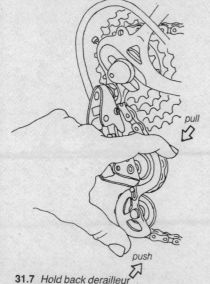

31.7 *Hold back derailleur*

pull

push

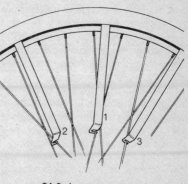

31.9 *Insert tyre-levers*

8. Do the same with the second tyre-lever about two spokes further along.

9. Repeat with the third tyre-lever.

10. The lever in the middle will fall out; use it as a fourth if this is needed.

11. Place your fingers under the bead and pull the tyre off the rim at the side where the tyre-levers were used.

12. Push the valve through and pull the tube out from under the tyre-cover.

13. Reassemble the valve if necessary and inflate the tube; listen carefully around the circumference to establish where the hole is. Check that there is not more than one hole. Mark the location.

14. If you can't hear anything, you may have a slow leak that can be located by submerging the tube in water a section at a time and watching for bubbles. Wipe dry.

15. Clean the area around the hole with the sandpaper from the repair kit, and then wipe the tube clean.

16. Find a patch of the right size and apply a thin layer of rubber solution to the tyre around the hole, over an area slightly bigger than the patch.

17. Allow the solution to dry for three to four minutes. Meanwhile check the inside of the tyre-cover for sharp protrusions and remove them.

18. Remove the foil from the adhesive surface of the patch and place the patch over the hole within the treated ('sticky') area. Apply pressure to improve bonding. Sprinkle talcum powder over the treated area.

19. Partially inflate the tube to check whether it will hold air. If it does, let the air out again and insert the valve through the valve hole. Then reassemble the valve if necessary and pump up very slightly.

20. Work the tube back, under the tyre-cover and pull the cover back over the rim with your bare hands. Push the bead into the centre of the rim as in step 6 to ease this process – *never* use a tyre-lever.

21. Inflate slightly and knead the tyre to ensure that the tube is not stuck and that the cover is seated evenly. Inflate completely. Put the wheel back and check every adjustment affected before setting off again.

Note: As an alternative to this procedure, punctures can be mended by injecting a pressurized sealant. Although it works for many punctures and actually makes the entire tube more or less 'puncture-proof', it won't do the trick when the puncture is big. Moreover, the sealant is very expensive.

DUMPED CHAIN (BICYCLE WITH DERAILLEUR GEARS)

This is what will happen when the derailleur is not properly adjusted: it will shift the chain beyond the furthest chainwheel or sprocket and it will get caught between the fixed and moving parts of the bicycle. It costs no more than a pair of greasy

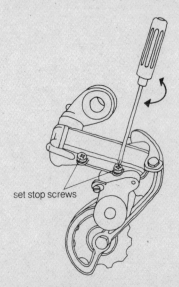

set stop screws

31.10 *Derailleur adjustment*

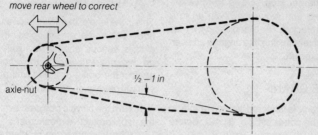

31.11 *Checking chain tension*

hands to put the chain back where it belongs, but that won't solve the problem – it will happen again next time you try to shift. It's quite easy to do the job properly:

1. Determine which derailleur is to blame and whether the chain was pushed over on the inside or the outside. Then put the chain back on.

2. Find the set stop or limit screw (fig. 31.10) that limits derailleur travel in that direction. You may have to push the shift lever back and forth a little to find it; it is the one which is approached by a little cam as the shift-lever is pushed in the direction in which the chain was dumped.

3. Screw the set stop screw in just a little – maybe half a turn.

4. Check the operation of all the gears. If the chain is still pushed off, you will have to turn the screw in a little further. If the chain does not quite 'reach' the last gear, you'll have to back off very slightly.

DUMPED CHAIN (BICYCLE WITHOUT DERAILLEUR GEARS)

If the chain comes off on a bicycle without a derailleur, it is simply too loose. This may mean that the chain should be replaced, but for the time being it will suffice to tighten it:

1. Turn the bicycle upside-down, taking the customary precautions.

2. Loosen the rear-wheel axle-nuts and any other items that may hold the wheel (for example, the gear-control chain or hub-brake parts).

3. Push the wheel forward until the chain can be replaced on the chainwheel or sprocket.

4. Now pull the wheel back again until the chain tension corresponds to that shown in fig. 31.11, making sure the wheel is not off-centre.

5. Hold the wheel carefully in exactly this position and tighten the axle-nuts and any other parts that have been loosened. Check the operation of the gearing and any other system that may have been affected and then adjust if necessary.

BROKEN CONTROL CABLE

A broken inner cable can be replaced if you carry one with you, which is not a bad idea for a long trip. You simply pull out the old cable and weave the new one through, starting at the control lever. Make the necessary adjustment at the other end, but don't try to shorten the protruding end of cable unless you have the right (very sharp) pinching tool for the job.

If you don't have a spare, you can maintain a certain amount of control over a rear derailleur even with a broken cable. Left alone, the derailleur engages the highest gear (the smallest rear sprocket). To obtain a more 'sympathetic' gear, you can adjust the set stop screws to force the cage over and move the chain on to a middle sprocket. For a long ascent, it may be worth readjusting it to engage an even larger sprocket.

LOOSE CRANK

If the crank is cottered you will have to tighten the cotter pin (fig. 31.12). Before

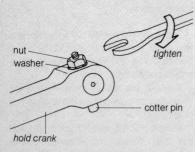

31.12 *Tightening a cottered crank*

doing that, it may be worth first hammering the pin in a little further. Pick up a couple of stones if you can't find a hammer – use the bigger stone to support the crank while you hammer the pin down with the other one.

A cotterless crank may come loose during the first hundred miles or so. Always carry the special crank-extractor, which has a spanner to fit the bolt inside the recess in the crank (fig. 31.13) so you can tighten up on the bolt.

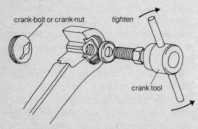

31.13 *Tightening a cotterless crank*

BUCKLED WHEEL

This is the kind of thing that happens if you ride over kerbs or pot-holes. It is not always serious enough to justify repair on the spot. However, if the wheel rubs against the brake or a part of the frame, you will have to do something:

1. Turn the bicycle upside-down, taking the usual protective measures.
2. Check whether the problem can be alleviated by simply loosening the wheel and twisting it a little at the drop-outs or by opening up the brakes a little further. However, make sure that the brake still works and that everything is tightened again.
3. If that doesn't do the trick, get out your small adjustable spanner (or a special spoke-nipple tool if you have one) and tighten and loosen the spokes in the area of the buckle as shown in fig. 31.14. First,

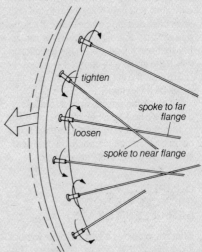

31.14 *Straightening a buckled wheel*

turn the wheel and check at the brake-shoe where the buckle is and in which direction it lies. Then loosen the nipples of the spokes on the 'high' side of the buckle, maybe only a quarter of a turn at a time. Finally, tighten those on the other side by about the same amount.

4. Continue adjusting the tension of the spokes until the buckle is sufficiently relieved to allow safe operation of the bicycle.

BATTERY-LIGHTING PROBLEMS

This will be due either to the bulb, the battery, the metal contact-strip or the switch. Check them in that order. Carry spares of the first two items. Scrape or bend the metal contact-strip and make a provisional contact, by-passing the switch if necessary – aluminium foil will do the job.

DYNAMO-LIGHTING PROBLEMS

When your dynamo lighting fails, one of a large number of things may have happened. A cool head and a systematic approach are usually all you need to see the light again. Start by isolating the problem:

1. If neither front nor rear light works, it's bound to be the dynamo itself:

(a) Check the earth contact (the little pinch-screw) and scrape off rust if necessary.

(b) Check whether the roller slips off the tyre; it may do when it's wet. This can be corrected by bending in the clamp attachment or by reversing the tyre or the wheel. If you have a Dyno-Hub, there'll be no earth contact or slippage to worry about.

(c) Check the contact of the flexible cable – there are two contacts in the case of a Dyno-Hub.

2. If it's only the front or the rear light, consider the following points for the faulty light only:

(a) Check the earth contact.

(b) Check the cable connection and the cable itself.

(c) Check the bulb. Make sure you use the right bulb and don't ride with only one light operating, since that will subject the remaining one to a higher voltage and cause it to burn out too.

Knowing how to avoid the problem from the outset is at least as useful as knowing how to fix a bicycle once it has broken down. A brief introduction to the essentials of bicycle maintenance – the subject of the present chapter – will ensure that your bicycle is as free from trouble as is humanly possible. Though punctures, falls and collisions cannot always be avoided, you will find that you'll encounter very few mishaps with a well-maintained, adjusted and lubricated machine.

I shall outline a simple maintenance schedule to help you to check for any possible deficiencies systematically and regularly – perhaps once a month or more often if you do a lot of riding. The lubrication and adjustment procedures required will be described in detail, although you always have the option of having the actual work done by a professional – if you can find one. You already have most of the equipment needed to do the job yourself – the few simple tools listed in the previous chapter.

In addition to these basic tools, you will need the following lubricants and cleaning aids:

(a) A small can of thin mineral oil (either special bicycle oil or SAE 30 motor oil but *not* household oil, since that is usually a vegetable-based oil and will congeal).

(b) A spray containing a powerful penetrating oil (WD–40 is one popular make but there are others).

(c) A small jar of acid-free Vaseline (petroleum jelly) – ordinary household Vaseline is fine.

(d) Some soft brushes or cloths in various sizes to clean the bike (one large duster and a ½-in brush for hidden corners will do).

(e) Lots of rags – clean ones and a greasy one; replace them when they get dirty.

(f) Paraffin oil to clean off greasy dirt such as that found on the chain.

CLEANING THE BICYCLE

Since dirt is perhaps the greatest hindrance to the smooth operation of many of the bicycle's controls, the following cleaning operation should always precede any inspection or adjustment work.

1. Brush off any loose dirt, taking particular care to get into all the tight little places.

2. If necessary, wash the bike with water, ordinary soap (not a detergent) and a soft cloth; wipe with another soft cloth to dry.

3. Using a cloth with solvent, remove caked dirt and grease from around the chain, chainwheels and sprockets, derailleur, wheel hubs, pedals and bottom bracket.

4. With a little Vaseline on a clean, soft cloth, lightly grease all exposed, unpainted metal surfaces. Points that can't be reached this way may be treated by dabbing them with a brush dipped in a

mixture of a few spoonfuls of oil and a cupful of paraffin oil; wipe away the excess.

5. If this is to be a big cleaning operation, you may use car wax, chrome polish and silver polish (for bare aluminium parts).

INSPECTION

A minimal inspection should be carried out before every ride and should cover at least the following important points:

1. Check the brakes for effectiveness; adjust them if necessary.

2. Check the tyre pressure; inflate them if necessary.

3. Check whether the wheels turn freely; correct them if necessary.

4. Check whether the saddle and handlebars are firm and correctly adjusted; adjust and fasten them if necessary.

5. Check the operation of the lights; make any replacements or repairs if necessary.

Although this quick inspection will often detect the most serious deficiencies, a more extended and thorough inspection will still be required regularly, at least once a month. When the bicycle has been cleaned, proceed as follows:

1. Check all nuts and bolts, as well as any other fasteners and connections; tighten everything that needs tightening.

2. Check the frame, the wheels and the front forks for distortion and alignment (figs. 32.1, 32.2 and 32.3). Consult a bicycle mechanic about any repairs that may be needed.

3. Carry out the checks listed as steps 1 to 5 in the quick inspection above.

4. Place the bicycle upside-down (or better still, hang it up by the saddle and handlebars – chapter 40 shows you how

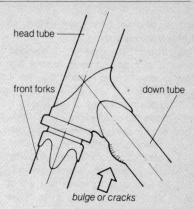

head tube

front forks

down tube

bulge or cracks

32.1 *Frame damage*

32.2 *Checking wheel alignment*

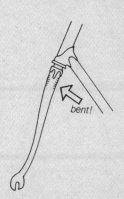

bent!

32.3 *Bent front forks*

this can be done), taking care not to damage any protrusions.

5. Inspect the tyres for embedded objects, damage and wear; remove any foreign objects and replace the tyre if necessary.

6. Check the spokes of the wheels – they must all be equally tight; correct them if necessary, using a spoke-nipple spanner or a small adjustable spanner.

7. Check for play in the wheel hubs (by attempting to push the wheel sideways) and for excessive tightness (the wheel must come to rest with the valve at the lowest point).

8. Check the brake shoes for correct alignment (fig. 32.4) and wear; adjust or replace them if necessary.

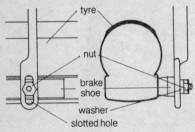

32.4 *Checking brake-shoe alignment*

9. Check the operation of all controls and control cables or rods; adjust the cables (fig. 32.7) or replace them if necessary.

10. Check the operation of the hub gear if you have one; adjust it as needed.

11. Check the bearings at the bottom bracket and pedals for play or tightness.

12. Check the head-set bearing by lifting the front end by the fork and moving it with one hand while holding the head tube with the other.

13. Check the chain tension; adjust as described in chapter 31 if it does not correspond to fig. 32.5.

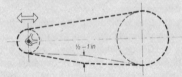

32.5 *Checking chain tension*

14. Check all electrical cables and the alignment of the dynamo (fig. 32.6); replace cables and correct the dynamo if required.

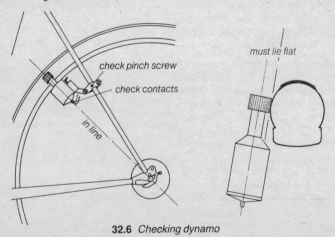

32.6 *Checking dynamo*

ADJUSTING CABLES AND CONTROLS

The major adjustments on a bicycle – brakes, derailleurs or hub gears – are easily made by means of barrel-adjusters on the cables (fig. 32.7). To take up slack

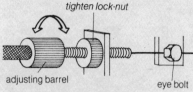

tighten lock-nut

adjusting barrel

eye bolt

32.7 *Adjusting cables*

in the inner cable, the adjuster is screwed out further and then held with one hand while the knurled lock-nut is tightened with the other hand. When the end of the adjustment-range is reached, the adjuster must be screwed in as far as it will go, the eye-bolt must be loosened and the cable pulled up, after which the eye-bolt is tightened again. Rod-brake controls are ad-

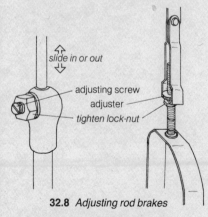

slide in or out

adjusting screw
adjuster
tighten lock-nut

32.8 *Adjusting rod brakes*

justed by means of the sliding joints in the rods.

For details of how to adjust derailleur travel, refer to chapter 31. To adjust a Sturmey–Archer three-speed hub, you should do the following:

1. Set the control lever in the 'N' (normal) position.

2. Check by looking from behind the rear-wheel axle-nut to see whether the view through the hole in the nut (where the little control chain enters the hub) corresponds to the one shown in fig. 32.9.

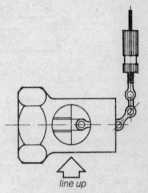

line up

engage second gear ('normal') before adjusting

32.9 *Adjusting a three-speed Sturmey–Archer hub gear*

3. Make any corrections necessary with the adjuster in the usual manner.

LUBRICATION

Lubrication is important, but two things must be kept in mind: parts to be lubricated must be thoroughly cleaned first and the *correct* lubricant must be selected and used sparingly and accurately. Cleaning can be done with a dry rag, with a rag soaked in paraffin oil or by dipping the entire part in paraffin oil, depending on the condition of the parts to be cleaned. Use the following as a guide when selecting the correct lubricant:

(a) Ball-bearings (hubs, pedals, etc.) must usually be taken apart and packed with bearing grease. However, if an oil nipple is installed, you can use mineral oil.

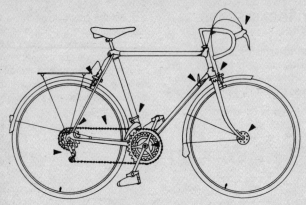

32.10 *Lubrication points*

(b) The chain likes to run on graphite or molybdenum-disulphide ('moly') grease, although this attracts dirt like nothing else on earth. Soaking the chain in light oil or synthetic oil will do, provided it's done frequently.

(c) Control cables can be taken apart and greased or you can use a spray can with a long, tubular nozzle.

Although minor adjustments and cleaning work can be done with a minimum of equipment almost anywhere, the cyclist who wants to do more work on his bicycle will soon find he needs something better – a permanent workshop. It is neither very expensive nor very difficult to set up such a workshop. The bicycle is not demanding and can be maintained in the smallest and most unlikely quarters – an attic, a basement, a pantry, a garden shed, even the corner of an ordinary room screened off by means of a curtain or a room divider will do to accommodate the mere six feet of bicycle and enough elbow room for you to work on it.

By way of equipment, all you'll need is a work bench, some tools and some apparatus to hold the bicycle. Most of the necessary tools you already have, although there are many more which are used for special jobs and are described below. The work bench need be only provisional – an old kitchen table, dresser or sideboard. Anything will do as long as it is sturdy and has a level top that can be used as a working surface. Two possible methods of holding the bike, both preferable to merely putting it upside-down, are detailed in chapter 40.

You will also need something to sit on – a piano stool is perfect but any stool will do. On the wall you can attach some shelves and hooks to store parts and tools. A blackboard allows you to jot down notes and make sketches should the work become complicated. Install a light over the work bench and one over the bike, or use an inspection-light which you can hold or hang wherever you need it. A wash-basin will qualify your workshop for the luxury league but some rags and a hand-cleansing lotion will do instead.

TOOLS

In addition to the contents of your road-side repair kit, you will need only a few tools to solve maybe ninety per cent of all the problems your bike presents. The other ten per cent are going to be expensive. Those special tools usually need not be bought until you encounter the particular difficulty that demands their use – in some cases this may never happen. Equipping yourself will therefore probably be a slow and gradual process that never demands really great expense at any one time.

Tools can be separated into two distinct categories – general tools and specific bicycle tools. The general tools are those that can be bought at any good ironmonger's or tool shop. Specific bicycle tools are bought – or at least are ordered and arrive perhaps after some delay – at bicycle shops and from reputable mail order catalogues. These tools are intended for very specific purposes, and their use is often restricted to the particular make of component for which they are designed. Others can be considered as general bicycle tools – these are made for bicycle-use only, but are suitable for any make.

In the sections that follow, the commonest tools for use on a bicycle, both general and specific, will be described with a picture and a few brief words. The ones most frequently used should probably be bought at once; the others can wait until they are needed. In the category of specific bicycle tools, I have noted whether or not the tools are usually suited to any make of component. Let me emphasize one thing: don't skimp on the quality of your tools; you'll do better with a few good tools than with a cartload of cheap junk.

General Tools

Vice This is mounted on the work bench and used to hold firmly the items you're working on. It should be the type used for metalwork which has accurately square jaws; any size that opens up to at least 1½ ins (38 mm) will be adequate. To protect

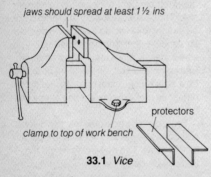

jaws should spread at least 1½ ins

clamp to top of work bench

protectors

33.1 *Vice*

the parts you work on, some soft metal angle-pieces (aluminium or copper) should be used over the jaws.

Fixed Spanners These are for use on the bolts and nuts on the bicycle, many of which are hexagonal-headed but some of which are square or octagonal-headed. You will need metric sizes in the range from 7 mm to 15 mm. There are three major types of fixed spanner:

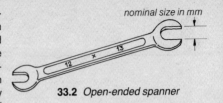

nominal size in mm

33.2 *Open-ended spanner*

(a) *Open-ended spanner* (fig. 33.2) with the two ends of different sizes; very handy for most repairs since it requires little room to work and may also be used on square and octagonal nuts or bolts.

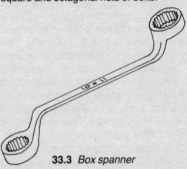

33.3 *Box spanner*

(b) *Box spanner* (fig. 33.3) again with a different size at each end; requires a little more room to work but is more precise and less likely to damage the head of the nut or bolt. A little more expensive than the open-ended spanner.

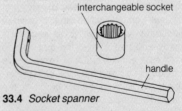

interchangeable socket

handle

33.4 *Socket spanner*

(c) *Socket-spanner set* (fig. 33.4) comes in a whole set with one or two different-sized handles and a whole range of different-sized socket-inserts. Requires even more room, works as well as the box spanner but is less expensive.

Adjustable Spanner This is a bigger version of the one I recommended for your roadside repair kit – 8 or 10 ins long. This tool will hold almost anything on your bike with reasonable accuracy. On long trips it can even double as an emergency vice (fig. 33.5).

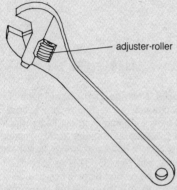

adjuster-roller

33.5 *Adjustable spanner*

Allen-key I have already mentioned this in chapter 31; you may need several sizes or none at all, depending on the components used on your bike – the more ornate the bicycle, the more likely you are to have Allen screws or bolts with hexagonal recesses which these fit (fig. 33.6).

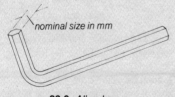

nominal size in mm

33.6 *Allen-key*

Screwdrivers You should have two or three screwdrivers in various sizes; ideally, the width and thickness of the blade should correspond to the saw-cut in the head of the screw. Get one or two Phillips-head screwdrivers as well for the cross-headed screws often found on minor accessories (fig. 33.7).

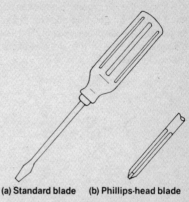

(a) Standard blade   (b) Phillips-head blade

33.7 *Screwdriver*

Hammers You'll probably need two: a mallet with a soft, plastic head and an ordinary steel hammer (fig. 33.8); don't get them too big.

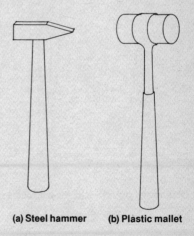

(a) Steel hammer   (b) Plastic mallet

33.8 *Hammers*

Pliers These are useful provided you use them only when no other more precise tool can do the job in hand; pliers often do more harm than good. In addition to the small needle-nose pliers, you may find the diagonal cutters and the arc-joint pliers useful (fig. 33.9).

(a) Needle-nose pliers

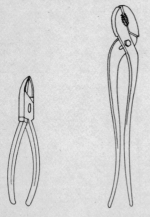

(b) Diagonal cutters   **(c) Arc-joint pliers**

33.9 *Pliers*

Hacksaw A saw should be used only when all else fails – to cut off a rusted bolt or to make a new saw-cut in the head of an abused screw. Get the small, cheap and handy 'Eclipse' saw (fig. 33.10).

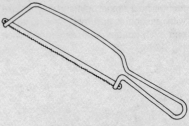

33.10 *'Eclipse' saw*

Punch, Drift and Cold Chisel These are not characters in a comic opera, but useful tools for hammering out items which no available tool seems to fit – cotter pins, bottom-bracket lock-rings, freewheel cones, etc. (fig. 33.11). The cold chisel should be ground blunt, since you don't want it to split the metal but to turn the whole part in one piece.

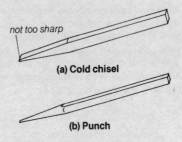

not too sharp

(a) Cold chisel

(b) Punch

33.11 *Punch and cold chisel*

Special Bicycle Tools

Most of the bicycle tools in this category are suitable only for one specific make of component, although even amongst these some individual tools may be found to fit one or two other makes as well. However, the first few tools covered (marked with an *) fit any make of component or bicycle.

Cone Spanner* This is no more than a very flat open-ended spanner used exclusively for bearing work (e.g., disassembly and adjustment of the wheel bearings). They usually come in sets of two for sizes of 13, 14, 15 and 16 mm; at a pinch the 15-mm size will also serve to remove or install pedals (fig. 33.12).

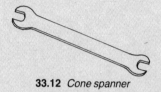

33.12 *Cone spanner*

Pedal Spanner* This tool is simply a longer and slightly thicker version of the preceding spanner, though often only single-ended (fig. 33.13).

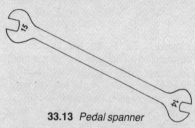

33.13 *Pedal spanner*

Nipple Spanner* These are used to adjust the spoke nipples. They're cheap and light, but be sure you use the right size cut-out for the nipples at hand or you'll ruin them (fig. 33.14). A small adjustable spanner will serve the same purpose.

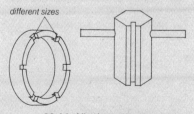

different sizes

33.14 *Nipple spanners*

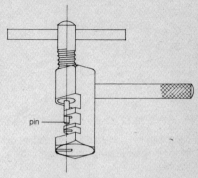

pin

33.15 *Chain-rivet extractor*

Chain-rivet Extractor* This device is used to open up a chain without a master-link and to connect the ends of such a chain (fig. 33.15); it is always necessary for a derailleur bicycle and is also needed to shorten the chain on a non-derailleur model.

'Third Hand'* It is possible to do without this device (fig. 33.16), though it does make life easier. It holds the brake-arms of a calliper brake together while you adjust the cable.

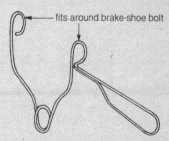

fits around brake-shoe bolt

33.16 *'Third hand' (brake-clamp)*

Cable Cutters* The clean way to shorten a Bowden inner cable is to use a pair of these (fig. 33.17), though the job can be

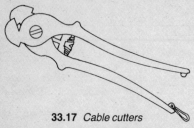

33.17 *Cable cutters*

done with very sharp diagonal cutters or even with a large sharp pair of carpenter's pinchers.

*Sprocket Remover** These are used to exchange the sprockets on a freewheel of a derailleur bicycle (fig. 33.18). In chapter 40, I'll show you how to make your own.

use two

33.18 *Sprocket remover*

Crank-extractor Already mentioned in chapter 31, this tool is required for work on the bottom bracket of a bicycle which has cotterless cranks. Make sure you get the correct make and model for the crank-set in question (fig. 33.19).

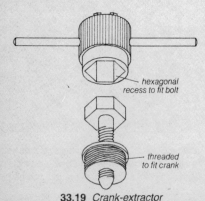

hexagonal recess to fit bolt

threaded to fit crank

33.19 *Crank-extractor*

Freewheel-extractor This is not always required to repair the freewheel itself (you can usually leave that on the wheel), but it is essential to replace a broken spoke on the right-hand side of the rear wheel on a derailleur bicycle (fig. 33.20).

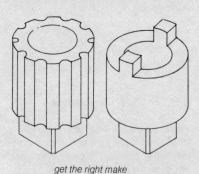

get the right make

33.20 *Freewheel-extractors*

Special tools These are available to accomplish all sorts of specialized tasks including brake adjustment, bottom-bracket work and head-set overhaul. They are helpful but usually not essential; almost all such jobs can be completed after a fashion with the more common tools described above. Perhaps the most useful of all these special tools is the *calliper-brake spanner*, a very thin 10-mm open-ended spanner which allows you to get hold of the lock-nut on a side-pull brake while tightening the main mounting bolt. They are difficult to obtain and if you can't find one take a regular 10-mm spanner and have it ground down to fit.

LUBRICANTS

In addition to the light oil, spray can and Vaseline listed in chapter 32, the following lubricants will be useful:

(a) *Bearing grease* to lubricate the ball-bearings. Perhaps the best quality grease is the lithium-based variety, although special bicycle grease may be slightly less viscous, resulting in even easier rolling. If at all possible, get it in a tube; that way it never gets dirty.

(b) *Chain lubricant* – either the messy but very durable Castrol Motorcycle Chain Grease (in which the chain is dipped after being heated in hot water) or one of the modern spray-can chain lubricants. The first kind contains graphite; the second usually contains molybdenum-disulphide. Both these compounds are 'dispersed particulates' which means that they act like tiny ball-bearings.

(c) *Paraffin oil* is not actually a lubricant but is equally important in maintaining lubrication efficiency. Use it to clean all parts that are to be lubricated. Let me add one warning though – used oil and other such substances do not belong in the national water supply – don't throw them down the drain or out in the back yard; take them in a closed container to the nearest garage or petrol station to be disposed of properly.

WORKSHOP PROCEDURE

Your approach to the work done in your workshop is possibly as important as the equipment you have accumulated. The following chapters will give brief directions for carrying out most of the repairs and maintenance operations which are regularly required. However, there is more to workshop procedure than simply following directions.

In the first place, all directions are general descriptions of a typical situation – they don't tell you what to do if the bolt is so tight that it won't come off with the proper tool and they can never be so comprehensive as to apply to every conceivable make and model. What you will need as much as good instructions is imagination, a systematic approach, common sense and a great deal of patience.

In fact, those will be the only things at your disposal for many of the jobs you'll encounter that aren't described in this manual or in any other bicycle book. To tackle that kind of job, a systematic approach is possibly the most important requirement. Begin on one side of the component you want to take apart (on wheel or transmission parts this will usually be the side opposite the chain), keep a record of the order in which things are removed, and clean and inspect each part as you take it off. Don't try to re-assemble any part that is obviously damaged or seriously worn. Finally, remember the golden rule of bicycle maintenance: don't tackle more than one job at a time!

In this and the following three chapters we will run through the major repair and maintenance jobs on the bicycle, beginning here with what might be considered to be its backbone – the frame, the steering mechanism and the saddle. The descriptions will be kept to a minimum, so this is not entertaining reading but bare step-by-step working procedures. Even so, not every description can be foolproof and the reader is expected to have read the preceding chapters which explain the way things work – both components and tools – as well as to think for himself.

THE FRAME

Unless you are involved in a serious accident, the frame is unlikely to be damaged. If such a thing has occurred, you can check the frame for misalignment and strained tubes as follows.

Checking for Frame Damage
(see figs. 34.1, 34.2 and 34.3)

Tools and equipment A 10-ft length of twine and a straight-edge marked in millimetres.

Procedure
1. Have someone hold the bike up with the handlebars straight.
2. Look along the rear wheel and try to get the two wheels in line; if you see something like fig. 34.1, either the frame or the fork is bent.

34.1 *Checking wheel-alignment*

3. To check whether the frame itself is bent, remove the rear wheel (see chapter 36) and place the twine around the frame and the rear fork-ends as shown in fig. 34.2, keeping the twine taut.

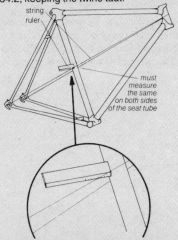

string
ruler

must measure the same on both sides of the seat tube

34.2 *Checking frame-alignment*

4. Measure the distance between the seat tube and the twine on both sides; if they differ by more than about 2 mm, you're in trouble. Seek the advice of a bicycle mechanic about the need and possibilities for repair or frame replacement.

5. Check the down tube and the top tube for any signs of a bulge or buckle, usually just behind the lower head-lug. If you find signs as shown in fig. 34.3 – or

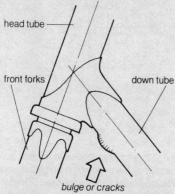

34.3 *Checking for frame damage*

even cracked paint in that area – you will again need professional advice. On a really good frame, it is often worth having a frame-builder replace the damaged tube.

6. The steering and the forks must also be checked; for a description see below.

THE STEERING SYSTEM

Smooth and accurate operation of the steering system is essential if the bike is to handle safely. A fall or a collision may damage both the forks and the head-set, so these items must be checked as well as the frame if an accident has occurred. The handlebars can usually be bent straight without much risk. The forks may break at the shaft – a very disconcerting

experience – if the handlebar stem is not set far enough into the steerer tube and an obstacle is hit at high speed. Finally, the head-set bearings themselves are subject to considerable wear, so they must be checked and overhauled regularly – maybe twice yearly with normal use.

Checking for Bent Forks
(see fig. 34.4)

Tools and equipment Metal straight-edge.

Procedure

1. Look at the forks from the side; the head tube and upper portion of the fork-blade should be in line.

2. If what you see resembles fig. 34.4, you'll either need new forks or you'll have to have the bent ones straightened out by someone who knows what he's doing and has the right tool.

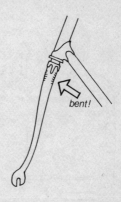

34.4 *Checking for bent front forks*

3. Even if evidence is not as strong as that shown in fig. 34.4, check that the steering is smooth by turning the handlebars as far as they will go to the left and to the right with the wheel off the ground. If it feels tight all the way or (more usually) for part of the way, the fork-shaft will be bent, which you can verify with the aid of the straight-edge once the forks have been

removed (description below). You will need to replace the forks.

Checking and Straightening Handlebars
(see fig. 34.5)

Tools and equipment Straight-edge marked in millimetres or sixteenths of an inch.

Procedure

1. Measure to check that the distance from the end of each handlebar-bend to the centre of the bar is identical. Unless there are serious visible signs of strain, the bend can be straightened by hand.

2. To straighten, remove the bar from the bike (described below) and bend as shown in fig. 34.5. Replace the bar (described below).

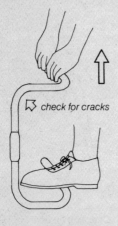

check for cracks

34.5 *Bending handlebars out*

Removing Handlebars
(see figs. 34.6 and 34.7)

Tools and equipment Spanners to fit expander-bolt and (if required) binder-bolt; heavy screwdriver if the handlebar-bend has to be removed; mallet or hammer.

Procedure

1. Loosen expander-bolt by about four turns.

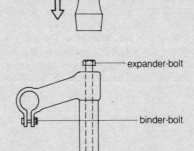

expander-bolt

binder-bolt

34.6 *Loosening handlebars*

2. If this has not loosened the bar, hold the bike by the handlebars and tap the bolt with the mallet; protect the head of the bolt with a block of wood if you use a steel hammer.

3. Lift out the bar and remove cables, brake-levers, tape and end-plugs if necessary.

4. If the handlebar-bend itself has to be removed, you will have to unscrew the binder-bolt and spread the clamp with your largest-sized screwdriver.

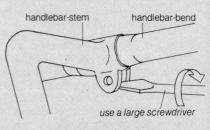

handlebar-stem   handlebar-bend

use a large screwdriver

34.7 *Opening clamp to move handlebar-bend*

Installing Handlebars
(see figs. 34.8 and 34.7)

Tools and equipment Spanners to fit expander-bolt and binder-bolt; large screwdriver if the handlebar-bend is to be installed in the stem.

Procedure

1. Check that the stem fits the fork-shaft (is it French, English or Italian?) and that the handlebar-bend fits the stem (matching make and model).

2. Loosen the expander-bolt enough to free the expander-cone or the wedge.

3. Slide the stem at least 65 mm (2½ ins) into the headset and tighten the expander-bolt.

4. If a new handlebar-bend is to be installed in the stem, open up the clamp with the large screwdriver as in fig. 34.7 and tighten the binder-bolt when the bend is in the right position and at the right angle.

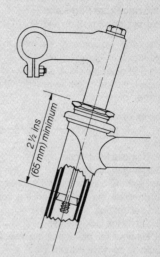

34.8 *Depth of handlebar-stem installation*

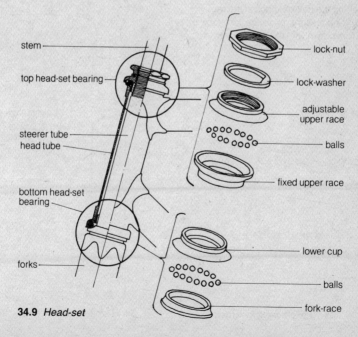

stem

top head-set bearing

steerer tube

head tube

bottom head-set bearing

forks

lock-nut

lock-washer

adjustable upper race

balls

fixed upper race

lower cup

balls

fork-race

34.9 *Head-set*

Removing Front Forks and Head-set (see figs. 34.9 and 34.10)

Tools and equipment Spanner to fit expander-bolt; large spanner or pliers to fit head-set lock-nut (or better still, special head-set tools); large screwdriver; hammer; rags.

Procedure

1. Remove handlebar as described above.
2. Remove front wheel.
3. Remove front brake.
4. Rest the bike on the front fork-ends and unscrew the lock-nut on the upper head-set bearing.
5. Lift off the lock-washer.
6. Remove the upper bearing race; this should be possible without a tool.
7. Remove the ball-bearings.
8. Hold the rag around the lower head-set bearing at the fork crown and lift the frame up from around the fork shaft, catching the ball-bearings in the rag.
9. If necessary, prize the fork-race off the fork crown with the screwdriver.

10. If necessary, remove the cups which are pressed into the head tube by hammering them out from the opposite end with the screwdriver and hammer, working around gradually and carefully.

Installing Front Forks and Head-set (see figs. 34.9, 34.11 and 34.12)

Tools and equipment The same as for removal of forks and head-set (but, if fork-race and cups must be installed, you will need a length of copper tubing about 12 ins long and 1¼ ins internal diameter, a block of wood and a hammer or mallet); rags; bearing grease.

Procedure

1. Make sure the forks and head-set have matching screw-threads and that the fork-shaft is the correct length.
2. Install new bearing cups and fork-race if necessary (it *will* be necessary if

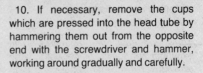

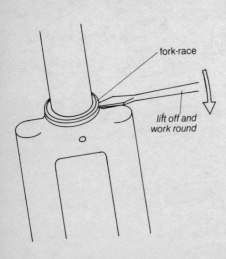

fork-race

lift off and work round

34.10 *Removing fork-race*

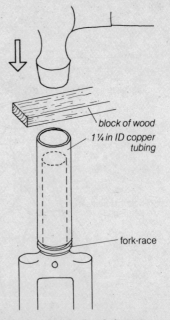

block of wood

1¼ in ID copper tubing

fork-race

34.11 *Installing fork-race*

the old ones show signs of pitting and uneven wear).

3. Place the frame upside-down and fill both bearing races with grease.

4. Insert the ball-bearings (usually the $^5/_{32}$-in size) into the bottom race, which will now be facing upwards. If the ball-bearings are contained in a retainer, insert them as in fig. 34.12.

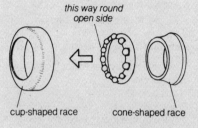

this way round
open side

cup-shaped race   cone-shaped race

34.12 *Installing bearing retainer*

5. Insert the fork-shaft through the head tube, hold the forks tightly at the lower bearing and the crown and turn the whole thing over (i.e., the right way up) and support the bike at the fork-ends.

6. Insert the balls into the upper race.

7. Screw the upper adjustable cup on to the fork-shaft – but not *too* tightly.

8. Install the lock-washer so that the groove matches the projection.

9. Install the lock-nut tightly while holding the adjustable cup.

10. Check the operation of the steering. If necessary, adjust the head-set by loosening the lock-nut a little, then lifting the lock-washer, screwing the adjustable race in or out and finally tightening the lock-nut again.

THE SADDLE

Maintenance of the saddle is simply a question of occasionally treating the underside of the leather cover with Proofide or a similar preservative and checking and correcting the tension of the cover (fig. 34.13). Here are instructions for the removal, adjustment and installation of the saddle and the seat pin.

Removing the Saddle

These instructions apply to a conventional tubular seat pin (see fig. 34.13).

Tools and equipment A spanner to fit the saddle clamp-nuts.

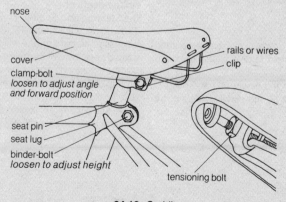

nose

cover

clamp-bolt
*loosen to adjust angle
and forward position*

seat pin

seat lug

binder-bolt
loosen to adjust height

rails or wires

clip

tensioning bolt

34.13 *Saddle*

Procedure

1. Loosen the saddle clamp-nuts until the clamp can be spread to slip over the saddle wires or rails and lift the saddle off, either with or without the clamp.

2. If the saddle has an alloy adjustable seat pin, you have to establish just how the task is done with the model in question.

Installing the Saddle
These instructions apply to a conventional seat pin (see fig. 34.13).

Tools and equipment As for the removal of a saddle.

Procedure

1. Open the clamp-bolt to spread the clamp over the rails or wires of the saddle.

2. Push the clamp over the seat pin and tighten the clamp-nuts. Make sure the clamp is positioned correctly – usually as in fig. 34.13 (i.e., with the clamp-bolt *behind* the seat pin).

3. Alloy adjustable seat pins require individual attention, depending on the make and model.

Removing the Seat Pin
(see fig. 34.14)

Tools and equipment Spanner to fit binder-bolt.

Procedure

1. Do this only with the saddle mounted on the seat pin to give yourself enough leverage.

2. Loosen the binder-bolt and pull the seat pin out by the saddle, twisting it if necessary.

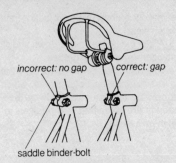

incorrect: no gap   correct: gap

saddle binder-bolt

34.14 *Installing the seat pin*

Installing the Seat Pin (see fig. 34.14)

Tools and equipment As for the removal of a seat pin.

Procedure

1. Make sure that the seat-pin diameter matches the inside diameter of the seat tube. If they don't match, you must get one that fits. The binder-bolt must leave some space between the two halves of the split seat lug when tightened; don't fiddle around with shims or drilling holes and installing pins!

2. Open the binder-bolt and insert the seat pin to the correct depth; hold it there and tighten the binder-bolt.

**Adjustments of
the Steering and Saddle**
The various adjustments required are all discussed elsewhere and will not be repeated here. You will find them as follows: Saddle height, angle and forward position on pages 34–5; handlebar height, angle and position on pages 35–6; head-set (ease and accuracy of steering) under the heading 'Installing Front Forks and Head-set' on pages 214–15.

Since the bicycle drive-train – the trans-mission and gearing mechanisms – con-sists of a large number of separate com-ponents which may be of various designs, it is not possible to present maintenance instructions with as much attention to de-tail as was given in the preceding chapter. Instead, I will take the major components and systems one at a time and describe how they are taken apart and put back together again, pointing out as we go along what is likely to need replacing and what to look out for.

THE PEDALS

On most bicycles the pedals are a peren-nial weak spot, since they are subjected to high forces and are asymmetrically loaded on small ball-bearings which are poorly sealed against dirt and moisture. You may be able to solve your problems with bearing maintenance but often the pedal may have to be replaced. When you do replace it, make sure the new one is a high-quality model – one of the varieties in which the entire central section, including ribs and bearing housings, is constructed in one piece.

Pedal Maintenance (see fig. 35.1)

Tools and equipment Needle-nose pliers; small spanner to fit internal bearing lock-nut; small screwdriver or spanner to fit bearing-cone; rags; bearing grease.

Procedure

1. Remove dust-cap; there is no need to remove pedal from crank.

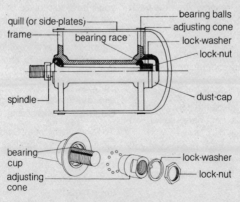

35.1 *Pedal*

2. Remove lock-nut and lock-washer and check that the projection in the lock-washer is intact; if the washer slips it must be replaced or you will not be able to adjust the bearing properly.

3. Remove outer bearing-cone; replace it if severely pitted.

4. Catch the ball-bearings from both sides; replace them if necessary (usually the $5/32$-in size).

5. Clean and inspect the bearing races and the inner cone which forms one piece with the axle. If it is severely grooved or pitted, it is usually best to replace the entire pedal; the same is true if the axle is bent.

6. Pack the bearing races with grease and insert the new ball-bearings.

7. Re-assemble in the reverse order to this.

To adjust: loosen the lock-nut slightly, raise the lock-washer, tighten or loosen the adjustable cone, then re-tighten the lock-nut.

Pedal Replacement

Tools and equipment Pedal spanner or another thin spanner which will fit (on some cheap bicycles, you will need an Allen-key to fit the recess in the back of the threaded stub, reached from the back of the crank).

Procedure
1. Hold the opposite crank with one hand and place the spanner on the flats of the pedal.

2. Think for a moment – if this is a left-hand pedal you loosen it by turning to the right; if it is a right-hand pedal you must turn to the left.

3. Loosen the pedal. If necessary, you can restrain the opposite crank with a length of wood held through the rear triangle of the frame.

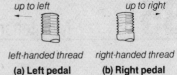

left-handed thread   right-handed thread
(a) Left pedal   **(b) Right pedal**
35.2 *Left or right pedal?*

4. To install the new pedal, make absolutely sure that:

(a) you have a pedal with a thread-type that corresponds to that of the crank;

(b) you know which pedal goes on the left and which on the right; turn the right-hand pedal to the right and the left-hand pedal to the left.

THE CRANKS

Two things may happen to a crank – it may work loose or it may get bent. A bent crank gives a strange pedalling action and can only be straightened by a bicycle mechanic with the appropriate tool; it only takes a second and saves you breaking your back and ruining your bike by trying to perform the feat yourself. A loose crank is a sign of a loose cotter-pin (cottered crank), a loose cotterless crank-bolt or a split cotterless crank. In the latter case, you'll have to replace the crank – as you will if the square hole in the cotterless crank has worn so much that the crank slips too far over the axle (you'll notice this if a straight crank or chainwheel hits the chain stay).

Removing and Installing a Cottered Crank (see fig. 35.3)

Tools and equipment Spanner to fit cotter-pin nut; hammer; small block of wood.

Procedure
1. Loosen the cotter-pin nut by two or three turns only.

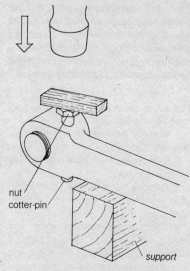

35.3 *Loosening a cotter-pin*

2. Supporting the end of the crank on something solid and protecting the nut with the piece of wood, hammer the cotter-pin out until the nut touches the crank.

3. Remove the nut and the washer and push the cotter-pin out the rest of the way.

4. Inspect the condition of the threads; replace the cotter-pin if necessary, but make sure that you get the same size – there are at least three different sizes!

5. To install, make sure that:

(a) you put the right-hand crank on the right-hand side and the left crank on the left;

(b) you push the cotter-pin in from the larger side of the tapered hole in the crank;

(c) you don't forget the washer and tighten the nut as firmly as possible.

Removing and Installing a Cotterless Crank (see fig. 35.4)

Tools and equipment Crank-extractor tool to match the make and model of crank.

Procedure

1. Remove dust-cap.

2. Remove cotterless nut or bolt *and the washer*, holding the crank tight.

3. Make sure that the extractor tool is withdrawn and screw it as far as it will go into the threaded hole in the crank.

4. Now turn the extractor inwards so that the crank is pushed off the tapered square axle; remove the tool.

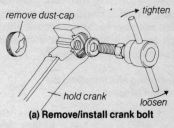

(a) Remove/install crank bolt

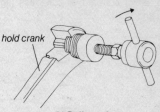

(b) Pull crank

35.4 *How to use a crank-extractor*

5. To install, make sure that:

(a) you put the right crank on the right side;

(b) you off-set the cranks by 180 degrees;

(c) you clean the mating surfaces and don't reinstall a cracked crank;

(d) you tighten the bolt or the nut, not forgetting the washer and the dust-cap;

(e) you re-tighten everything after at least the first twenty-five miles of riding;

(f) if you replace the crank, it must have the appropriate pedal threading as well as being the right length.

BOTTOM BRACKET

This component also gets a great deal of wear, especially if you often ride in bad weather. However, all you normally need to do is to overhaul it once every six months, the procedure for which is described below. The same instructions apply when replacing the entire crank-set or any part of it. The Thompson crank-set, found on some cheaper imported bicycles, probably needs more frequent attention but will work very well if cleaned, greased and adjusted regularly.

Removing and Installing the Bottom Bracket

These instructions apply to the BSA type, either cottered or cotterless (figs. 35.5 and 35.6).

Tools and equipment Assuming that the cranks have been removed, you'll need special bottom-bracket tools correct for the make and model, or a large adjustable spanner; hammer, cold chisel, punch and similar equipment; rags; bearing grease.

Procedure (assuming that the cranks have been removed):

1. Remove the lock-nut on the adjustable side (i.e., left).

2. Remove the adjustable cup; remove the ball-bearings.

3. Remove the axle. This is only possible if you've also removed the right-hand crank.

4. Catch all ball-bearings; clean and inspect all surfaces; replace parts if necessary (the ¼-in balls are cheap and always worth replacing). If balls come in a retainer, reinstall as shown in fig. 35.6.

5. If the right-hand side fixed cup has to be replaced, remember that the English and Swiss versions have a left-handed thread (loosen by turning to the right; fasten by turning to the left), whereas

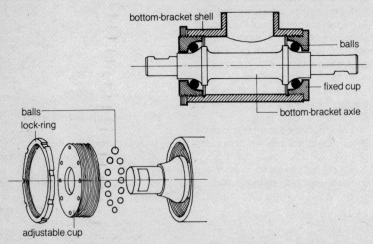

bottom-bracket shell

balls

fixed cup

bottom-bracket axle

balls
lock-ring

adjustable cup

Adjusting detail

35.5 *Bottom bracket (BSA or conventional type)*

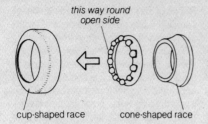

*this way round
open side*

cup-shaped race   cone-shaped race

35.6 *Installing bearing retainer*

French and Italians standards have a right-handed thread.

6. When replacing a bottom bracket or any other part, consider the following:

(a) the threading must match the threading in the frame (British, French, Italian, Swiss or Raleigh proprietory);

(b) axles come in two different lengths even for a normal double chainwheel – not to mention triples and tandem parts!

(c) clean every part you install and grease the bearing surfaces.

To adjust: loosen the lock-ring, tighten or loosen the adjustable cup and re-tighten the lock-ring.

Overhauling a Thompson Bottom Bracket (fig. 35.7)

Tools and equipment Assuming that the left-hand crank has been removed: large adjustable spanner; rags; bearing grease.

Procedure (assuming that the left-hand crank has been removed):

1. Remove the lock-nut on the left side – it has a left-handed thread so you must turn it to the right!

2. Remove the washer.

3. Remove the adjustable cone by turning the dust-cap to the right (left-handed thread).

4. Pull out the axle from the opposite side, catching all the ball-bearings.

5. Clean, inspect and lubricate all parts; use new ball-bearings (¼ in).

6. Re-assemble in the reverse order.

To adjust: loosen lock-nut, lift lock-washer and turn dust-cap with cone in or out.

CHAINWHEELS

On a good quality crank-set the chainwheels can be replaced. How that's done will be revealed by looking closely for attachment screws, bolts or nuts. These must also be checked for tightness and must be fastened or replaced when necessary. The only other job you're likely to encounter – apart from the ever-necessary cleaning – is straightening a bent chainwheel, which can be recognized by scraping sounds and poor shifting. If only a few teeth are bent you can do this as in fig. 35.8 (overleaf); if the entire chainwheel is warped you may try hitting it

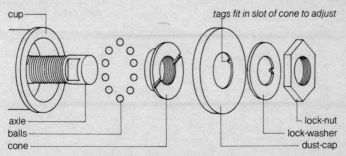

cup

tags fit in slot of cone to adjust

axle
balls
cone

lock-nut
lock-washer
dust-cap

35.7 *Thompson bottom bracket*

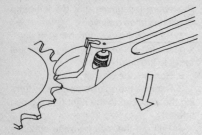

35.8 *Straightening chainwheel teeth*

gently with a wooden or plastic mallet while supporting the rest of the chainwheel with something solid. You may be better off buying a new chainwheel (of the right size, make and model), as you must when the teeth are clearly worn. You can prevent wear by replacing the chain frequently – say at every 3,000 miles.

FREEWHEEL AND SPROCKETS

The most likely thing you'll ever have to do to a freewheel and sprocket cluster on a derailleur bicycle is to remove it in order to replace a spoke. Sometimes, however, the freewheel mechanism itself breaks down or you may want to replace the individual sprockets because they are worn (you'll find that the chain will 'jump', especially on the smallest sprocket) or to achieve a better combination of gears.

Repair of the mechanism and a number of sprocket replacements are possible without removing the freewheel from the hub.

To remove a freewheel, you must use a special freewheel-extractor as shown in fig. 35.9. Make sure it is of the right make and model for your freewheel and restrain it with the axle-nut or quick-release lever – but not too tightly: leave enough room free to give the extractor at least one complete turn and loosen up as you go along. A repair to the mechanism is carried out by removing the outer ring with the two indents; this is in fact the bearing cone and has a left-handed thread. It hides a large number of ball-bearings ($\frac{1}{8}$-in size). You can now lift out the mechanism itself and you will find another fifty or

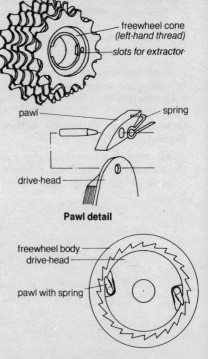

freewheel cone
(left-hand thread)

slots for extractor

pawl — spring

drive-head

Pawl detail

freewheel body
drive-head

pawl with spring

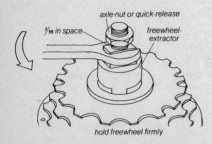

axle-nut or quick-release

$\frac{1}{16}$ in space

freewheel-extractor

hold freewheel firmly

35.9 *How to use a freewheel-extractor*

35.10 *Freewheel*

so ball-bearings. Your problem will probably be that the little pawls or their springs (fig. 35.10) are broken. When reinstalling, hold everything together using twelve inches of twine or heavy yarn, wrapped around the parts and withdrawn only after the drive-head is in place inside the freewheel body.

When replacing sprockets, it is important to buy ones of the correct make and model for your freewheel and to use the appropriate tool (which can be home-made as shown on page 248 or shop bought as shown on page 208). Check what kind of threading is involved – left or right. Some models are not screwed but are held on splines. When the complete freewheel is installed, it is done so by hand, after the threads have been carefully cleaned and greased. Again, there are differences between British, French and Italian threading – make sure you use the right one!

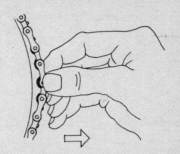

35.11 *Checking for chain wear*

THE CHAIN

There is nothing the chain needs more than cleaning and lubrication at regular intervals. To check for chain wear and stretch, you must try to lift the chain off the front chainwheel as shown in fig. 35.11. If it can be lifted by more than 3 mm (⅛ in) you'd do well to replace it. If you have allowed chain wear to progress so far that

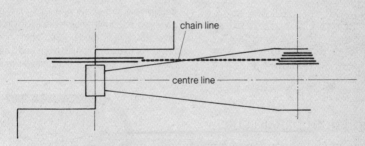

35.12 *Checking chain line (ten-speed)*

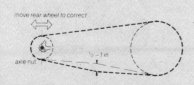

35.13 *Checking chain tension*

a (new) chain jumps or slips off the (old) sprocket, the rear sprocket will also need replacing. The other important thing to watch is the correct alignment of the chain line (fig. 35.12). A bicycle without derailleur gearing must have the correct chain tension (fig. 35.13). Lengthen or shorten the chain with the chain-rivet tool (fig. 35.14) or by removing the master link for

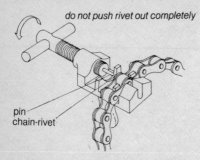

do not push rivet out completely

pin
chain-rivet

35.14 *How to use a chain-rivet extractor*

the wider chain on a bike without a derail-leur, putting it back on the right way (fig. 35.15). You may need to adjust the tension by moving the rear wheel-axle in the rear fork-ends or by removing an even number of links if the chain is far too long. A derailleur chain is routed as in fig. 35.17.

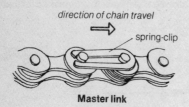

direction of chain travel

spring-clip

Master link

35.15 *Chain master link*

THE FRONT DERAILLEUR

There are far too many different types of derailleur to do justice to them all in a repair manual, so I merely advise you to clean, adjust, align and lubricate the one you have. Fig. 35.16 shows the correct position, although simply listening ought to tell you whether the cage is properly aligned (it must be parallel to the chain). Adjustment has been dealt with in chapters 31 and 32 which also contain advice on how to keep the control cables free and the control levers tightened.

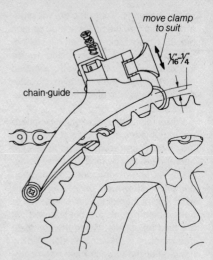

move clamp to suit

$\frac{1}{16}" - \frac{1}{4}"$

chain-guide

35.16 *Chain-guide clearance at front derailleur*

THE REAR DERAILLEUR

What is true of the front derailleur is doubly true of the rear one – no one can give you adequate maintenance instructions for every model. So, again, the advice is to clean, adjust, align and lubricate. The little pulleys in particular must

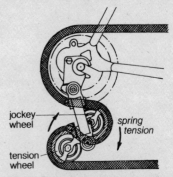

jockey wheel

spring tension

tension wheel

35.17 *Path of chain at rear derailleur*

be cleaned regularly, while all of the many pivot-points need a few drops of light oil (preferably of the spray-can variety) from time to time. Adjustment instructions have been given in chapter 31. Good sources of instructions for other work on the derailleur are *Richard's Bicycle Book* and *Glenn's Handbook*; both are listed in the bibliography (page 273).

THE HUB GEAR

Sturmey–Archer hub gears are almost indestructible. Usually, the only work which is needed is cleaning and lubricating with a teaspoonful of light oil about once a month. You may decide to change the sprocket for one with fewer or more teeth. This can be done once the wheel has been removed from the bike and the round spring-steel clip has been prised off (fig. 35.18). Some sprocket sizes are dished, which allows you to make adjustments to the chain line by reversing the sprocket.

If you have to work on the interior of a hub gear, you may find the *Raleigh Book of Cycling* (for Sturmey–Archer hubs) and *Glenn's Manual* quite useful. However, it is not impossible to approach and successfully complete the overhaul of such a mechanism without any instructions other than the following: begin on the left, work systematically, keep the parts in their order and refer to the paragraph in this

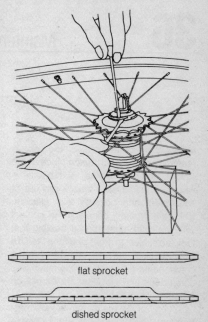

flat sprocket

dished sprocket

35.18 *Replacing a three-speed sprocket*

chapter on freewheel repair. You will be surprised and delighted to find that it all fits back together again and still works! Adjustments have been dealt with in chapter 32, while a few more hints on the maintenance of the controls will be found in chapter 37.

Probably no other parts of the bicycle require such frequent maintenance as the wheels and the brakes. The brakes – whatever their type – easily slip out of adjustment and become less efficient, while the wheels, constantly in contact with the road, take such a beating that they are subject to great wear and tear. If it is not checked, the wear and tear on these components will make cycling much less comfortable and a lot less safe than it is on a well-maintained bicycle.

Several of the maintenance jobs most frequently necessary with these components have been described in chapters 31 and 32, but one major job – wheel-building – is considered to be so specialized that it merits a chapter to itself (see chapter 38). The remaining problems will be discussed here in some detail, taking each component separately.

THE WHEELS

Work on the wheels must itself be broken down according to the various components that make up the wheel: the hub, the spokes, the rim and the tyre. Most jobs on the wheel require it to be removed from the bicycle first. The procedure differs according to the kind of attachment used – axle-nuts or quick-release levers. Although anyone with at least one hand can more or less manage to remove and install a bicycle wheel, I've discovered that many people do not use the correct technique, and this results in poor adjustment

and often makes the job more difficult than it need be. Here's the correct way to do it.

Removing and Installing a Wheel with Quick-release Levers

Tools and equipment For the rear wheel only, a rag is all you need.

Procedure
To remove:

1. If it's a rear wheel, turn the bicycle upside-down or hang it up.

2. Twist the quick-release lever to the 'open' position as shown in fig. 36.1.

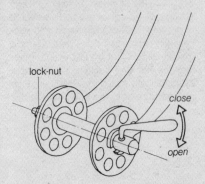

36.1 *How the quick-release lever works*

3. It should now be possible to lift the wheel out; if not you may have to loosen the quick-release lock-nut by one or two turns.

4. With a rear wheel, hold the chain back with a rag. If you have a derailleur,

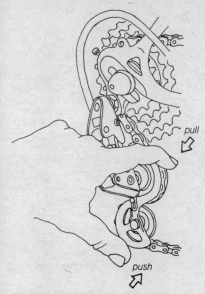

36.2 *Holding back the derailleur*

push it back as shown in fig. 36.2. Lift the wheel out.

To install:

1. Make sure the quick-release lever is in the 'open' position.

2. If this is the rear wheel, turn the bike upside-down.

3. Push the wheel into the fork-ends, holding back the chain or the derailleur with a cloth if it is a rear wheel. Check the seating of the chain. If the wheel does not fit through the brakes, you can either loosen them or let the air out of the tyre. If the hub does not fit, loosen the quick-release lock-nut by one or two turns.

4. Place the wheel in the centre of the forks. Tighten the lock-nut just enough to leave a little play – but *not* all the way.

5. Tighten the quick-release lever by twisting it to the 'closed' position.

6. Check the operation of the wheel and re-adjust the brakes if necessary. If the wheel is not tight enough or the lever

cannot be pushed over completely, loosen the lever and then adjust the lock-nut as required before tightening again.

7. If the rear wheel has adjusters, screw them in to match the position of the wheel.

8. Correct any adjustments which have been disturbed.

Removing and Installing a Wheel with Axle-nuts

Tools and equipment Spanner to fit axle-nuts; rag (if rear wheel).

Procedure
To remove:

1. If it's the rear wheel, turn the bike upside-down.

2. Loosen the various attachments – the control cable of a hub gear, the brake cable and attachment in the case of a hub brake or stirrup brake.

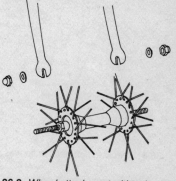

36.3 *Wheel attachment with axle-nuts*

3. Loosen both axle-nuts – if other items such as mudguards or a luggage carrier are held under the nut, remove the nuts completely and bend these items out of the way.

4. Hold back the chain and derailleur if necessary and lift the wheel out.

To install:

1. Make sure both axle-nuts are loose enough or remove them altogether.

2. Push the wheel into its correct position, holding back anything that may interfere, including the brake and the derailleur.

3. Centre the wheel and check that the positions of chain and brake are correct.

4. Tighten the axle-nuts first by hand; check again and then tighten them fully.

5. Replace any parts removed and make any adjustments required.

Checking the Tension of the Spokes

This should be done occasionally to prevent spokes from breaking and the wheel from losing its roundness. To make the necessary adjustments to the spoke tension, refer to the section on straightening a wheel in chapter 31. Check the tension by pushing the spokes together in pairs as shown in fig. 36.4. To tighten them you

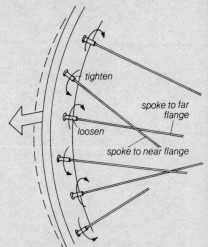

36.5 *Straightening the wheel*

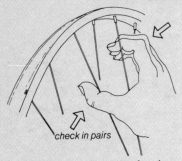

36.4 *Checking tightness of spokes*

need either a spoke-nipple spanner or a small adjustable spanner. Replace any broken spokes immediately to avoid more serious problems. Make sure that you have the correct length and file away the end if it protrudes through the head of the nipple.

Overhauling the Hub

Tools and equipment Cone spanners; spanner to fit lock-nuts; bearing grease; rags.

Procedure (after the wheel has been removed from the bicycle):

1. Loosen the lock-nut on one side only, using a cone spanner to hold the bearing cone, and remove the lock-nut.

2. Lift off the lock-washer and unscrew the cone, preferably while holding the opposite cone with a second cone spanner.

3. Remove the axle from the opposite side.

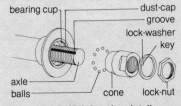

36.6 *Hub-bearing detail*

4. Remove the ball-bearings; clean and inspect all parts. Replace the balls and any damaged parts, including the lock-washer if the internal key (fig. 36.6) is so worn or damaged that it cannot hold the

washer fixed on the groove in the axle. If the axle is bent, buy a new one.

5. Pack the bearing races with bearing grease and insert new balls (the sizes can be found from table 9 on page 262).

6. Insert the axle with the cone and nut from the same side as before and screw on the other cone, followed by the lock-washer and the lock-nut. Tighten the lock-nut against the cone on the same side – *not* against the lock-nut or the cone on the opposite side!

To adjust: loosen the lock-nut slightly, lift the lock-washer and tighten or loosen the cone against the opposite cone; you'll need two cone spanners of the same size. If all is well, the axle should project equally on either side (fig. 36.7).

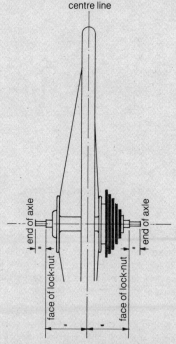

centre line

36.7 *Checking that the rear wheel is centred*

Repairing a Tubular Tyre

Anybody foolish enough to use tubular tyres should at least learn how to repair them. This is not an impossible task and some cyclists consider it well worth the trouble in order to gain the sensation and prestige that come from riding the 'real thing'. However, I would seriously advise anybody with little time, patience or money to try the excellent, modern, high-pressure wired-ons instead; you'll hardly know the difference and races have been won on these tyres! Rebuilding a wheel for different tyres is described in chapter 38 (you'll need a different type of rim and a different spoke-length). Here, very briefly, is the procedure for repairing a tubular tyre, assuming that it has already been removed from the wheel.

Tools and equipment Tubular-tyre repair kit; very sharp knife. (In addition to patches and cement, the repair kit should include a needle, a thimble, twine, talcum powder and sandpaper.)

Procedure

1. Establish where the leak is by pumping up, listening, looking and if necessary dipping the tyre in water. Throw away a tyre that is torn in the area of the tread profile – almost anything else can be repaired (after a fashion).

2. Remove 4–6 ins of the backing tape from around the hole using a screwdriver or similar narrow object (fig. 36.8).

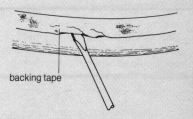

backing tape

36.8 *Removing backing tape*

3. Draw a number of lines across the stitching. Cut about 3 ins of stitching, push the interior tape out of the way and pull the tube out (fig. 36.9).

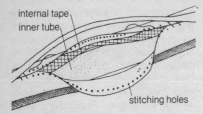

internal tape
inner tube
stitching holes

36.9 *The inner tube exposed*

4. Repair the puncture as normal (see chapter 31).

5. Put some talcum powder on and around the patch. Tuck the tube back in.

6. Sew the tyre back together, using the lines you drew for orientation and taking great care not to prick into the tube. Use

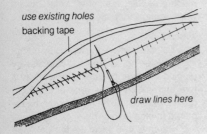

use existing holes
backing tape
draw lines here

36.10 *Sewing up the tyre*

the old stitching holes and do not pull too tightly or the finished seam will not lie flat. Work the end of the twine in under the stitching.

7. Cement the outside tape back on. Store the tyre with some air in it, preferably around an old rim in a cool, dry place.

Installing a Tubular Tyre

The easiest way is to use two-sided adhesive tape rather than shellac or the special cement. Whatever you use, clean the rim-bed first – using either paint thinner, petrol or another solvent (do this outside in the open air!). The best way to get the messy cement off your hands is with a water-less hand cleanser like 'Swarfega'.

Saving a Buckled Rim

This is not recommended as a permanent solution unless you have hub brakes, in which case it does not make much difference how smooth the rim is. For emergency repairs, however, you can try to salvage a buckled rim following the method shown in fig. 36.11.

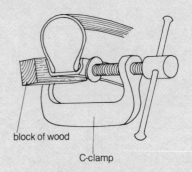

block of wood
C-clamp

36.11 *Correcting buckled rim*

THE BRAKES

Brake maintenance is essentially a matter of adjustment. Here are the things to watch out for in the case of calliper brakes:

1. The brake blocks must make contact with the side of the rim over their entire length and width, although the front of the block may be adjusted to touch slightly (perhaps 2 mm or 1/16 in) before the rear.

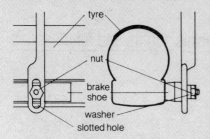

36.12 *Brake-shoe alignment*

2. The rims must be smooth and clean.

3. The blocks must be replaced when worn and installed as shown in fig. 36.13.

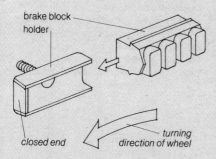

36.13 *Installing a brake shoe*

4. The springs at the pivot-points must open the brake segments well away from the rim. If not, check the pivot-points, the cable, the lever and the spring itself to see whether they are free; adjust and lubricate if required.

5. The entire brake assembly and the individual parts must be bolted tightly enough to minimize unwanted movement while still being free to operate smoothly.

Stirrup brakes are operated by a complex set of pull-rods and pivot mechanisms. Provided these are properly cared for and are not bent or loose, the only maintenance required is the same as that listed above for calliper brakes. They simply touch another part of the rim.

Internally expanding hub brakes (drum brakes) must be kept effective by occasional inspection and, if necessary, by re-lining the brake shoes. Be particularly careful not to get oil or solvents inside these brakes since such substances will harm the brake linings. Keep the frame attachment tight.

Back-pedalling brakes seem to require no maintenance other than that required to keep the bearings of the hub operating smoothly, the chain properly adjusted and the attachment to the frame tightened.

More exotic brakes like the disc brake, the contracting brake and the even rarer contracting and expanding hub brake made by the Japanese Bridgestone company are basically subject to the same maintenance procedures as the hub brake – providing you can find somebody to re-line them!

Quite often it is not a major component of the bicycle that is at fault when the machine does not perform as it should, but an apparently insignificant little thing. Brake cables, levers and other minor parts are only too frequently the cause of malfunctioning equipment. Badly mounted and poorly maintained accessories can seriously reduce the pleasure of cycling, not to mention the irritation and danger that defective lighting causes. These are the things to which this chapter is devoted.

BRAKE LEVERS

Your brake levers must be free to move without noticeable friction and must have enough travel to contract the brakes fully without 'bottoming out'. If there is not at least 2 cm (¾ in) between the lever and the handlebars when the brakes are pulled, either the adjustment of the cable (or pull-rod) or the position of the lever must be modified. Most levers can be moved by loosening the hidden pull-bolt which appears when the lever is pulled (fig. 37.1). Don't unscrew it completely, since it will be hard to get it back in the nut again. The way in which cable tension is adjusted was shown in chapter 32; fig. 37.2

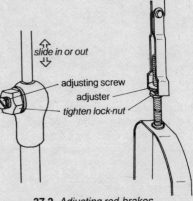

37.2 *Adjusting rod-brakes*

shows typical pull-rod adjusters. If the brake system has a quick-release, it will be easier to adjust the brakes with the quick-release open – only don't forget to tension it again after the adjustment has been made.

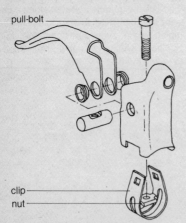

37.1 *Brake lever*

GEAR-SHIFT LEVERS

The only thing that is likely to go wrong with most shift-levers for derailleur gearing is that the screw or nut which holds the various parts together and keeps enough tension on the spring-washers inside comes loose. Check it occasionally and

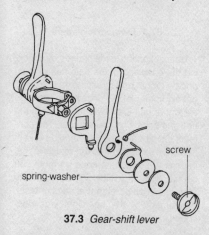

37.3 *Gear-shift lever*

tighten it until the shifting seems positive, without excessive friction. If everything comes to pieces, make sure that you still have all the parts – the spring-washers are necessary to ensure controlled gear-shifting.

CONTROL CABLES

The Bowden cables used to transmit movements to the brakes and gear-changer are effective but rather delicate

and are sensitive to corrosion, abuse and neglect. To avoid corrosion and to minimize friction, it is wise to lubricate the inner cable with a light non-gummy grease – the special bearing grease sold under the brand names of some component manufacturers is particularly suitable. A cable that has not been lubricated in this way should occasionally be treated with a spray-can lubricant at either end.

When replacing an inner cable, it should be cut without fraying the end (preferably with special cable cutters). Allow about one inch beyond the point where it is clamped (fig. 37.4) to facilitate adjustment in excess of the range of the barrel adjuster. Replace the inner cable when it shows signs of fraying (fig. 37.5).

this one is about to break!

37.5 *Frayed cable*

The outer cable must be kept as short as possible and free from any sharp bends. Cut it in such a way that there is no 'hook' at the end to interfere with the inner cable. Make sure that the outer cable is not too tight for the thickness of the inner cable – brake cables are often thicker than those used for derailleur controls. Refer to chapter 32 for adjustment procedures.

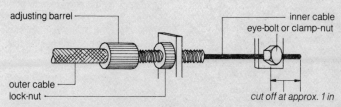

37.4 *Barrel adjuster*

LIGHTING

The bicycle's lighting system seems such a mystery to most cyclists that they give up any hope of ever maintaining it. This is sad when one considers the vital role it plays in the effort to keep cycling reasonably safe. It is worth reading through chapter 18 again to remind yourself of the very simple principles involved in the electrical and optical components of this major safety system.

If your bicycle is equipped with dynamo lighting, the most important thing to watch is that the various cables are intact – not damaged, not loose and not pinched anywhere. In addition, all the components should be kept properly fastened – the earth-contact pinch screws, the cable contacts, the bulbs and the mounting hardware. Finally, the adjustment of the generator and of the headlight should be checked regularly. Figs. 37.6 and 37.7 show the major points to watch.

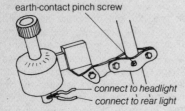

earth-contact pinch screw

connect to headlight
connect to rear light

Tyre-driven dynamo

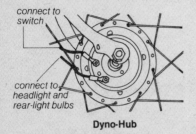

connect to switch

connect to headlight and rear-light bulbs

Dyno-Hub

37.6 *Dynamo connections*

must lie flat

in line

37.7 *Dynamo alignment*

Battery lighting is maintained by checking the condition of the batteries at least once a month and by replacing a drained battery immediately, since it may damage the entire unit if allowed to remain in the housing once it has burned out. The contacts inside battery lights should be kept free from oxidation and the moisture that causes it, so at least once a month you should spread a little Vaseline on the surfaces of all parts that act as contacts. Adjustment of the headlight was described in chapter 18.

REFLECTORS

Reflectors can add enormously to the night-time safety of the cyclist – provided that they are correctly installed and maintained. Keep them free from dirt and replace them if they are damaged. Their operation can be checked by simply placing the bicycle about 30 m (100 ft) ahead of a car headlight. If the reflector 'lights up' brightly when the bike is directly in line with the car, it is working adequately; replace it if it is not. The only other thing you need to do is to make sure that it is firmly mounted at the correct angle and that it does not become obstructed.

THE LOCK

Bicycle locks are often exposed to the elements and need some lubrication to keep them working. Don't simply pour oil into the mechanism; instead, occasionally put one or two drops on the key and on each end of the shackle, and then open and close the lock a few times. It will last for ever this way!

THE PUMP

If you avoid using the bicycle pump as a weapon – some writers suggest that you use it to beat off attacking dogs – it will not get damaged. All you need to check is the little leather, rubber or plastic plunger inside. If it is of leather, you can put some grease on it occasionally; any other material seems to be unaffected by good care, so just replace the thing whenever needed – making your own (out of greased leather) if necessary. The other item that needs to be watched is the leather or rubber washer at the head – it too can be easily replaced.

ALL OTHER ACCESSORIES

Short of giving a detailed maintenance description of every individual type of every possible bicycle accessory, the best I can do here is to offer some general rules on care:

(a) Keep accessories clean and protected: clean with water and soap; protect with Vaseline if made of bare metal.

(b) Keep accessories tight; at least two bolts are usually required to hold anything on the bike. Once one bolt is gone the other one will rattle loose in no time at all.

(c) If it moves, lubricate it. However, be careful to use the *right* lubricant: clean water for nylon, PTFE and other plastics; grease for anything that runs on ball-bearings; mineral oil for other items.

(d) If it's worn or damaged, remove or replace it. A broken accessory is worse than no accessory at all since it is likely to get caught in a moving part of the bicycle and perhaps cause a serious accident.

Building your own bicycle wheel, which is necessary when the hub or rim has to be replaced, is like riding tubular tyres: you can't justify it in conventional terms of practical benefit versus cost. It's more a question of enthusiasm. Let an expert build your wheel and he'll take about twenty minutes to produce one that's perfectly round, whereas if you're attempting the job for the first time you may work at it all afternoon before your wheel begins to look like anything at all.

However, the next wheel you build will be considerably easier to get right. With the right tools, the cost will be repaid after the first ten wheels or so, and you will eventually match the expert's speed and accuracy. Your gain is the pride of achievement and the therapy that comes from doing fiddly work in general, and in particular, fiddly work you enjoy. However, if you lack the time and patience, you'd do better to leave this job to someone who earns his living by it. If you do want to build your own wheel, it's a good idea to begin with one that can be copied exactly and easily – for example, a front wheel with thirty-six spokes in a three-cross pattern (see chapter 14 for an explanation of the terms used here).

A CLOSE LOOK AT WHEEL-BUILDING

There are five possible spoke patterns as shown in fig. 38.1. To find your way out of

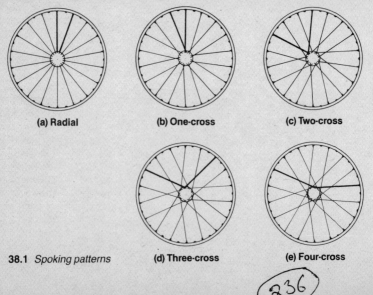

(a) Radial   **(b) One-cross**   **(c) Two-cross**

38.1 *Spoking patterns*   **(d) Three-cross**   **(e) Four-cross**

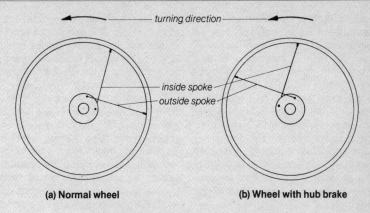

(a) Normal wheel   **(b) Wheel with hub brake**

38.2 *Orientation of inside and outside spokes*

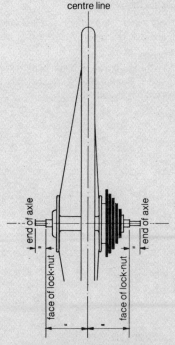

38.3 *Long and short spokes on a 'dished' rear wheel*

the maze, I have shown only the near-side spokes and in each example I have highlighted one pair of adjacent spokes – one inside and one outside spoke on the same hub flange. Though some wheels are built asymmetrically, which means that they are identical when viewed from either side, a good rear wheel should be symmetrically built, which means that all the spokes on the inside of either flange point the same way in relation to the direction of travel.

Inside spokes tend to break more easily than outside spokes; for this reason it is important to make sure that the outside spokes are the ones which take the higher forces. The higher forces are those developed when accelerating or climbing and – in the case of the hub brake – when braking. The direction of these forces is shown in fig. 38.2a for rear wheels with rim brakes and in fig. 38.2b for wheels with hub brakes. You can avoid a lot of broken spokes by correct orientation of the inside and outside spokes: unless your wheel has a hub brake, the outside spokes should 'point backwards' from the hub to the rim on the rear wheel.

A rear wheel is usually 'dished', which means that the rim is centred over the combination of hub and freewheel rather than over the hub flanges. To achieve this, the spokes on the freewheel side should ideally be about 3 mm (⅛ in) shorter than the ones on the opposite side. Unfortunately, the different angles also cause higher tension forces on the spokes on the freewheel side; the spokes that are the most difficult to replace are therefore often the first ones to break. Fig. 38.3 shows the orientation of the rear-wheel spokes in a cross-section of the wheel.

Nowadays most wheels are built with thirty-six spokes of no. 14 gauge thickness (2 mm) in a three-cross pattern. The instructions in this chapter will be based on this configuration, though adjustments can easily be made for other configurations if you first make a sketch of them. The required spoke-lengths can be taken from table 11 (page 264), together with some indication of the spoke-thickness preferable for various uses. Stainless-steel spokes are not actually as strong as the cruder looking galvanized models but

these shiny items have their advantages if the bicycle is often exposed to the elements, since galvanized spokes may in time become difficult to adjust due to the build-up of rust in the nipple threads and may break when forced.

To do the job itself requires no tools other than the usual ones, and centring can be done with reasonable ease and accuracy employing nothing more unusual than the front or rear fork of a bicycle – provided it is designed for the size of the wheel in question. Calliper brakes can be used as guides to aid the centring and alignment processes although the work is easier if you use a 'wheel-truing stand' (fig. 38.4a) which can be made following the instructions in chapter 40.

Lacing the Wheel

Tools and equipment Spoke-nipple spanner; screwdriver; Vaseline; rag.

Procedure
1. Choose the appropriate pattern from fig. 38.1 (page 236); refer constantly to this pattern as you proceed.

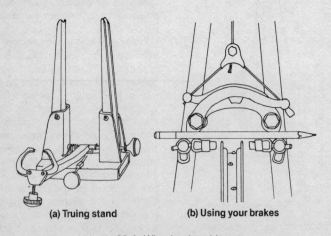

(a) Truing stand   (b) Using your brakes

38.4 *Wheel-truing aids*

38.5 *Spoking procedure*

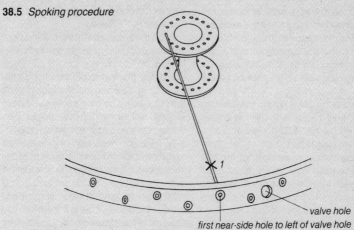

first near-side hole to left of valve hole

valve hole

(a) The first spoke

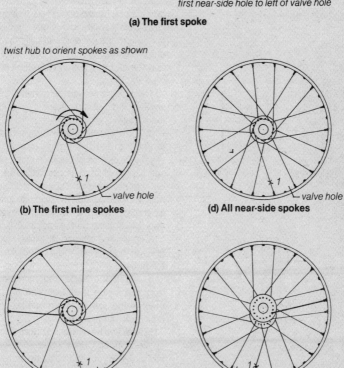

twist hub to orient spokes as shown

(b) The first nine spokes

valve hole

(d) All near-side spokes

valve hole

(c) The first crossing spoke

valve hole

valve hole

**(e) Wheel turned over –
the first spoke on the other side**

2. Dip the threaded ends of the spokes in Vaseline, then wipe away the excess.

3. Place the rim and the hub on the table in front of you, the threaded end of a rear hub pointing upwards. Note that alternate spoke holes are off-set to either side of the rim.

4. Locate the valve hole in the rim. Call the first hole to the left which is off-set upwards hole no. 1 and mark it with a felt-tip pen (fig. 38.5a).

5. Take nine spokes and put them in every alternate hole in the hub flange facing you – inserting them from the inside to the outside. If the holes in the hub are not all counter-sunk, make sure you select the holes that have the counter-sinking on the outside (fig. 38.6).

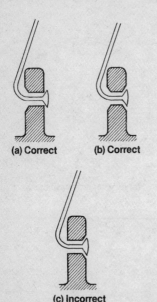

(a) Correct   (b) Correct

(c) Incorrect

38.6 *Spoke-bend in counter-sunk hole*

6. Attach one of these nine spokes to a nipple through hole no. 1 (not too tightly, it only needs a few turns). Use a nipple washer if the rim is of aluminium and if the holes are not ferruled.

7. Do the same with the remaining eight spokes, using every fourth spoke hole in the rim.

8. Twist the hub in the direction of the arrow in fig. 38.5b so that the spokes point the right way. The nine spokes you have inserted will be the 'tension spokes' (i.e., the spokes that take the highest forces).

9. Take another batch of nine spokes and thread them from the outside to the inside through the remaining holes in the same hub flange.

10. Take any one of these spokes and insert it through the hole in the rim that you reach when you have crossed the desired number of tension spokes (our example is three-cross, so the spoke goes under the first, under the second and over the third one), leaving one rim hole free between it and the last neighbouring tension spoke (see fig. 38.5c).

11. Do the same with the remaining eight spokes (fig. 38.5d), again using every fourth hole.

12. Turn over the entire wheel and locate the hole in the hub flange that lies just slightly clockwise of the hole in the opposite flange which was connected to hole no. 1 in the rim. Put a spoke through this hole from the outside to the inside and run it parallel to one of the inside spokes in the opposite hub flange (see fig. 38.5e).

13. Insert the other eight inside spokes and run them to every fourth spoke hole in the rim.

14. Insert the remaining nine spokes from the inside to the outside and lace them in the same pattern as that on the other side of the wheel.

15. Now you have a loose but completely spoked wheel. Check whether it does in fact look like your example and correct it if necessary.

16. Tighten all spoke nipples equally with the screwdriver, using the amount of

exposed thread as a guide, but do not tighten them so that any spokes are under tension.

17. Place the wheel in the frame or the truing stand and check which corrections have to be made, using the brake shoes for reference if necessary. Now follow the same procedure as outlined in chapter 31 for wheel-truing. This way you can get the rim round and remove any side wobble (fig. 38.7). Tighten the spokes all round with the nipple spanner.

18. Check whether all the spokes are equally tensioned and make sure that no spokes protrude where they might damage the tube of the tyre; file them flush if necessary.

19. Check the wheel after you've ridden on it for a few miles and tension the spokes again, since they will have 'seated'. Once the spokes have worked a little and have been tightened again, the wheel will keep its shape remarkably well. Don't use a brand new, untested wheel for a demanding race or a heavy tour; give it a chance to settle first.

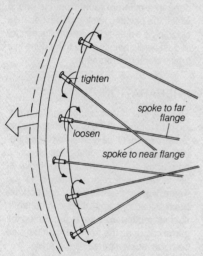

tighten

spoke to far flange

loosen

spoke to near flange

38.7 *Straightening a buckled wheel*

39

There is hardly any job more tempting than repainting an old bicycle in the hope of making it 'look like new'. Nor is there any other job so often utterly botched. Repainting is extremely demanding work which requires great devotion, patience, precision, care and experience. So even someone who fulfils every requirement must still regard his first attempt as a way of gaining experience; the result will be less than perfect under even the best of conditions and a total disaster if even some of the minor conditions are imperfect. But don't despair; your next product will probably look a lot better – and one day you may even be satisfied.

Of course, painting is another of those jobs that can't be justified on a basis of cost–benefit. You can get a frame-builder or a paint shop to do the work for you, producing a good or an excellent finish at a price totally out of proportion (on the low side) with the enormous effort you'd have to put in to do it yourself. Let's be quite frank – you're insane to re-paint a frame yourself. However, for pride of achievement and occupational therapy it can't be beaten.

The job really consists of four stages: preparation, priming, finishing and curing. Preparatory cleaning varies according to the state of the bicycle before painting; a new, bare frame requires a different treatment to one which has been previously painted or a rusty, neglected old bicycle. But don't fool yourself: this, the least attractive part of the entire job, is the most essential process and must be carried out with painstaking precision. It must also be done in a different room from the one in which the painting itself is done, because cleaning is a messy job and produces a lot of dust, while painting has to be done in a totally clean environment.

PREPARATION

The very first step in preparation for painting is to remove all the parts which are *not* to be painted. Usually, this involves stripping the bike down until there is only a bare frame left. You must also remove all the objects which are attached to the frame, like head-set bearings and bottom-bracket cups. If any other components, such as mudguards, are to be painted the same colour as the frame, they must also be removed and treated separately.

If you begin with a newly built, unpainted frame, the only completely satisfactory process is sand-blasting with 0.5-mm grit, which gives an excellent surface for the adhesion of the primer and yet leaves it smooth enough to require no further treatment. You'll have to have this done by professionals – if you can find any who will undertake such a small job. If you can't, you'll be stuck with a great deal of work – you will have to clean the whole thing to sand-blasting standards using nothing but sandpaper and elbow grease.

To do this, get 'wet-or-dry' sandpaper (preferably used wet), cut in strips 1–1½ ins wide. Cut the strip into 12-in-long

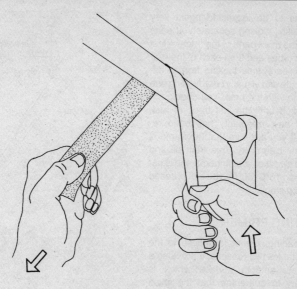

39.1 *Sanding frame tubes*

sections and use them as shown in fig. 39.1 for the main portions of the frame tubes. To get into the many little nooks and crannies, you must cut narrower strips – maybe ⅜–½ in wide – applied in the same way or else wrapped around a finger. Sand until the last trace of scale,

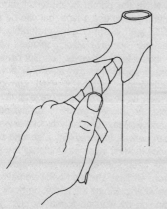

39.2 *Sanding tight spots*

brazing metal and flux has been removed. I do not recommend tapering the lugs down too much, since the result rarely looks very good.

If the frame has previously been painted, the first operation should be washing, followed by drying, and then the application of a chemical paint-remover. Read the instructions on the container of this highly caustic chemical carefully and observe them meticulously for your own safety and to avoid damage to other items. After the paint-remover has been allowed to penetrate the old paint, scrape the softened paint away with a thin, flexible metal object such as a putty knife. Wash off the remains carefully and apply once more to those areas where the paint has not been fully removed. Follow this with another wash after which the whole frame should be dried.

The next step is a thorough inspection, followed by the same kind of sandpaper action as described above. Then everything has to be inspected again very meticulously, looking separately at each of the three main parts of the frame – first the main tubes and then each of the rear triangles, each time looking from a different angle and visually coordinating one inspection with the next. You should not be satisfied until the last trace of rust, paint or any irregularity has been removed. If you are sure that the frame is absolutely clean, dry, free from oil and acid (the sweat of your fingers!) and is not colder than 10°C (50°F), you can proceed to the next stage.

APPLYING PRIMER

After cleaning, primer is applied to the bare metal for two reasons: it provides a completely smooth surface which is necessary to guarantee that the finish coat will also look perfectly smooth, and it increases the adhesion between the different finish layers and the bare metal. The place where you do the priming work will be the same as the one used for finish painting – a clean, fairly warm, well-lit and well-ventilated room. A sheltered outside area may be ideal for your purposes.

Suspend the frame by means of a spoke fixed through the rear fork-end adjuster eyelet as shown in fig. 39.3. A piece of wood through the head tube will enable you to turn the frame while working on it. All other areas not to be painted can be protected by stuffing them with rolls of paper (inside the frame tubes) or sticking masking tape over them (e.g., the chromed areas of tubes and lugs).

The kind of primer you use depends on the kind of paint you intend to apply finally; check with the paint supplier for compatibility and also buy a compatible thinner. The first thing you use is the thinner – wash down the entire frame with it, drying it afterwards with a perfectly clean, lint-free cloth. This will ensure that no reaction

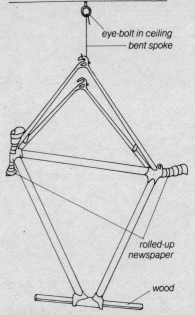

eye-bolt in ceiling
bent spoke
rolled-up newspaper
wood

39.3 *Frame suspended for painting*

occurs between the paint used and any unknown substance remaining on an otherwise clean frame to spoil the smoothness of the paint-work.

Next, the primer is applied. I recommend you to use a type that can be applied with a spray gun, preferably the 'airless' variety which splutters and bubbles less. However, aerosol cans or brush application can also give a very satisfactory surface if used correctly. When using spray paint, several layers must be applied; brushing, on the other hand, will leave one fairly thick layer which can only be followed with a second coat once the first layer is completely dry and has been sanded down and wiped free from all dust. Proceed as systematically as when cleaning the frame, perhaps beginning by working round the lugs and then tackling the main tubes of each section of the frame from several overlapping angles.

Once the primer is completely dry (which may take several days), sand the surface with very fine wet or dry paper, check for pits and irregularities and fill these with car bodywork filler. These areas must be re-primed when they are smooth; you may even have to do the entire frame again. Sand down the frame once more with very fine sandpaper ('600 grit' is best) and wipe again, if possible blowing it clean with compressed air. You are now ready for the finish coat.

FINISH COAT PAINTING

This job is again done in your dust-free painting room using the same procedure as for priming. Of the several types of paint available, I would normally recommend an epoxy finish. This is a paint with two components which are mixed shortly before painting. It hardens as a result of the chemical reaction occurring between the components instead of by the much slower drying process of a solvent (as is the case with most lacquers and enamels). However, it is important to note that many of these epoxy enamels must be painted on in a single application consisting of several thin layers applied perhaps within one hour at the most. Touching up or re-painting later will almost inevitably look dreadful.

Other kinds of paint fall into two categories – enamels and lacquers. Enamel is quite thick and covers in one or, at most, two coats, while lacquer requires numerous layers. However, since lacquer contains much greater percentages of volatile components, it dries much faster and often gives a smoother finish. Enamel takes ages to harden fully and is more likely to result in an uneven surface.

Whatever you use, don't do anything else until the finish coat is perfectly hard – which may take several months in the case of brushed enamel!

A final operation is usually only necessary in the case of enamels, since they harden with a slightly uneven 'orange-peel' surface. You can cure this effect by polishing the frame with rubbing compound or paint polish, taking great care not to cut too deeply into the paint since this would ruin the entire job. Once washed off and wiped, you may consider finishing your work with a layer of compatible transparent lacquer. This will provide a high-gloss, chip-resistant top surface to a bicycle finished with conventional enamel or lacquer. For epoxy enamels, I do not know of any compatible transparent lacquer so you'd probably be wiser not to attempt such an operation.

If you want to decorate your newly painted frame with pin-stripes, emblems, labels and transfer lettering, you should do that before applying this final coating of transparent lacquer. This will ensure that these decorations stay on the bike for as long as possible and will continue to look at least fairly presentable. To apply transfer lettering, etc., you should first make a reverse-image pattern on a piece of masking tape, to ensure that it is correctly lined up and spaced. Another strip of masking tape is then placed on the frame to outline the correct position of the final transfer. If all goes well and the paint has been adequately cured before you started, you should be able to remove all those pieces of masking tape without damaging either the paint or the transfer once it has properly adhered to the frame. Personally, I think the most attractive frames are those with a minimum of frills – just plain, simple paint looks great!

40

Finally, here are a number of suggestions for simple projects in connection with the bicycle which any handyman can do for himself. They are divided into two general categories: sewing and workshop projects. (I hope you take no offence at the term 'handyman' – both types of work are performed equally well by men and women. Throughout this book I have applied the masculine to both sexes, not for discriminatory reasons, but simply to avoid complication.)

The instructions that follow are kept to an absolute minimum; you should be guided rather by the drawings. Even these drawings, however, can be no more than suggestions which you will need to vary and complement as necessary. The dimensions are at best approximate suggestions and always need to be checked against the actual sizes of the components that are used. Look on these project descriptions as mere hints and sketches, not as foolproof plans.

SEWING PROJECTS

Tool Bag

Materials Canvas, pack cloth or 8-oz coated nylon; heavy-duty yarn; tape.

This will help to organize the tools you take on a longer trip. Spread them out on the material and leave enough space to enable you to roll it up once it's sewn together.

Bike Cover

Materials Waterproof coated nylon or canvas; heavy-duty yarn; tape.

This is a garage for your bicycle; if you intend to take it with you on a camping tour, choose very light coated nylon. You can modify the design by putting elastic tape around the bottom to hold it together without needing to fiddle with pieces of tape or a string.

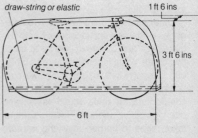

40.2 *Bicycle cover*

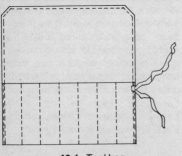

40.1 *Tool bag*

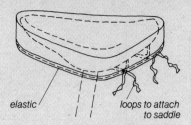

elastic   *loops to attach to saddle*

40.3 *Saddle cover*

Saddle Cover

Materials Waterproof coated nylon or canvas; heavy-duty yarn; tape.

Make this just like the bike cover. You can tie it to the saddle to keep it handy when travelling.

Bike Bag

Materials Light coated nylon or pack cloth; heavy-duty yarn; zip; webbing.

This will enable you to take your bike on trains and other forms of public transport when it cannot be taken as it is. The secret of the light-weight and safe construction lies in the fact that the bike is carried directly on the webbing straps and the bag is fitted around it. Any design that attaches the handles to the bag rather

than to the bike will be enormously heavy. Tie the wheels to the side of the frame and lower both the saddle and the handlebars, turning the bars around.

WORKSHOP PROJECTS

Maintenance Hanger

Materials Metal wire ⅛ in (3 mm) thick; eye-bolts or screws; string; nails.

This is a simple contraption that enables you to hang the bicycle up while working on it. Make sure there is enough room between the cycle and the wall to allow you to work on both sides of the bicycle.

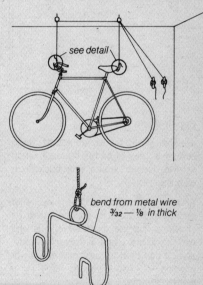

see detail

bend from metal wire ³⁄₃₂ — ⅛ in thick

Hook detail

40.5 *Maintenance hanger*

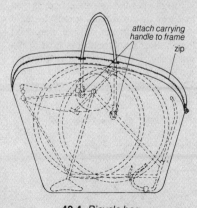

attach carrying handle to frame
zip

40.4 *Bicycle bag*

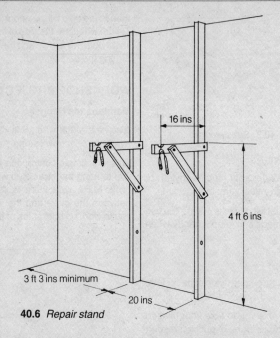

16 ins

4 ft 6 ins

3 ft 3 ins minimum

20 ins

40.6 *Repair stand*

Repair Stand

Materials 4 × 2 ins wooden struts; wood scraps; scraps of carpet material; wood screws; leather straps with buckles or webbing.

Another device to hold the bicycle for maintenance work. It can be made as shown or can be mounted against the wall. If you make one of the arms removable, it can then be attached at a lower position to enable you to hang up a women's frame.

Sprocket Remover

Materials Steel strip (12 ins long by 3/16 in thick by 1¼ ins wide); section of bicycle chain (15 ins long).

This tool can be used to unscrew a single sprocket while the freewheel body is held in a vice by the biggest sprocket. Use a chain-rivet extractor to put the short length of chain through the hole in the metal strip. Don't bother if your sprockets are held on to the freewheel with splines. This only works on screwed sprockets!

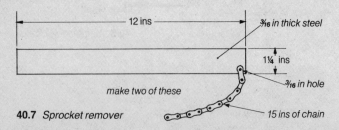

12 ins

3/16 in thick steel

1¼ ins

3/16 in hole

make two of these

40.7 *Sprocket remover*

15 ins of chain

Wheel-truing Stand

Materials An old but straight pair of bicycle forks; screws or bolts; you will also need the use of an electric drill and a tap to cut the screw-thread.

Use this device to true a wheel. Set the screws at the right height to correspond to the sides of the rims and use the bracket to check for the roundness of the wheel.

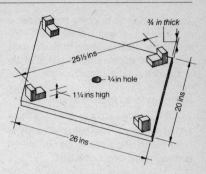

40.9 *Wheel-spoking aid*

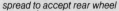

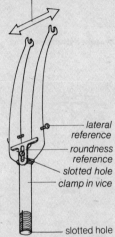

40.8 *Wheel-truing stand*

Wheel-spoking Aid

Materials Pieces of wood as shown; screws.

This device will hold a rim and a hub while you build a wheel. It can be constructed so that either a (centred) front wheel or a (dished) rear wheel can be pre-assembled to a fairly high standard before it is trued.

Dynamo Lighting Tester

Materials 6 volt lamp with fixture; 6 volt battery (or 4.5 volt flat battery); contact strip; flexible insulated wires; crocodile clips; board.

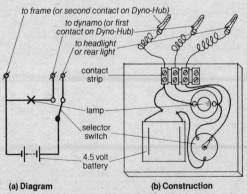

40.10 *Lighting tester*

This will help you to locate any problems in a dynamo lighting system. Make sure you do not store it with the crocodile clips unprotected since a short-circuit will drain your battery and may cause a fire.

Rechargeable Lighting System

Materials Sturmey–Archer Dyno-Hub; NiCad 4.8 or 6 volt battery; matching bulbs; electronic parts as shown; switch and wiring; headlight; rear light.

This system makes the best use of your Dyno-Hub, providing a continually burning light as long as you ride enough by day to keep the batteries charged and don't forget to turn the switch off!

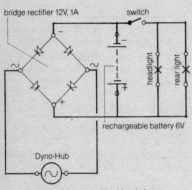

insulate all parts touching bicycle frame

40.11 *Wiring diagram for rechargeable lighting system*

Ideas for Bicycle Storage

Finally here are a few suggestions for storing your bicycle. The drawings should be self-explanatory.

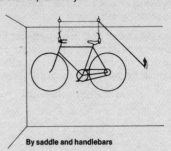

By saddle and handlebars

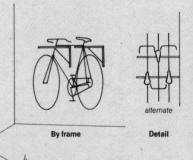

alternate

By frame   **Detail**

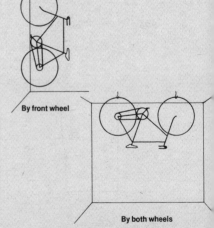

By front wheel

By both wheels

40.12 *Bicycle storage*

Part 5

APPENDIX

Table 1. *Frame-size and Seat-height*

| Inside-leg measurement | | Maximum frame-size | | Recommended seat-height | |
cm	inches	cm	inches	cm	inches
73		50	19	80.5	
	29	51	19.5		31.6
74		52	20	81	
75		52	20	82	
76		53	20.5	83	
	30	53	20.5		32.7
77		54	21	84	
78		55	21	85	
	31	56	21.5		33.8
79		56	21.5	86	
80		57	22	87.5	
81		58	22.5	88.5	
	32	58	22.5		34.9
82		59	23	89.5	
83		60	23	90.5	
84	33	61	23.5	92	36.0
85		62	24	93	
86		63	24.5	94	
	34	63	24.5		37.1
87		64	25	95	
88		65	25	96	
89	35	66	25.5	97	38.1
90		67	26	98	
91		68	26.5	99.5	
	36	68	26.5		39.2
92		69	27	100.5	

Notes

1. Inside-leg measurement is taken as shown in fig. 1b.

2. Frame-size is measured as shown in fig. 1a. These figures are for maximum frame-sizes; optimum frame-size is about 2 cm less.

3. Seat-height is measured as shown in fig. 1a.

4. Further explanation in chapter 5.

1a

1b

Table 2. Gear Numbers (in inch-gear sizes) for 27-in, 700-mm and Other-sized Wheels

In each cell: the upper (bold) figure is the gear number in inch-gear size; the lower figure is the ratio. Columns are the number of teeth on the rear sprocket (12–24); rows are the number of teeth on the front chainwheel (60–32).

Chainwheel \ Sprocket	12	13	14	15	16	17	18	19	20	21	22	23	24
60	135 / 5.00	125 / 4.62	116 / 4.29	108 / 4.00	101 / 3.75	95 / 3.53	90 / 3.33	85 / 3.16	81 / 3.00	77 / 2.86	74 / 2.73	70 / 2.61	68 / 2.50
59	133 / 4.92	123 / 4.54	114 / 4.21	106 / 3.93	100 / 3.69	94 / 3.47	88 / 3.28	84 / 3.11	80 / 2.95	76 / 2.81	72 / 2.68	69 / 2.57	66 / 2.46
58	130 / 4.83	120 / 4.46	112 / 4.14	104 / 3.87	98 / 3.62	92 / 3.41	87 / 3.22	82 / 3.05	78 / 2.90	75 / 2.76	71 / 2.64	68 / 2.52	65 / 2.42
57	128 / 4.75	118 / 4.38	110 / 4.07	103 / 3.80	96 / 3.56	91 / 3.35	86 / 3.17	81 / 3.00	77 / 2.85	73 / 2.71	70 / 2.59	67 / 2.48	64 / 2.37
56	126 / 4.67	116 / 4.31	108 / 4.00	101 / 3.73	94 / 3.50	89 / 3.29	84 / 3.11	80 / 2.95	76 / 2.80	72 / 2.67	69 / 2.55	66 / 2.43	63 / 2.33
55	124 / 4.58	114 / 4.23	106 / 3.93	99 / 3.67	93 / 3.44	87 / 3.24	82 / 3.06	78 / 2.89	74 / 2.75	71 / 2.62	68 / 2.50	65 / 2.40	62 / 2.29
54	122 / 4.50	112 / 4.15	104 / 3.86	97 / 3.60	91 / 3.38	86 / 3.18	81 / 3.00	77 / 2.84	73 / 2.70	69 / 2.57	66 / 2.45	63 / 2.35	61 / 2.25
53	119 / 4.42	110 / 4.08	102 / 3.79	95 / 3.53	89 / 3.31	84 / 3.12	80 / 2.94	75 / 2.79	72 / 2.65	68 / 2.52	65 / 2.41	62 / 2.30	60 / 2.21
52	117 / 4.33	108 / 4.00	100 / 3.71	94 / 3.47	88 / 3.25	83 / 3.06	78 / 2.89	74 / 2.74	70 / 2.60	67 / 2.48	64 / 2.36	61 / 2.26	58 / 2.17
51	115 / 4.25	106 / 3.92	98 / 3.64	92 / 3.40	86 / 3.19	81 / 3.00	76 / 2.83	72 / 2.68	69 / 2.55	66 / 2.43	63 / 2.32	60 / 2.22	57 / 2.12
50	112 / 4.17	104 / 3.85	96 / 3.57	90 / 3.33	84 / 3.12	79 / 2.94	75 / 2.78	71 / 2.63	68 / 2.50	64 / 2.38	61 / 2.27	59 / 2.17	56 / 2.08
49	110 / 4.08	102 / 3.77	94 / 3.50	88 / 3.27	83 / 3.06	78 / 2.88	74 / 2.72	70 / 2.58	66 / 2.45	63 / 2.33	60 / 2.23	58 / 2.13	55 / 2.04
48	108 / 4.00	100 / 3.69	93 / 3.43	86 / 3.20	81 / 3.00	76 / 2.82	72 / 2.67	68 / 2.53	65 / 2.40	62 / 2.29	59 / 2.18	56 / 2.09	54 / 2.00
47	106 / 3.92	98 / 3.62	91 / 3.36	85 / 3.13	79 / 2.94	75 / 2.76	70 / 2.61	67 / 2.47	63 / 2.35	60 / 2.24	58 / 2.14	55 / 2.04	53 / 1.96
46	104 / 3.83	96 / 3.54	89 / 3.29	83 / 3.07	78 / 2.88	73 / 2.71	69 / 2.56	65 / 2.42	62 / 2.30	59 / 2.19	56 / 2.09	54 / 2.00	52 / 1.92
45	101 / 3.75	93 / 3.46	87 / 3.21	81 / 3.00	76 / 2.81	71 / 2.65	68 / 2.50	64 / 2.37	61 / 2.25	58 / 2.14	55 / 2.05	53 / 1.96	51 / 1.87
44	99 / 3.67	91 / 3.38	85 / 3.14	79 / 2.93	74 / 2.75	70 / 2.59	66 / 2.44	63 / 2.32	59 / 2.20	57 / 2.10	54 / 2.00	52 / 1.91	50 / 1.83
43	97 / 3.58	89 / 3.31	83 / 3.07	77 / 2.87	73 / 2.69	68 / 2.53	64 / 2.39	61 / 2.26	58 / 2.15	55 / 2.05	53 / 1.95	50 / 1.87	48 / 1.79
42	94 / 3.50	87 / 3.23	81 / 3.00	76 / 2.80	71 / 2.62	67 / 2.47	63 / 2.33	60 / 2.21	57 / 2.10	54 / 2.00	52 / 1.91	49 / 1.83	47 / 1.75
41	92 / 3.42	85 / 3.15	79 / 2.93	74 / 2.73	69 / 2.56	65 / 2.41	62 / 2.28	58 / 2.16	55 / 2.05	53 / 1.95	50 / 1.86	48 / 1.78	46 / 1.71
40	90 / 3.33	83 / 3.08	77 / 2.86	72 / 2.67	68 / 2.50	64 / 2.35	60 / 2.22	57 / 2.11	54 / 2.00	51 / 1.90	49 / 1.82	47 / 1.74	45 / 1.67
39	88 / 3.25	81 / 3.00	75 / 2.79	70 / 2.60	66 / 2.44	62 / 2.29	58 / 2.17	55 / 2.05	53 / 1.95	50 / 1.86	48 / 1.77	46 / 1.70	44 / 1.63
38	86 / 3.17	79 / 2.92	73 / 2.71	68 / 2.53	64 / 2.38	60 / 2.24	57 / 2.11	54 / 2.00	51 / 1.90	49 / 1.81	47 / 1.73	45 / 1.65	43 / 1.58
37	83 / 3.08	77 / 2.85	71 / 2.64	67 / 2.47	62 / 2.31	59 / 2.18	56 / 2.06	53 / 1.94	50 / 1.85	48 / 1.76	45 / 1.68	43 / 1.61	42 / 1.54
36	81 / 3.00	75 / 2.77	69 / 2.57	65 / 2.40	61 / 2.25	57 / 2.12	54 / 2.00	51 / 1.89	48 / 1.80	46 / 1.71	44 / 1.64	42 / 1.57	40 / 1.50
35	79 / 2.92	73 / 2.69	68 / 2.50	63 / 2.33	59 / 2.19	56 / 2.06	52 / 1.94	50 / 1.84	47 / 1.75	45 / 1.67	43 / 1.59	41 / 1.52	39 / 1.46
34	76 / 2.83	71 / 2.62	66 / 2.43	61 / 2.27	57 / 2.12	54 / 2.00	51 / 1.89	48 / 1.79	46 / 1.70	44 / 1.62	42 / 1.55	40 / 1.48	38 / 1.42
33	74 / 2.75	69 / 2.54	64 / 2.36	59 / 2.20	56 / 2.06	52 / 1.94	50 / 1.83	47 / 1.74	45 / 1.65	42 / 1.57	40 / 1.50	39 / 1.43	37 / 1.37
32	72 / 2.66	66 / 2.46	62 / 2.29	58 / 2.13	54 / 2.00	51 / 1.88	48 / 1.78	45 / 1.68	43 / 1.60	41 / 1.52	39 / 1.45	38 / 1.39	36 / 1.33

Number of teeth on front chainwheel

Rear \ Chainwheel	32	33	34	35	36	37	38	39	40	41	42	43	44	45	46	47	48	49	50	51	52	53	54	55	56	57	58	59	60
25	**35** 1.28	**36** 1.32	**37** 1.36	**38** 1.40	**39** 1.44	**40** 1.48	**41** 1.52	**42** 1.56	**43** 1.60	**44** 1.64	**45** 1.68	**46** 1.72	**48** 1.76	**49** 1.80	**50** 1.84	**51** 1.88	**52** 1.92	**53** 1.96	**54** 2.00	**55** 2.04	**56** 2.08	**57** 2.12	**58** 2.16	**59** 2.20	**60** 2.24	**62** 2.28	**63** 2.32	**64** 2.36	**65** 2.40
26	**33** 1.23	**34** 1.27	**35** 1.31	**36** 1.35	**37** 1.38	**38** 1.42	**39** 1.46	**41** 1.50	**42** 1.54	**43** 1.58	**44** 1.62	**45** 1.65	**46** 1.69	**47** 1.73	**48** 1.77	**49** 1.81	**50** 1.85	**51** 1.88	**52** 1.92	**53** 1.96	**54** 2.00	**55** 2.04	**56** 2.08	**57** 2.12	**58** 2.15	**59** 2.19	**60** 2.23	**61** 2.27	**62** 2.31
27	**32** 1.19	**33** 1.22	**34** 1.26	**35** 1.30	**36** 1.33	**37** 1.37	**38** 1.41	**39** 1.44	**40** 1.48	**41** 1.52	**42** 1.56	**43** 1.59	**44** 1.63	**45** 1.67	**46** 1.70	**47** 1.74	**48** 1.78	**49** 1.81	**50** 1.85	**51** 1.89	**52** 1.93	**53** 1.96	**54** 2.00	**55** 2.04	**56** 2.07	**57** 2.11	**58** 2.15	**59** 2.19	**60** 2.22
28	**31** 1.14	**32** 1.18	**33** 1.21	**34** 1.25	**35** 1.29	**36** 1.32	**37** 1.36	**38** 1.39	**39** 1.43	**40** 1.46	**41** 1.50	**41** 1.54	**42** 1.57	**43** 1.61	**44** 1.64	**45** 1.68	**46** 1.71	**47** 1.75	**48** 1.79	**49** 1.82	**50** 1.86	**51** 1.89	**52** 1.93	**53** 1.96	**54** 2.00	**55** 2.04	**56** 2.07	**57** 2.11	**58** 2.14
29	**30** 1.10	**31** 1.14	**32** 1.17	**33** 1.21	**34** 1.24	**34** 1.28	**35** 1.31	**36** 1.34	**37** 1.38	**38** 1.41	**39** 1.45	**40** 1.48	**41** 1.52	**42** 1.55	**43** 1.59	**44** 1.62	**45** 1.66	**46** 1.69	**47** 1.72	**47** 1.76	**48** 1.79	**49** 1.83	**50** 1.86	**51** 1.90	**52** 1.93	**53** 1.97	**54** 2.00	**55** 2.03	**56** 2.07
30	**29** 1.07	**30** 1.10	**31** 1.13	**32** 1.17	**32** 1.20	**33** 1.23	**34** 1.27	**35** 1.30	**36** 1.33	**37** 1.37	**38** 1.40	**39** 1.43	**40** 1.47	**41** 1.50	**41** 1.53	**42** 1.57	**43** 1.60	**44** 1.63	**45** 1.67	**46** 1.70	**47** 1.73	**48** 1.77	**49** 1.80	**50** 1.83	**50** 1.87	**51** 1.90	**52** 1.93	**53** 1.97	**54** 2.00
31	**28** 1.03	**29** 1.06	**30** 1.10	**30** 1.13	**31** 1.16	**32** 1.19	**33** 1.23	**34** 1.26	**35** 1.29	**36** 1.32	**37** 1.35	**37** 1.39	**38** 1.42	**39** 1.45	**40** 1.48	**41** 1.52	**42** 1.55	**43** 1.58	**44** 1.61	**44** 1.65	**45** 1.68	**46** 1.71	**47** 1.74	**48** 1.77	**49** 1.81	**50** 1.84	**51** 1.87	**51** 1.90	**52** 1.94
32	**27** 1.00	**28** 1.03	**29** 1.06	**30** 1.09	**30** 1.13	**31** 1.16	**32** 1.19	**33** 1.22	**34** 1.25	**35** 1.28	**35** 1.31	**36** 1.34	**37** 1.38	**38** 1.41	**39** 1.44	**40** 1.47	**41** 1.50	**41** 1.53	**42** 1.56	**43** 1.59	**44** 1.63	**45** 1.66	**46** 1.69	**46** 1.72	**47** 1.75	**48** 1.78	**49** 1.81	**50** 1.84	**51** 1.88
33	**26** 0.97	**27** 1.00	**28** 1.03	**29** 1.06	**29** 1.09	**30** 1.12	**31** 1.15	**32** 1.18	**33** 1.21	**34** 1.24	**34** 1.27	**35** 1.30	**36** 1.33	**37** 1.36	**38** 1.39	**38** 1.42	**39** 1.45	**40** 1.48	**41** 1.52	**42** 1.55	**43** 1.58	**43** 1.61	**44** 1.64	**45** 1.67	**46** 1.70	**47** 1.73	**47** 1.76	**48** 1.79	**49** 1.82
34	**25** 0.94	**26** 0.97	**27** 1.00	**28** 1.03	**29** 1.06	**29** 1.09	**30** 1.12	**31** 1.15	**32** 1.18	**33** 1.21	**33** 1.24	**34** 1.26	**35** 1.29	**36** 1.32	**37** 1.35	**37** 1.38	**38** 1.41	**39** 1.44	**40** 1.47	**41** 1.50	**41** 1.53	**42** 1.56	**43** 1.59	**44** 1.62	**44** 1.65	**45** 1.68	**46** 1.71	**47** 1.74	**48** 1.76

Number of teeth on rear sprocket

Notes

1. The larger, bold figures in the table are the gear numbers (in inch-gear sizes) for different chainwheel and sprocket combinations on a bicycle fitted with 27-in wheels.

2. Continental wheels with a diameter of 700 mm and 26-in wheels are so similar to 27-in wheels that the same figures may be used.

3. To calculate gear numbers for bikes with wheels of other sizes, take the second, smaller figure and multiply it by the wheel-size.

4. For further explanation, see chapter 7.

Table 3. Development (in metres) for 27-in and 700-mm Wheels

Number of teeth on rear sprocket

Number of teeth on rear sprocket	Number of teeth on front chainwheel										
	12	**13**	**14**	**15**	**16**	**17**	**18**	**19**	**20**	**21**	**22**
56	9.97	9.20	8.54	7.97	7.47	7.03	6.64	6.29	5.98	5.69	5.43
55	9.78	9.03	8.39	7.83	7.33	6.90	6.52	6.16	5.87	5.59	5.34
54	9.61	8.87	8.23	7.69	7.20	6.78	6.40	6.07	5.76	5.49	5.24
53	9.43	8.70	8.08	7.54	7.07	6.66	6.29	5.95	5.66	5.39	5.14
52	9.25	8.54	7.93	7.40	6.94	6.53	6.17	5.84	5.55	5.29	5.04
51	9.07	8.38	7.78	7.26	6.81	6.40	6.05	5.73	5.44	5.18	4.95
50	8.90	8.21	7.63	7.12	6.67	6.28	5.93	5.62	5.34	5.08	4.85
49	8.72	8.05	7.47	6.97	6.54	6.15	5.81	5.50	5.23	4.98	4.75
48	8.54	7.88	7.32	6.83	6.40	6.03	5.69	5.39	5.12	4.88	4.66
47	8.36	7.72	7.17	6.69	6.27	5.90	5.57	5.28	5.02	4.78	4.56
46	8.18	7.55	7.01	6.55	6.14	5.78	5.45	5.17	4.91	4.67	4.46
45	8.01	7.39	6.86	6.40	6.00	5.65	5.34	5.05	4.80	4.57	4.37
44	7.83	7.23	6.71	6.26	5.87	5.52	5.22	4.94	4.70	4.47	4.27
43	7.65	7.06	6.56	6.12	5.74	5.40	5.10	4.83	4.59	4.37	4.17
42	7.47	6.90	6.40	5.98	5.60	5.27	4.98	4.72	4.48	4.27	4.07
41	7.30	6.73	6.25	5.84	5.47	5.15	4.86	4.61	4.37	4.17	3.98
40	7.12	6.57	6.10	5.69	5.34	5.02	4.74	4.50	4.27	4.07	3.88
39	6.94	6.40	5.94	5.55	5.21	4.90	4.62	4.38	4.16	3.96	3.79
38	6.77	6.23	5.80	5.41	5.07	4.78	4.50	4.27	4.06	3.86	3.70
37	6.58	6.07	5.75	5.27	4.93	4.65	4.38	4.16	3.95	3.76	3.59
36	6.40	5.90	5.49	5.12	4.80	4.53	4.27	4.05	3.85	3.66	3.49
35	6.22	5.74	5.34	4.98	4.67	4.40	4.16	3.94	3.75	3.56	3.39
34	6.04	5.57	5.19	4.84	4.53	4.27	4.04	3.83	3.63	3.45	3.29
33	5.87	5.41	5.04	4.69	4.40	4.14	3.92	3.71	3.52	3.35	3.20
32	5.69	5.24	4.89	4.55	4.27	4.02	3.80	3.59	3.41	3.25	3.10
31	5.51	5.08	4.73	4.41	4.14	3.89	3.68	3.48	3.31	3.15	3.01
30	5.34	4.92	4.58	4.27	4.01	3.77	3.56	3.36	3.20	3.05	2.91
29	5.14	4.76	4.42	4.12	3.88	3.64	3.44	3.25	3.09	2.94	2.81
28	4.98	4.59	4.27	3.98	3.75	3.51	3.32	3.14	2.99	2.84	2.71

Front chainwheel ↓ \ Rear sprocket →	28	29	30	31	32	33	34	35	36	37	38	39	40	41	42	43	44	45	46	47	48	49	50	51	52	53	54	55	56
23	2.60	2.68	2.76	2.84	2.92	3.00	3.09	3.17	3.25	3.34	3.42	3.62	3.71	3.80	3.90	3.98	4.08	4.18	4.27	4.36	4.45	4.55	4.64	4.73	4.83	4.92	5.01	5.10	5.20
24	2.48	2.57	2.68	2.75	2.84	2.93	3.02	3.11	3.20	3.29	3.38	3.47	3.56	3.64	3.75	3.82	3.91	4.00	4.09	4.18	4.27	4.36	4.45	4.54	4.62	4.71	4.80	4.89	4.98
25	2.39	2.47	2.55	2.64	2.72	2.81	2.90	2.99	3.08	3.17	3.25	3.33	3.42	3.50	3.58	3.67	3.76	3.84	3.93	4.01	4.10	4.18	4.27	4.36	4.44	4.52	4.61	4.70	4.78
26	2.30	2.38	2.46	2.54	2.62	2.71	2.79	2.87	2.95	3.03	3.11	3.20	3.28	3.36	3.45	3.53	3.61	3.69	3.78	3.86	3.94	4.02	4.10	4.19	4.27	4.35	4.43	4.51	4.59
27	2.21	2.29	2.36	2.44	2.52	2.60	2.69	2.76	2.84	2.92	3.00	3.08	3.16	3.24	3.32	3.40	3.48	3.56	3.64	3.72	3.80	3.87	3.95	4.03	4.11	4.19	4.27	4.34	4.42
28	2.13	2.21	2.29	2.36	2.44	2.52	2.60	2.68	2.75	2.83	2.90	2.97	3.05	3.13	3.20	3.28	3.36	3.43	3.51	3.59	3.66	3.75	3.82	3.89	3.97	4.04	4.12	4.19	4.27
29	2.06	2.13	2.20	2.28	2.35	2.42	2.49	2.57	2.64	2.72	2.79	2.86	2.94	3.01	3.08	3.16	3.24	3.31	3.39	3.46	3.53	3.60	3.68	3.75	3.82	3.90	3.97	4.04	4.12
30	1.99	2.06	2.13	2.21	2.28	2.35	2.42	2.48	2.56	2.63	2.70	2.77	2.84	2.92	2.99	3.06	3.13	3.20	3.28	3.35	3.42	3.49	3.56	3.63	3.70	3.77	3.85	3.92	3.98

Number of teeth on rear sprocket

Number of teeth on front chainwheel

Notes

1. 'Development' indicates how far a bicycle travels (in metres) for each crank revolution.

2. To determine the development for other wheel-sizes, refer to table 5 which gives equivalent development values for inch-gears.

3. For further explanation, see chapter 7.

Table 4. *Gear Numbers (in inch-gear sizes) for Hub Gearing*

(a) 27-in and 700-mm wheel-sizes

Number of teeth on rear sprocket

Number of teeth on front chainwheel	14	16	18	20	22
42	108 81 61	95 71 53	84 63 47	76 57 43	69 52 38
44	113 85 64	99 74 56	88 66 50	79 59 45	72 54 40
46	118 89 67	104 78 58	92 69 52	83 62 47	75 56 42
48	124 93 70	108 81 61	96 72 54	87 65 49	79 59 44
50	128 96 72	112 84 63	100 75 56	91 68 51	81 61 46

(b) Other wheel-sizes (multiply the figures below by the wheel-size in inches)

Number of teeth on rear sprocket

Number of teeth on front chainwheel	14	16	18	20	22
42	4.00 3.00 2.25	3.51 2.63 1.97	3.11 2.33 1.75	2.80 2.10 1.58	2.55 1.91 1.43
44	4.19 3.14 2.36	3.67 2.75 2.06	3.25 2.44 1.83	2.93 2.20 1.65	2.67 2.00 1.50
46	3.05 3.29 2.47	3.84 2.88 2.16	3.41 2.56 1.92	3.07 2.30 1.73	2.79 2.09 1.57
48	4.57 3.43 2.57	4.00 3.00 2.25	3.56 2.67 2.00	3.20 2.40 1.80	2.91 2.18 1.64
50	4.76 3.57 2.68	4.17 3.13 2.35	3.71 2.78 2.09	3.33 2.50 1.88	3.03 2.27 1.70

Notes

1. The values shown are for Sturmey–Archer AW three-speed hubs. The three figures are for the high, normal and low gear numbers.

Example:

$$72 \text{———high gear}$$
$$\text{normal gear———}54$$
$$40 \text{———low gear}$$

2. For other hubs, use tables 2 or 3 to find the normal gear and calculate the other gear numbers by multiplying by the figures below:

Make	Model	No. of gears	Gear ratios (normal = 1.0)				
F & S	Torpedo (all 3-speeds)	3	0.74	1.0	1.35		
"	Torpedo (all 2-speeds)	2	1.0	1.35			
Shimano	(all 3-speeds)	3	0.74	1.0	1.35		
Sun-Tour	(all 3-speeds)	3	0.75	1.0	1.33		
Sturmey–Archer	S5	5	0.67	0.79	1.0	1.26	1.50
"	AC	3	0.92	1.0	1.67		
"	AM	3	0.84	1.0	1.13		
"	SW	3	0.72	1.0	1.38		
"	FC	4	0.75	0.90	1.0	1.09	
"	FM	4	0.67	0.86	1.0	1.13	
"	FW	4	0.67	0.79	1.0	1.27	

3. For development values in metres, refer to table 5.
4. For further explanation, see chapter 7.

Table 5. *Gear Number and Development Conversion*

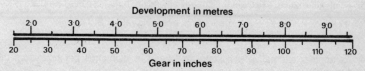

Development in metres

Notes

1. The graph shows the relationship between development (in metres) and gear numbers (in inch-gear sizes).
2. For development, see table 3; for gear numbers, see tables 2 and 4.
3. For further explanation, see chapter 7.

Table 6.   *Riding Speeds for Various Pedalling Rates in Different Gears*

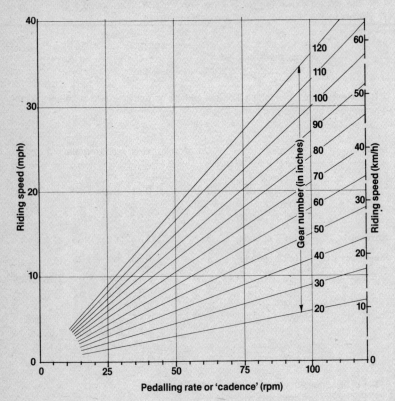

Notes

1. The table shows the riding speeds that correspond to different pedalling rates in different gears.

2. Obtain gear values from tables 2, 3 or 4.

3. As an alternative, calculate the speed in miles per hour from this formula:

$$\text{speed} = \frac{\text{gear no.} \times \text{pedalling rate} \times 3}{1,000}$$

4. As another alternative, calculate the speed in kilometres per hour from this formula:

$$\text{speed} = \text{development (metres)} \times \text{pedalling rate} \times 0.06$$

5. For further explanation, see chapter 7.

Table 7. *Equivalent Tyre-sizes*

Nominal wheel-size	Rim-shoulder circumference	ETRTO international standard	British denomination	French denomination	British rim-size
inches (mm)	mm	mm	inches	mm	
14 (350)	939	32–299	14 × 1⅜		E2J
	911	37–290		350A	
16 (400)	1096	32–349	16 × 1⅜		E3J
	1068	37–340		400A	
18 (450)	1253	32–399	18 × 1⅜	450 × 32A	E4J
	1225	37–390		450A	
20 (500)	1417	32–450	20 × 1⅜	500 × 32A	E5J
	1382	37–440		500A	
22 (550)	1574	32–501	22 × 1⅜	550 × 32A	F2
	1539	37–490		550A	
24 (600)	1728	32–550	24 × 1⅜	600 × 32A	F8
	1700	37–541		600A	
26 (650)	1876	32–597	26 × 1⅜	600 × 32A	E3
	1854	37–590		600A	
	1835	40–584		600B	
27 (675)	1979	30–630	27 × 1¼		K2
28 (700)	1954	32–622		700C	
	2017	37–642	28 × 1⅜	700A	F5
	1995	40–635		700B STD	

Notes

1. The basis for interchangeability is the rim-shoulder diameter, determined by dividing the measured circumference of the rim-shoulder by 3.14.

2. In several foreign countries, tyre-sizes expressed in British units are available which differ from the British standardized sizes. Always check the international standard rim-shoulder diameter (the three-digit number in the combination **–***).

3. For further explanation, see chapter 14.

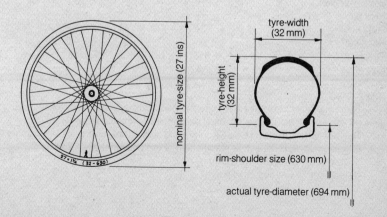

Table 8. *Recommended Minimum Tyre Pressures*

Tyre-width		Pressure in psi (pounds per square inch)	Pressure in bar
inches	mm		
1	25	110	7.5
1⅛	28	90	6.1
1¼	32	80	5.4
1⅜	37	60	4.1
1½	40	45	3.1
1¾	44	35	2.4

Note
These are recommended values for the front tyre of a normally loaded bicycle; the rear tyres and both tyres of a heavily loaded bicycle may be inflated by about another 10 to 15 per cent.

Table 9. *Ball-bearing Sizes*[1]

Bearing location	Ball-bearing size	
	inches	approx. mm equivalent[2]
Bottom bracket	¼	6.4
Rear hub	¼	6.4
Front hub[3]	3/16	4.8
Head-set[3]	5/32	4.0
Pedals	5/32	4.0
Freewheel	⅛	3.2

Notes
1. Some manufacturers have introduced models with pre-assembled sealed bearing units – these are not adjustable and must be completely replaced when worn.
2. The millimetre equivalent is not accurate and is given only as an aid to measuring.
3. Campagnolo and some other manufacturers use different sizes for some models:
    Front hub: 7/32 in (approx. 5.6 mm)
    Head-set: 3/16 in (approx. 4.8 mm).

Table 10.   *Threading Standards*

Thread location	BCI-standard (British)	ISO-standard (French)	Italian standard
Bottom-bracket fixed cup (right-hand side)	1.370 × 24 tpi (L)	32 × 1 mm (R)	36 mm × 24 tpi-F (R)
Bottom-bracket adjustable cup (left-hand side)	1.370 × 24 tpi (R)	35 × 1 mm (R)	36 mm × 24 tpi-F (R)
Pedal (left)	⁹⁄₁₆ in × 20 tpi (L)	14 × 1.25 mm (L)	BCI-standard
Pedal (right)	⁹⁄₁₆ in × 20 tpi (R)	14 × 1.25 mm (R)	BCI-standard
Head-set	1.000 × 24 tpi	25 × 1 mm	1.000 × 24 tpi-F
Freewheel	1.370 × 24 tpi	34.7 × 1 mm	35 mm × 24 tpi
Derailleur attachment	(French standard)	10 × 1 mm	10 mm × 26 tpi

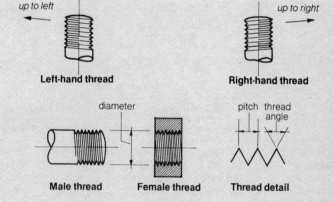

Left-hand thread   Right-hand thread

Male thread   Female thread   Thread detail

Notes

1. Abbreviations: tpi is the 'pitch' measured in threads per inch; L indicates a left-handed thread; R indicates a right-handed thread. For further explanation, see chapter 2.

2. Raleigh and some foreign manufacturers use different standards for some of their simple bicycles; in the case of Raleigh:

Bottom-bracket fixed cup (right-hand side): 1.375 × 26 tpi (L)
Bottom-bracket adjustable cup (left-hand side): 1.375 × 26 tpi (R)
Head-set: 1.000 × 26 tpi.

3. The country of origin does not necessarily coincide with the standards that are used. For complete bicycles manufactured abroad, the following table can be used as a guide:

Table 10. *Continued*

Country of origin	Usual standard	Remarks
Austria	British	Sometimes French
Belgium	French	Sometimes British
France	French	Sometimes British
Germany	British	
Holland	British	
Italy	Italian	
Japan	British	
Spain	French	
Switzerland	French or Italian	Sometimes a Swiss bottom bracket made to French dimensions but with a left-handed thread on the fixed cup

Table 11. *Spoke-lengths*

Tyre-size	Hub-type and spoking pattern			
	Small flange hub		Large flange hub	
	Three-cross	Four-cross	Three-cross	Four-cross
27 × 1¼ ins	303 mm	310 mm	298 mm	308 mm
27-in tubulars	300 mm	306 mm	296 mm	305 mm
700C (French)	296 mm	305 mm	294 mm	303 mm
26 × 1⅜ ins	282 mm	288 mm	277 mm	287 mm

Notes

1. These spoke-lengths are for wheels with thirty-six spokes.

2. Small flange hubs are those with a hub-flange diameter of less than 45 mm; large flange hubs are those with a diameter of 45 mm or more.

3. Spokes may not be available in all the lengths shown, in which case the figures can be rounded up or down by 2 mm.

4. For wheel-sizes and spoking patterns not shown here, consult a bicycle mechanic or refer to *Sutherland's Handbook* (see bibliography).

5. For further explanation, see chapter 38.

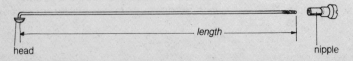

head   — length —   nipple

Table 12. *Spoke-thicknesses*

Thickness in mm	British gauge number	French gauge number	Application
1.4	17	10	Light time-trial work
1.6	16	11	Light racing
1.8	15	12	Racing and training
2.0	14	13	Normal use
2.3	13	15	Heavy touring or tandem use
2.6	12	15	Heavy tandem use

Notes

1. Butted spokes have two or three gauge numbers; select the larger of these numbers from the table above.

2. Check that the spoke holes in the hubs will take the thickness of the spokes you choose.

3. The spokes and nipples of different manufacturers may not always be interchangeable.

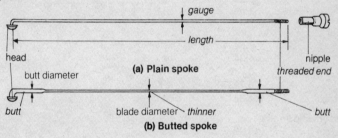

(a) Plain spoke

(b) Butted spoke

Table 13. *Conversion Factors*

Multiply	by	to obtain
Length		
mm	0.039	in
cm	0.394	in
m	3.28	ft
km	0.621	mile
in	25.4	mm
ft	0.305	m
mile	1.61	km
Mass and weight		
gm	0.035	oz
kg	2.20	lb
N (Newton)	0.225	lbf
lbf (force)	4.45	N
lbm (mass)	0.454	kg

Table 13.   *Continued*

Multiply	*by*	*to obtain*
Volume		
cu cm	0.061	cu in
l	61.0	cu in
l	0.220	gal (imp.)
cu inch	16.4	cu cm
l	1.76	pint (imp.)
gal (imp.)	4.55	l
pint (imp.)	0.57	l
Work		
kgm	7.25	ft lb
kWh	367×10^3	kgm
kJ	0.948	Btu
kcal	3.97	Btu
ft lb	0.138	kgm
Btu	1.054	kJ
Power		
kgm/sec	7.22	lb ft/sec
kW	1.34	hp
hp	0.746	kW
Nm/sec	0.723	lb ft/sec
lb ft/sec	1.38	kgm/sec
Pressure and stress		
kg/sq cm	14.22	psi
N/sq mm	142.5	psi
bar	0.070	psi
psi	14.22	bar

Temperature
$$°C = 0.56 \times (°F - 32)$$
$$°F = (1.8 \times °C) + 32$$

Speed		
km/h	0.622	mph
mph	1.609	km/h

Table 14. *Typical Weights of Bicycle Components*

	Weight in grams	Weight in lb and oz
Frame without front forks		
(a) Seamless carbon steel	2,800–3,200	6 lb 2 oz −7 lb
(b) Plain-gauge steel alloy	2,400–2,800	5 lb 4 oz −6 lb 2 oz
(c) Butted steel alloy	1,800–2,400	4 lb −5 lb 4 oz
(d) Aluminium alloy or titanium alloy	1,200–1,800	2 lb 10 oz–4 lb
Front forks		
Carbon steel	800–1,000	1 lb 12 oz–2 lb 7 oz
Steel alloy	700– 900	1 lb 8 oz −2 lb
Aluminium or titanium	600– 700	1 lb 5 oz −1 lb 8 oz
Wheels without tyres and freewheel		
(a) With aluminium hub and steel rim	1,200–1,400	2 lb 10 oz–3 lb 1 oz
(b) With aluminium hub and rim	900–1,100	2 lb −2 lb 7 oz
(c) For tubular tyre	600– 900	1 lb 5 oz −2 lb
Tyres		
(a) Wired-on with tube (27 × 1¼ ins)	500– 700	1 lb 2 oz −1 lb 8 oz
(b) High-pressure wired-on	450– 600	1 lb −1 lb 5 oz
(c) Tubular for track use	120– 200	4 oz −7 oz
(d) Tubular for road use	250– 400	9 oz −14 oz
Brakes		
(a) Set of alloy side-pulls with controls	500– 700	1 lb 2 oz −1 lb 8 oz
(b) Set of alloy centre-pulls with controls	600– 800	1 lb 5 oz −1 lb 12 oz
Gearing		
(a) Aluminium rear derailleur	150– 300	5 oz −10 oz
(b) Steel rear derailleur	300– 400	10 oz −13 oz
(c) Front derailleur	150– 200	5 oz −7 oz
(d) Set of controls	200– 300	7 oz −10 oz
Crank-sets		
(a) Steel crank-set with chainwheels	1,300–1,500	2 lb 12 oz–3 lb 5 oz
(b) Alloy crank-set with chainwheels	900–1,000	2 lb −2lb 7 oz
Pedals		
(a) Set of steel pedals	500– 600	1 lb 2 oz −1 lb 5 oz
(b) Set of aluminium pedals	350– 500	12 oz −1 lb 2 oz
Freewheel block with sprockets		
(a) Steel (up to 22 teeth)	400– 450	14 oz −1 lb
(b) Steel (over 22 teeth)	450– 500	1 lb −1 lb 2 oz
(c) Alloy or titanium (up to 22 teeth)	250– 350	9 oz −12 oz
Chain		
(a) Steel	350– 400	12 oz −14 oz
(b) Titanium	250– 300	9 oz −10 oz
Saddle		
(a) Leather	450– 600	1 lb −1 lb 5 oz
(b) Nylon	350– 450	12 oz −1 lb
(c) Steel seat pin	200– 250	6 oz −9 oz
(d) Alloy (adjustable) seat pin	250– 350	9 oz −12 oz

Table 14.   *Continued*

	Weight in grams		Weight in lb and oz	
Handlebars				
(a) Aluminium bend	300–	350	10 oz	–12 oz
(b) Steel bend	450–	500	1 lb	–2 oz
(c) Aluminium extension	220–	300	8 oz	–10 oz
(d) Steel extension	350–	400	12 oz	–14 oz
Head-set				
Steel	180–	200	6 oz	–7 oz
Aluminium, titanium or nylon	100–	150	3 oz	–5 oz
Luggage carrier				
Steel	600–	700	1 lb 5 oz	–1 lb 8 oz
Aluminium	250–	400	9 oz	–14 oz
Mudguards (set of two)				
Plastic	300–	350	10 oz	–12 oz
Aluminium	350–	450	12 oz	–1 lb
Steel	500–	600	1 lb 2 oz	–1 lb 5 oz

BRITISH GOVERNMENT AGENCIES AND PUBLIC SOCIETIES

British Waterways Board: (1) PO Box 9, 1 Dock Street, Leeds LS1 1HH;
   (2) Willow Grange, Church Road, Watford, Herts WD1 3QA; (3) Dock Office,
   Gloucester GL1 2EJ.
Countryside Commission: John Dower House, Crescent Place, Cheltenham,
   Gloucester GL50 3RA.
Forestry Commission Headquarters: 231 Corstorphine Road, Edinburgh EH12 7AT.
National Trust: 42 Queen Anne's Gate, London SW1H 9AS.
National Trust of Scotland: 5 Charlotte Square, Edinburgh 2.
Royal Society for the Prevention of Accidents: Cannon House, The Priory, Queensway,
   Birmingham B4 6BS.

BRITISH AND IRISH CYCLING ORGANIZATIONS

Association of Cycle and Lightweight Campers: 11 Grosvenor Place, London
   SW1W 0EY.
AUDAX (UK): 188 Runcorn Road, Moore, Warrington WA4 6SY.
Bicycle Association of Great Britain Ltd: Starley House, Eaton Road, Coventry
   CV1 2FH.
Bicycle Polo Association of Great Britain: 10 Priestley Drive, Tonbridge, Kent.
British Cycling Bureau: Stanhope House, London W2 2HH.
British Cycling Federation: 70 Brompton Road, London SW3 1EN.
British Cyclo-Cross Association: 8 Bellam Road, Hampton Magna, Warwickshire.
British Professional Cycle Racing Association: 4 Lane Top, Queensbury, Bradford,
   West Yorkshire.
Cycle Speedway Council: 391 Wimborne Road, Poole, Dorset BH15 3EE.
Cycling Council of Great Britain: 69 Meadrow, Godalming, Surrey GU7 3HS.
Cyclists' Touring Club: 69 Meadrow, Godalming, Surrey GU7 3HS.
English Schools Cycling Association: 8 Lady's Meadow, Beccles, Suffolk
   NR3 9DR.
Friends of the Earth: 9 Poland Street, London W1V 3DG.
Irish Cycling Federation: 9 Casement Park, Finglas West, Dublin 11.
London Cycling Campaign: Colombo Street Centre, London SE1.
L'Ordre des Cols Durs: 39 Delahays Road, Hale, Altrincham, Cheshire WA15 8DT.
National Association of Cycle and Motor Cycle Traders: 31a High Street,
   Tunbridge Wells, Kent.

Northern Ireland Cycling Federation: 9a Great Northern Street, Belfast.
Road Records Association: 58 Tintern Road, Carshalton, Surrey.
Road Time-Trials Council: Dallacre, Mill Road, Yarwell, Peterborough PE8 6PS.
Rough Stuff Fellowship: 4 Archway Avenue, Callander, Perthshire FK17 8JZ.
Scottish Cyclists' Union: 293 Rosemount Place, Aberdeen.
Tandem Club: c/o Peter Hallowell, 25 Hendred Way, Abingdon, Oxfordshire OX14 2AN.
Tricycle Association: 37 York Close, Market Bosworth, Nuneaton, Warwickshire.
UKBMX: 47 Cuxton Road, Strood, Kent.
Veteran Time-Trials Association: 137 Glenwood Avenue, Westcliff-on-Sea, Essex.
Women's Cycle Racing Association: 129 Grand Avenue, Surbiton, Surrey.
Women's Road Records Association: 45 Juniper Road, Langley Green, Crawley, West Sussex.
The Youth Hostel Association: Trevelyan House, 8 St Stephens Hill, St Albans, Herts AL1 2DY; Travel and Services Dept: 29 John Adam Street, London WC2.

INTERNATIONAL AND FOREIGN CYCLING ORGANIZATIONS

Alliance Internationale de Tourisme (Dept de Cyclisme): Quai Gustave Ador 2, CH–1207 Geneva, Switzerland.
Amateur Bicycle League of America: Box 669, Wall Street Station, New York, NY 10005, USA.
Australian Amateur Cyclists' Association: 20 Patterson Crescent, Morphettville 5043, South Australia, Australia.
Australian Cycling Council: 153 The Kingsway, Cronulla, Sydney 2230, New South Wales, Australia.
Bicycle Manufacturers' Association: 1101 15th Street, Washington D C 20005, USA.
Bikecentennial, PO Box 8308, Missoula, Montana 59807, USA.
Canadian Cycling Association: 333 River Road, Vanier, Ottawa, Ontario, Canada.
Fédération Cyclotouriste Provinciale: 4305 Bossuet, Montreal 431, Quebec, Canada.
Fédération Internationale Amateur de Cyclisme (FIAC): Viale Tiziano 70, I–0010 Rome, Italy.
Fédération Internationale du Cyclisme Professionnel (FICP): 26 Rue de Cessange, Leudelange, Luxemburg.
International Bicycle Touring Society: c/o Dr Clifford Graves, 2115 Paseo Dorado, La Jolla, California 92037, USA.
League of American Wheelmen: PO Box 988, Baltimore, Maryland 21203, USA.
New Zealand Amateur Cycling Association: PO Box 3104, Wellington, New Zealand.
Professional Racing Organization USA: 1524 Linden Street, Allentown, Pennsylvania 18102.
Union Cycliste Internationale (UCI): Rue Charles Humbert 8, CH–1205 Geneva, Switzerland.
United States Cycling Federation: 1750 East Boulder, Colorado Springs, Colorado 80909, USA.

CYCLING PUBLICATIONS

Bicycle Magazine: 11 Garrick Street, London WC2 9AR.
Cycletouring: Cyclists' Touring Club, 69 Meadrow, Godalming, Surrey GU7 3HS.
Cycling: IPC Specialist and Professional Press, Surrey House, 1 Throwley Way,
    Sutton, Surrey SM1 4QQ.
International Cycling Sports: Kennedy Bros. (Publishing) Ltd, Howden Road,
    Silsden, Keighley, West Yorkshire.
Bicycle Forum: Box 8311, Missoula, Montana 59801, USA.
Bicycling: 33 East Minor Street, Emmaus, Pennsylvania 18049, USA.
Freewheeling Australia: PO Box 57, Broadway, New South Wales 2007, Australia.
Radmarkt: Bielefelder Verlagsanstalt KG, Postfach 1140, 4800 Bielefeld 1,
    West Germany.
Bike-Tech: 33 East Minor Street, Emmaus, Pennsylvania 18049, USA.

MAIL ORDER AND TRADE

Freewheel: 275 West End Lane, London NW6 1QS.
Andrew Hague: Cwm Draw Industrial Estate, Ebbw Vale, Gwent NP3 5AE.
Holdsworthy Company Ltd: 132 Lower Richmond Road, Putney, London SW15 1LN.
International Cycling Centre (Ron Kitching): Hookstone Park, Harrogate,
    West Yorkshire HG2 7BZ.
Ken Rogers: 71 Berkeley Avenue, Cranford, Hounslow, Middlesex TN4 6LF.
Edward Stanford Ltd (Maps): 12–14 Long Acre, London WC2E 9LP.
Bikecology: 2055 McKerny Street, Chandler, Arizona 85224, USA.
Bike Nashbar: PO Box 290, New Middletown, Ohio 44442, USA.
Palo Alto Bicycles: PO Box 1276, Palo Alto, California 94302, USA.

MUSEUMS WITH IMPORTANT BICYCLE EXHIBITS –
BRITAIN AND IRELAND

Belfast: *Transport Museum*, Witham Street, Belfast.
Biggleswade: *Shuttleworth Collection*, Old Warden Aerodome, Biggleswade.
Birmingham: *Museum of Science and Industry*, Newhall Street, Birmingham.
Coventry: *Herbert Museum and Art Gallery*, Jordan Well, Coventry.
Edinburgh: *Royal Scottish Museum*, Chambers Street, Edinburgh.
Glasgow: *Museum of Transport*, 25 Albert Drive, Glasgow.
Leicester: *Leicestershire Museum of Technology*, Corporation Road, Leicester.
London: *Science Museum*, Exhibition Road, South Kensington, London.
Maidstone: *Tyrrwhitt-Drake Museum of Carriages*, Archbishop's Stables, Mill Street,
    Maidstone.
Newcastle-upon-Tyne: *Science Museum*, Exhibition Park, Great North Road,
    Newcastle-upon-Tyne.
Nottingham: *Industrial Museum*, Wollaton Park, Nottingham; *The Raleigh Company's
    Museum*, Lenton Boulevard, Nottingham.

MUSEUMS WITH IMPORTANT BICYCLE EXHIBITS – OTHER COUNTRIES

Austria: *Technisches Museum für Industrie und Gewerbe*, Vienna.

Belgium: *Musée Belgique de motocyclette et du cycle*, Farmignoul, Namur.

Denmark: *Traffikmuseum*, Helsignør.

France: *Musée Français de l'automobile*, Rochetaillée-sur-Saône; *Musée de la voiture et du tourisme*, Compiègne.

Germany: *Deutsches Zweirad Museum*, Neckarsulm; *Germanisches Nationalmuseum*, Nürnberg; *Deutsches Museum*, Munich.

Holland: *Batavus Museum*, Heerenveen; *Museum de Waag*, Deventer.

Italy: *Museo Nazionale della Scienza e della Tecnica Leonardo da Vinci*, Milan; *Museo dell'automobile Carlo Biscaretti di Ruffia*, Turin.

Switzerland: *Velo Museum*, Wolfhausen; *Turn- und Sportmuseum*, Basle; *Verkehrsmuseum der Schweiz*, Lucerne.

USA: *Harah's Automobile Collection*, Reno, Nevada; *The Henry Ford Museum*, Dearborn, Michigan; *Museum of Science and Industry*, Chicago, Illinois; *Schwinn Bicycle Museum*, Chicago, Illinois; *Smithsonian Institution*, Cycle Collection, Washington DC.

Bibliography

Alth, Max, *All About Bikes and Bicycling*. Folkestone: Bailey Bros. & Swinfen, 1974.

Ayres, Martin, *Cycles and Cycling*. London: Butterworth, 1981.

Ballantine, Richard, *Richard's Bicycle Book*. London: Pan Books, 1979.

Balshone, Bruce L., and Deering, Paul L., *Bicycle Transit: Its Planning and Design*. New York: Praeger, 1975.

Bowden, Gregory H., *Story of the Raleigh Cycle*. London: W. H. Allen, 1975.

Coles, C. W., and Glenn, H. T., *Glenn's Complete Bicycle Repair Manual*. New York: Crown Publishers, 1973.

Cooper, K. H., *The New Aerobics*. New York: Bantam Books, 1970.

Crane, Nicholas (ed.), *International Cycling Guide* (Annual). London: A. S. Barnes & Co.

Cross, K. D., *Bicycle Safety Education – Facts and Issues*. Falls Church, Virginia: AAA Foundation for Traffic Safety, 1978. (Order from AAA Foundation for Traffic Safety, Falls Church, Virginia 22042, USA.)

Cross, K. D., and Fisher, G., *A Study of Bicycle/Motor Vehicle Accidents*, Vols. I and II. Washington DC: National Highway Traffic Safety Administration, 1977 and 1978. (Order from National Technical Information Service, Springfield, Virginia 22161, USA.)

Crowley, T. E., *Discovering Old Bicycles*. Aylesbury, Buckinghamshire: Shire Publications, 2nd ed., 1978.

Cuthbertson, Tom, *Anybody's Bike Book*. Berkeley, California: Ten Speed Press, 1979.

Cycling. Rome: Italian Cycling Federation's Central Sports School, CONI–FIAC, 1971.

DeLong, Fred, *DeLong's Guide to Bicycles and Bicycling*. Radnor, Pennsylvania: Chilton Book Co., 1978.

Duker, Peter, *The TI Raleigh Story*. Coventry: Midland Letterpress, 1979.

Durrey, Jean, *The Guinness Book of Bicycling*. Poole: Blandford Press, 1977.

Dyson, G. H. G., *The Mechanics of Athletics*. London: Hodder, 7th ed., 1977.

Evans, David, *The Ingenious Mr Pedersen*. Gloucester: Alan Sutton, 1979.

Evans, Ken, *The Young Cyclist's Handbook*. London: Hamlyn, 1979.

Faria, I. E., and Cavanagh, P. R., *The Physiology and Biomechanics of Cycling*. New York: Wiley, 1978.

Forester, John, *Cycling Transportation Engineering*. London and Cambridge (USA): MIT Press, 1983.

Forester, John, *Effective Cycling*. Palo Alto: Custom Cycle Fitments, 1975. (Order from Custom Cycle Fitments, 726 Madrone Avenue, Sunnyvale, California 94086, USA.)

Gausden, C., and Crane, N., *The CTC Route Guide to Cycling in Britain and Ireland.* Oxford: Oxford Illustrated Press, 1980; Penguin Books, 1981.

Hay, James G., *The Biomechanics of Sports Techniques.* Englewood Cliffs, New York: Prentice-Hall, 1973.

Henderson, N. G., *Continental Cycle Racing.* London: Pelham Books, 1970.

Hudson, Mike, *The Bicycle Planning Book.* London: Open Books, 1978.

Hudson, Mike, *Bicycle Planning, Policy and Practice.* London: The Architectural Press, 1982.

Hughes, Tom, *Adventure Cycling in Britain.* Poole: Blandford Press, 1978.

Illich, Ivan, *Energy and Equity.* London: Calder & Boyars, 1974.

Know the Game – Cycle Racing. Wakefield: E. P. Group, 1978.

Krausz, J., and Van der Reiz-Krausz, V. (eds.), *The Bicycling Book.* New York: Dial Press, 1982.

Luebbers, David J., *The Bicycle Bibliography.* (Annual, order from D. J. Luebbers, Route 3, Box 312, Columbia, Maryland 65201, USA.)

McGonagle, Seamus, *The Bicycle in Life, Love, War and Literature.* London: Pelham, 1968.

MacKenzie, Jeanne (ed.), *Cycling.* Oxford: Oxford University Press, 1982.

McPhee, Gribble, and Lancaster, *Bicycles, All About Them.* Sydney: Penguin Books Australia, 1978.

Nicholson, G., *The Great Bike Race.* London: Hodder & Stoughton, 1977.

Planning and Design Criteria for Bikeways in California. Sacramento: California Department of Transportation, 1978. (Obtain from Caltrans, Sacramento, California, USA.)

Rauch, S., and Winkler, F., *Fahrrad-Technik.* Bielefeld, West Germany: Bielefelder Verlagsanstalt, 1980.

Rauck, M. J. B., Volke, G., and Paturi, F. R., *Mit dem Rad durch zwei Jahrhunderte.* Aarau, Switzerland: AT Verlag, 1979.

Reed, Marshall F., Jr, *The Economic Cost of Commuting.* Washington DC: Highway Users Federation, 1975. (Obtain from Highway Users Federation, 1776 Massachusetts Avenue NW, Washington DC 20036, USA.)

Rennert, Jack, *100 Years of Bicycle Posters.* St Albans: Hart Davis, 1973.

Research on Road Safety. London: Her Majesty's Stationery Office, 1963.

Richards, Rey, *Cyclo-Cross.* Silsden: Kennedy Bros., 1973.

Ritchie, Andrew, *King of the Road.* London: Wildwood House, 1975.

Safe Cycling. London: Her Majesty's Stationery Office, 1957.

St Pierre, Roger, *Cycle Racing Tactics.* Silsden: Kennedy Bros., 1970.

St Pierre, Roger, *The Book of the Bicycle.* London: Ward Lock, 1973.

Schulz and Schulz, *Bicycles and Cycling: A Guide to Information Sources.* Detroit: Gale Research Co., 1980. (Order from Gale Research Co., Book Tower, Detroit, Michigan 48226, USA.)

Sharp, Archibald, *Bicycles and Tricycles – An Elementary Treatise on their Design and Construction* (Facsimile of original 1896 edition). London and Cambridge (USA): MIT Press, 1977.

Shaw, Reg. (ed.), *The Raleigh Book of Cycling.* London: Sphere Books, 1978.

Skilful Cycling: A Manual of Roadcraft. Purley: Royal Society for the Prevention of Accidents, 1975. (Order from RoSPA – Cycling Programme, Cannon House, The Priory, Queensway, Birmingham B4 6BS.)

Sloane, Eugene A., *The New Complete Book of Bicycling*. New York: Simon & Schuster, 1974.

Sumner, P., *Early Bicycles*. London: Hugh Evelyn, 1966.

Sutherland, H., and Hart, J. P., *Sutherland's Handbook for Bicycle Mechanics*. Berkeley: Sutherland's Publications, 3rd ed., 1981. (Order from Sutherland's Publications, Box 9061, Berkeley, California 94709, USA.)

Talbot, Richard P., *Designing and Building Your Own Frameset*. Boston: The Manet Guild, 1979.

Thomas, Vaughan, *Science and Sport*. London: Faber & Faber, 1970.

Velox, *Velocipedes, Bicycles and Tricycles. How to Make and How to Use Them* (Facsimile of original 1869 edition). East Ardley, Wakefield: S. R. Publishers, 1971.

Wadley, John Borland, *Cycling*. London: Macmillan, 1975.

Wagenvoord, James, *Bikes and Riders*. New York: Van Nostrand Reinhold, 1982.

Watson, R., and Gray, M., *The Penguin Book of the Bicycle*. Harmondsworth: Penguin Books, 1978.

Whitt, F. R., and Wilson, D. G., *Bicycling Science*. London and Cambridge (USA): MIT Press, 2nd ed., 1982.

Wiley, Jack, *The Bicycle Builder's Bible*. Blue Ridge Summit, Pennsylvania: TAB Books, 1980. (Order from the UK distributor: W. Foulsham & Co. Ltd, Yeovil Road, Slough, Berkshire SL1 4JH.)

Williamson, Geoffrey, *Wheels within Wheels – The Starleys of Coventry*. London: Bles, 1966.

Woodard, C. R., *Scientific Training for Cycling*. London: Temple Press, 3rd ed., 1967.

Woodforde, J., *The Story of the Bicycle*. London: Routledge & Kegan Paul, 1970.

Woodland, Les, *Cycle Racing: Training to Win*. London: Pelham Books, 1975.

FIND OUT MORE ABOUT PENGUIN BOOKS

We publish the largest range of titles of any English language paperback publisher. As well as novels, crime and science fiction, humour, biography and large-format illustrated books, Penguin series include *Pelican Books* (on the arts, sciences and current affairs), *Penguin Reference Books*, *Penguin Classics*, *Penguin Modern Classics*, *Penguin English Library* and *Penguin Handbooks* (on subjects from cookery and gardening to sport), as well as *Puffin Books* for children. Other series cover a wide variety of interests from poetry to crosswords, and there are also several newly formed series – *King Penguin*, *Penguin American Library*, *Penguin Diaries and Letters* and *Penguin Travel Library*.

We are an international publishing house, but for copyright reasons not every Penguin title is available in every country. To find out more about the Penguins available in your country please write to our U.K. office – Dept EP, Penguin Books Ltd, Harmondsworth, Middlesex UB7 0DA – unless you live in one of the following areas:

In the U.S.A.: Dept DG, Penguin Books, 299 Murray Hill Parkway, East Rutherford, New Jersey 07073.

In Canada: Penguin Books Canada Ltd, 2801 John Street, Markham, Ontario L3R 1B4.

In Australia: Marketing Department, Penguin Books Australia Ltd, P.O. Box 257, Ringwood, Victoria 3134.

In New Zealand: Marketing Department, Penguin Books (N.Z.) Ltd, P.O. Box 4019, Auckland 10.

In India: Penguin Overseas Ltd, 706 Eros Apartments, 56 Nehru Place, New Delhi 110019.

The Penguin Book of the Bicycle

Roderick Watson and Martin Gray

Richly illustrated, entertaining and packed with fascinating detail, this is a sparkling celebration of the bicycle, in all its forms and fashions. The authors have brought their immense enthusiasm and experience to bear on every aspect: the social and technical evolution of cycling, the dramatic complexities of cycle sport, the modern bicycle revival. There are behind-the-scenes visits to the cycle industry, and many practical insights into buying, assembling, maintaining and riding a bicycle. Above all, this is a book about the aesthetic and technical beauty of a mechanical contraption that is one of the simplest and most perfect (and harmless) that the human mind has devised.

A Hitch-hiker's Guide to Great Britain

Ken Lussey

Illustrated by Reg Piggott

Whether you're a beginner or an expert, this handbook provides the essential information to enable you to hitch safely and enjoyably from A to B, with the minimum of time, trouble and expense. Dividing Britain into ten regions for easy reference, the guide features

★ maps to show the best pick-up points on motorway junctions and A roads, rated according to a carefully devised grading system

★ large-scale maps giving hitching-ratings at spots in city and town centres throughout Britain

★ information on equipment, motorways and camping, and many more useful hints

The Walker's Handbook
Second Enlarged Edition

H. D. Westacott

Maps, tents, clothes, rights of way, National Parks, the law, hostels, farmers, gamekeepers, shoes, boots, safety and first aid – all you need to know to walk safely and happily, whether you take the low road or the high road. This new and enlarged edition also includes extra chapters on challenge walks and walking abroad.

The Town Gardener's Companion

Felicity Bryan

Former gardening columnist for the *Evening Standard*, Felicity Bryan has marshalled all her expertise and inventiveness in this month-by-month guide which includes sixteen pages of colour photographs. Here she demonstrates that lack of space offers a challenge of its own, and with ingenious planning the town gardener can produce a riot of flowers, foliage and vegetables the whole year round.

'An inspiring new book . . . a fertile source of ideas for turning a cat-ridden concrete backyard into a jungle of soothing green' – *Sunday Times*